D1165172

SPECIAL EDUCATION LAW

*A Guide for Parents,
Advocates, and Educators*

SPECIAL EDUCATION LAW

A Guide for Parents, Advocates, and Educators

STEVEN S. GOLDBERG

PLENUM PRESS • NEW YORK AND LONDON

Library of Congress Cataloging in Publication Data

Goldberg, Steven S. (Steven Selig), 1950–
  Special education law.

  (Critical topics in law and society)
  Includes bibliographical references and index.
  1. Handicapped children — Education — Law and legislation — United States.
I. Title. II. Series.
KF4210.G64 1982   344.73′0791   82-13190
ISBN 0-306-40848-1   347.304791

© 1982 Plenum Press, New York
A Division of Plenum Publishing Corporation
233 Spring Street, New York, N.Y. 10013

Printed in the United States of America

To
HARRY, RUTH, AND REBECKAH

Preface

To any professional concerned with exceptional children, it would be the greatest understatement to say that the courts and legislatures have had a tremendous impact on the field of special education. Especially in the last decade, a flood of litigation filed to develop and define the right to education of previously unserved handicapped children has left no special education teacher, school administrator, nurse, educational psychologist, or pediatrician unaffected—either because these professionals are daily called upon to help children, or because they may come forward as witnesses on behalf of children who are the subjects of special education meetings, individualized education programs, placement hearings, or judicial proceedings. Thus, for these people, questions regarding a student's legal rights are immediate and pervasive.

This book developed out of the need to provide nonlegal professionals with a lawyer's view of the huge body of court cases and federal laws and regulations that affect their practice as well as their students and clients. An introductory chapter provides the historical basis of the current interface between law and special education. The Education for All Handicapped Children Act of 1975 and Section 504 of the Rehabilitation Act of 1973, and their regulations promulgated in 1977, are the major national laws in the field and are therefore described in Chapters 2 and 3. To suggest how they operate, there is extensive commentary on each of these laws, and the important passages of those cases that lawyers in the field acknowledge as critical are provided to supplement the text. Professionals want to know how the law works in practice as well as how it affects them, and this need has been addressed at great length.

Chapter 4 focuses on the legal requirement that is perhaps most foreign to nonlegal professionals and that involves many of them with lawyers for the first time—the special education "placement" or "due process" hearing. These hearings are held to determine an appropriate program of special education and related services for each child whose needs are in dispute. For professionals and parents who must testify or who choose to present their cases without a lawyer (and for attorneys unfamiliar with these proceedings), this chapter suggests what to expect at the hearing. Legal advice, of course, must be sought from attorneys familiar with the facts of any individual case with which a reader may become personally involved.

The final chapter sets forth a legal view of the major issues that are developing in special education—year-round special education; legal concerns that arise when school officials and teachers seek to discipline mentally handicapped students, legal problems of children with special needs whose primary language is other than English; "educational malpractice" cases; and the emerging rights of mentally gifted students.

The Appendixes present for immediate reference P.L. 94-142, Section 504, and their regulations in full; as well as a list of legal organizations with addresses.

"Special education law" has become a distinct area of civil rights law. I have attempted to outline its major points and to describe some of its applications. My clients at the Education Law Center have provided me with much indispensable information. I also wish to thank my colleagues there, without whose influence this book would not have been attempted. The dozens of meetings with parents and professional groups I have had over the years have been critical to any understanding I may have of their needs. Especially outstanding in their advocacy and inspirational in their devotion to children's rights are members of the Pennsylvania and Montgomery County (Pennsylvania) Associations for Children with Learning Disabilities, including Anne Boyle and Mary Rita Hanley, as well as Audrey Coccia, parent and advocate. Finally, I acknowledge the technical and editorial assistance of Bruce Dennis Sales, professor and director of the Law-Psychology Program, University of Nebraska, and Betsy McPherrin who encouraged me to write this book.

STEVEN SELIG GOLDBERG

CONTENTS

SPECIAL EDUCATION LAW

A Guide for Parents,
Advocates, and Educators

Introduction

1.1. The Background

Despite laws in every state mandating universal free instruction for children entering public school, millions of students who require special education have been excluded from the programs they need. Although formal special education classes began almost eighty years ago, they were often of little value to their intended beneficiaries. Classified as "feebleminded," "imbeciles," or worse, mentally and physically handicapped children were segregated in rooms apart from the rest of the school population, received inferior educational services, and were very often institutionalized. Other such children were denied access to educational programs entirely.

It is incredible that until only the last decade these exclusions and mis-classifications remained commonplace. In the early part of the 1970s, parents of mentally and physically handicapped persons began to assert a legal right to an education similar to that offered other children. These parents based their claims on legal victories achieved by civil rights activists advocating on behalf of black students who had been similarly segregated and provided with inferior education or none at all. For at least thirty years before the Supreme Court's landmark desegregation decision in *Brown v. Board of Education*,[1] black students had gained a variety of small but critical victories allowing them access to programs, mostly in professional schools, that had previously been restricted to whites. But in *Brown*, the Court held that separate facilities for black students denied the Constitution's requirement that all persons be treated equally under the law. In language that is frequently cited by advocates representing children who require special education—known today as "exceptional children"—the Court in a unanimous opinion stressed the importance of education to society.

Today education is perhaps the most important function of state and local governments. Compulsory school attendance laws and the great expenditures for education both demonstrate our recognition of the importance of education to our demo-

cratic society. It is required in the performance of our most basic public responsibilities, even service in the armed forces. It is the very foundation of good citizen-
ship. Today it is a principle instrument in awakening the child to cultural values, in
preparing him for later professional training, and in helping him to adjust normally to
his environment. In these days, it is doubtful that any child may reasonably be
expected to succeed in life if he is denied the opportunity of an education. Such an
opportunity, where the state has undertaken to provide it, is a right which must be
made available to all on equal terms.[2]

Courts of law have increasingly come to accept the fact that handicapped
children have been in a disadvantaged position similar to that of other minorities
and that educational opportunity is their legal right.

The Pennsylvania Association for Retarded Children (PARC) successfully
brought a case[3] that is now considered a landmark and is utilized by other
advocates who claim a right to education for handicapped children. In the
Commonwealth of Pennsylvania, school law allowed children of "school age"
(six to twenty-one) to attend the local public schools. Children who were deemed
unable to benefit from education could be excluded from school upon the
certification of a psychologist. Furthermore, the compulsory attendance law,
which required children from eight to seventeen to attend school, was used to
exclude retarded persons who were outside that age group. Retarded children
who had been excluded either stayed home, were sent to private special schools
at enormous expense to their parents, or became institutionalized wards of the
Department of Public Welfare, where they were maintained for the most part
without appropriate schooling.

The PARC case resulted in an agreement (the "PARC Consent Decree")
recognizing the legal right to education for retarded children in Pennsylvania.
The agreement required that retarded children be provided with a free and
appropriate public education to meet their individual needs. State Board of
Education regulations resulting from the lawsuit required that "due process"
procedures be followed whenever any change in a retarded person's program was
proposed either by a child's parents or school district officials.[4] Thus parents
must be notified whenever school officials intend to increase, decrease, or eliminate any aspect of a child's curriculum, including teaching techniques or related
services such as transportation, speech, language, or occupational therapy. Similarly, parents have a right to propose programs they think will benefit their child.
When parents and school administrators disagree about a child's placement, and
if the problem cannot be resolved through an informal conference, a hearing
must be held. The hearing is set up by State Department of Education officials, who also appoint a hearing officer. The officer, who is an educator and
not a lawyer, is required to hear the concerns of both parties to the dispute;
persons presenting evidence may include experts in educational psychology,
doctors, therapists, or teachers. Both sides may be represented by legal or other

representatives of their choice, but a school district is not responsible for providing parents with an attorney or other advocate.

After the officer hears the evidence, which is recorded by a court reporter, he renders an opinion about the child's placement including the specific details for an appropriate program of special education and related services. This decision may be appealed by either party to the state secretary of education, and then to the courts.

These "PARC" procedures set a detailed model for future advocates. In another now-famous case, an attack was mounted on the exclusion of handicapped children from appropriate classes in the District of Columbia. Plaintiffs claimed and the judge agreed that Washington's exceptional children, including those classified as behavioral problems, mentally retarded, emotionally disturbed, learning disabled, and physically handicapped, had overwhelmingly been excluded from publicly supported education. According to the court, the U.S. Constitution had twice been violated: first, equal protection requires that plaintiffs and their nonhandicapped peers be provided with education on a similar basis; second, due process of law "requires a hearing prior to exclusion, termination, or classification into a special education program." The Court ordered District school administrators to develop (1) a plan for the identification, classification, and placement of handicapped children, and (2) due process procedures and services for such children. This lawsuit, known as *Mills v. Board of Education*,[5] remains under the supervision of the federal courts in Washington, as does PARC in Pennsylvania, to resolve remaining special education problems.

Mills and PARC provided a legal basis for numerous challenges to state and local policies denying equal educational opportunity for handicapped persons. In Pennsylvania, for example, another case was brought that resulted in the extension of procedures designed to protect retarded persons to *all* "exceptional" children in the State. Physically handicapped and socially and emotionally disturbed students were now covered by right-to-education laws (as were those students "thought-to-be" handicapped), as was a newly identified group requiring special education—children who are intellectually gifted or who are talented in art, music, creative writing, theater, and other fields.[6] Educators have discovered that school can be a waste of time for highly creative or remarkably bright children taught with materials and techniques prepared for typical children. Far more than other groups of exceptional children, students classified as gifted or talented remain without appropriate special education programs. As with handicapped students several years ago, advocacy groups on behalf of these children are increasing in number, and educators are required to confront the needs of gifted and talented persons.

After advocates achieved these initial paper victories, there remained the time-consuming and somewhat less glamorous task of enforcing the new rights in the classroom. In addition, litigation was still required to continually enforce hard-won cases and to ensure that all groups of exceptional children were served. For example, *Frederick L. v. Thomas*[7] was filed in federal court in Philadelphia to obtain special education programs for adolescents with specific learning disabilities in that city's school district. The court agreed with plaintiffs that this population was not properly identified or served, and ordered the Board of Education to promulgate guidelines and substantially expand its special education program so that these children could obtain appropriate instruction. After an appeal of the court's orders to the U.S. Court of Appeals for the Third Circuit, the higher court affirmed this decision, ensuring that screening, identification, and placement of learning-disabled children would continue.

These and other cases[8] led to congressional study and, eventually, to implementation of the Education for All Handicapped Children Act of 1975, known as P.L. 94-142. This law, together with its implementing regulations[9] promulgated in 1977, expanded on the previous Education of the Handicapped Act to provide substantial additional funding for states accepting funding under the law. It established procedural safeguards for parents and handicapped children and mandated an individualized program for each child requiring special education. In its first year of operation, some $200 million was appropriated by Congress to assist states in the funding of special education programs.

The second major federal law passed to protect the rights of disabled persons nationally, including those in elementary, secondary, and postsecondary programs, is Section 504 of the Rehabilitation Act of 1973. Section 504 is a corollary to Title IX (of the Education Amendments of 1972), the well-known law prohibiting discrimination based on sex in most federally funded education programs; it is also a direct descendant of Title VI (of the Civil Rights Act of 1964), the statute barring discrimination resulting from race or national origin. All three laws have in the past been monitored by the U.S. Office for Civil Rights, a division of the Department of Health, Education and Welfare. The new U.S. Department of Education has a Civil Rights Office to administer the education-related aspects of these laws.[10]

Section 504 outlaws discrimination against handicapped persons in any program receiving direct or indirect federal financial assistance; the protected person must be "otherwise qualified" to participate in the activity, whether employment, transportation, or education. In 1977, after a protracted battle between the federal bureaucracy and consumer activists resulted in a lawsuit seeking implementing regulations, HEW promulgated extensive guidelines describing the persons and programs covered by Section 504.

A third federal law, hardly as extensive as P.L. 94-142 and Section 504, was passed in 1978 to begin to provide for the special needs of gifted or talented exceptional children. The Gifted and Talented Children's Education Act (Title IX of the Education Amendments of 1978) does not allow for a uniform system of due process protections for these children; parents have no right to a hearing under the law, notice of testing or evaluations, nor any right to a specific program of special education or related services. Instead, this law increases national education funding for those states already developing and implementing programs in this area.[11] In addition, the Developmentally Disabled Assistance and Bill of Rights Act, Public Law 94-103 (42 U.S.C. § 6000 *et seq.*) sets forth certain rights for developmentally disabled individuals, contains specific requirements for habilitation plans, and requires states receiving funds under the act to establish a system to protect and advocate the rights of persons with developmental disabilities. The act also supports State Developmental Disabilities Councils and various programmatic activities. All these laws affect various groups of exceptional children. The full text of P.L. 94-142, Section 504 and their implementing regulations is set out in the appendixes.

1.2. THE RIGHT TO EDUCATION FOR RETARDED CHILDREN: PENNSYLVANIA ASSOCIATION FOR RETARDED CHILDREN V. COMMONWEALTH OF PENNSYLVANIA (343 F. SUPP. 279)

MASTERSON, District Judge.

This civil rights case, a class action, was brought by the Pennsylvania Association for Retarded Children and the parents of thirteen individual retarded children on behalf of all mentally retarded persons between the ages of 6 and 21 whom the Commonwealth of Pennsylvania, through its local school districts and intermediate units, is presently excluding from a program of education and training in the public schools. . . .

The exclusions of retarded children complained of are based upon four State statutes: (1) 24 Purd.Stat. Sec. 13-1375 which relieves the State Board of Education from any obligation to educate a child whom a public school psychologist certifies as uneducable and untrainable. The burden of caring for such a child then shifts to the Department of Welfare which has no obligation to provide any educational services for the child; (2) 24 Purd.Stat. Sec. 13-1304 which allows an indefinite postponement of admission to public school of any child who has not attained a mental age of five years; (3) Purd.Stat. Sec. 13-1330 which appears to *excuse* any child from compulsory school attendance whom a psychologist finds unable to profit therefrom and (4) 24 Purd.Stat. Sec. 13-1326 which defines compulsory school age as 8 to 17 years but has been used in practice to postpone admissions of retarded children until age 8 or to eliminate them from public schools at age 17.

Plaintiffs allege that Sections 1375 (uneducable and untrainable) and 1304 (mental age of 5 years) are constitutionally infirm both on their faces and as applied in three broad respects. First, plaintiffs argue that these statutes offend due process because they lack any provision for notice and a hearing before a retarded person is either excluded from a public education or a change is made in his educational assignment within the public system. Secondly, they assert that the two provisions violate equal protection because the premise of the statute which necessarily assumes that certain retarded children are uneducable and untrainable lacks a rational basis in fact. Finally, plaintiffs contend that because the Constitution and laws of Pennsylvania guarantee an education to all children, these two sections violate due process in that they arbitrarily and capriciously deny that given right to retarded children. Plaintiffs' third contention also raises a pendent question of state law, that is, whether the Pennsylvania Constitution as well as other laws of the Commonwealth already afford them a right to public education.

It is not alleged that Sections 1330 (excusal from compulsory attendance) or 1326 (definition of compulsory school age) are facially defective under the United States Constitution. Rather, plaintiffs contend that these provisions violate due process (lack of a prior hearing) and equal protection (no basis in fact to support exclusion) *as applied* to retarded children.

In addition, plaintiffs contend that the clear intent of Section 1330 is to forgive *parents* from any criminal penalty for what otherwise would be a violation of compulsory attendance requirements, and consequently, use of this provision to *exclude* retarded children constitutes an impermissible misinterpretation of state law. Likewise, plaintiffs assert that Section 1326 relates only to obligation of *parents* (under penalty of criminal sanctions) to place their children in public schools, and its use to *exclude* retarded children contravenes the obvious meaning of the statute.

. . . [T]he parties agreed upon a Stipulation which basically provides that no child who is mentally retarded or thought to be mentally retarded can be assigned initially (or re-assigned) to either a regular or special educational status, or excluded from a public education without a prior recorded hearing before a special hearing officer. At that hearing, parents have the right to representation by counsel, to examine their child's records, to compel the attendance of school officials who may have relevant evidence to offer, to cross-examine witnesses testifying on behalf of school officials and to introduce evidence of their own. . . .

On October 7th, 1971 the parties submitted a Consent Agreement to this Court which, along with the June 18th Stipulation, would settle the entire case. Essentially, this Agreement deals with the four state statutes in an effort to eliminate the alleged equal protection problems. As a proposed cure, the defendants agreed, *inter alia*, that since "the Commonwealth of Pennsylvania has undertaken to provide a free public education for all of its children between the ages of six and twenty-one years" (Paragraph 5), therefore, "it is the Commonwealth's obligation to place each mentally retarded child in a *free, public program of education and training appropriate to the child's capacity*." (Paragraph 7.) To effectuate this result without conceding the unconstitutionality of the foregoing statutes or upsetting the existing statutory scheme, the Attorney General of the Commonwealth agreed to issue Opinions declaring in substance that: (1) Section 1375 means that "insofar as the Department of Public Welfare is charged to arrange for the care, training and supervision of a child certified to it, the Department of Public Welfare must provide a program of education and training appropriate to the capacities of that child" (Paragraph 37); (2) Section 1304 means "*only* that a school district may refuse to accept into or retain in the lowest grade of the *regular* primary school [as contrasted with a *special* primary school] any child who has not attained a mental age of five years" (Paragraph 10); (3) Section 1330(2) means "*only* that a parent may be excused from liability under the compulsory attendance provisions of the School Code when, with the approval of the local school board and the Secretary of Education and the finding by an approved school psychologist, the parent elects to withdraw the child from attendance; Section 1330(2) may not be used by defendants, contrary to parents' wishes, to terminate or in any way deny access to a free public program of education and training to any mentally retarded child." (Paragraph 20); and (4) Section 1326 means "*only* that parents of a child have a compulsory duty while the child is between eight and seventeen years of age to assure his attendance in a program of education and training; and Section 1326 does not limit the ages between which a child must be granted access to a free public program of education and training [and may not be used as such]." (Paragraph 16.) Thus, possible use of these four provisions to exclude (or postpone) retarded children from a program of public education was effectively foreclosed by this Agreement. And on October 22, 1971, the Attorney General issued these agreed upon Opinions.

In addition, the Consent Agreement addresses itself to three other matters involving the education of retarded children which the plaintiffs did not specifically raise in their pleadings. First, in the area of pre-school education, the defendants agreed to cease applying 24 Purd.Stat. Sec. 13–1371 so as to deny retarded children below the age of six access to a free pre-school program of education and training appropriate to their learning capacities whenever the school districts provide such a pre-school program to *normal* children below the age of six. The Attorney General again issued an Opinion so interpreting Section 1371(1).

Next, the defendants agreed to cease applying 24 Purd.Stat. Sec. 13–1376 so as to deny tuition or tuition maintenance to any mentally retarded person. Basically, Section 1376 provides for the payment of tuition to private schools by the Commonwealth and local school districts (75% and 25% respectively) where, with the approval of the Department of Education, a child afflicted with blindness, deafness, cerebral palsy, brain damage or muscular dystrophy is attending a private school. Prior to the Consent Agreement, this statute was interpreted not to apply to retarded children unless they also suffered from one of the maladies mentioned above. Consequently, if the public sector excluded a retarded child (who lacked a multiple disability) under Section 1375, 1304, 1330 or 1326, his parents had to assume the full financial burden of educating and training him in a private school. Often, because of the special care required, this burden assumed formidable proportions. . . . Thus, the Attorney General issued an Opinion "construing the term 'brain damage' as used in Section 1376 . . . so as to include thereunder all mentally retarded persons, thereby making available to them tuition for day school and tuition and maintenance for residential school . . ." (Paragraph 27).

Finally, the defendants agreed to cease applying 24 Purd. Stat. Sec. 13-1372(3) so as "to deny [mentally retarded children] homebound instruction under that Section . . . merely because no physical disability accompanies the retardation or because retardation is not a short-term disability." (Paragraph 31.) Once again, the Attorney General issued an Opinion so construing this provision.

The lengthy Consent Agreement concludes by stating that "[e]very retarded person between the ages of six and twenty-one shall be provided access to a free public program of education and training appropriate to his capacities as soon as possible but in no event later than *September 1, 1972*." . . .

We then entered an *interim order*, without prejudice, pending notice to the class of plaintiffs and the class of defendants, which temporarily enjoined the defendants from applying (1) 24 Purd. Stat. Sections 13-1375, 1304, 1330 (2), and 1371(1) "so as to deny any mentally retarded child access to a free public program of education and training;" (2) Section 13-1376 "so as to deny tuition or tuition and maintenance to any mentally retarded person except on the same terms as may be applied to other exceptional children, including brain damaged children generally;" and (3) Section 13-1372(3) "[so as to deny] homebound instruction to any mentally retarded person merely because no physical disability accompanies the retardation or because it is not a short-term disability." . . .

1.3. Districtwide Relief for All Handicapped Students: Mills v. Board of Education, District of Columbia (348 F. Supp. 866)

WADDY, District Judge.

This is a civil action brought on behalf of seven children of school age by their next friends in which they seek a declaration of rights and to enjoin the defendants from exluding them from the District of Columbia Public Schools and/or denying them publicly supported education and to compel the defendants to provide them with immediate and adequate education and educational facilities in the public schools or alternative placement at public expense. They also seek additional and ancillary relief to effectuate the primary relief. They allege that although they can profit from an education either in regular classrooms with supportive services or in special classes adopted to their needs, they have been labelled as behavioral problems, mentally retarded, emotionally disturbed or hyperactive, and denied admission to the public schools or excluded therefrom after admission, with no provision for alternative educational placement or periodic reivew. The action was certified as a class action under Rule 23(b) (1) and (2 of Federal Rules of Civil Procedure by order of the Court dated December 17, 1971.

The defendants are the Board of Education of the District of Columbia and its members, the Superintendent of Schools for the District of Columbia and subordinate school officials, the Commissioner of the District of Columbia and certain subordinate officials and the District of Columbia.

THE PROBLEM

The genesis of this case is found (1) in the failure of the District of Columbia to provide publicly supported education and training to plaintiffs and other "exceptional" children, members of their class, and (2) the excluding, suspending, expelling, reassigning and transferring of "exceptional" children from regular public school classes without affording them due process of law.

The problem of providing special education for "exceptional" children (mentally retarded, emotionally disturbed, physically handicapped, hyperactive and other children with behavioral problems) is one of major proportions in the District of Columbia. The precise number of such children cannot be stated because the District has continously failed to comply with Section 31–208 of the District of Columbia Code which requires a census of all children aged 3 to 18 in the District to be taken. Plaintiffs estimate that there are "... 22,000 retarded, emotionally disturbed, blind, deaf, and speech or learning disabled children, and perhaps as many as 18,000 of these children are not being furnished with programs of specialized education." According to data prepared by the Board of Education, Division of Planning, Research and Evaluation, the District of Columbia provides publicly supported special education programs of various descriptions to at least 3880 school age children. However, in a 1971 report to the Department of Health, Education and Welfare, the District of Columbia Public Schools admitted that an estimated 12,340 handicapped children were not to be served in the 1971–72 school year.

Each of the minor plaintiffs in this case qualifies as an "exceptional" child. . . .

Plaintiffs' entitlement to relief in this case is clear. The applicable statutes and regulations and the Constitution of the United States require it.

Statutes and Regulations

Section 31–201 of the District of Columbia Code requires that:

> Every parent, guardian, or other person residing [permantly or temporarily] in the District of Columbia who has custody or control of a child between the ages of seven and sixteen years shall cause said child to be regularly instructed in a public school or in a private or parochial school or instructed privately during the period of each year in which the public schools of the District of Columbia are in session. . . .

Under Section 31–203, a child may be "excused" from attendance only when

> . . . . upon examination ordered by . . . [the Board of Education of the District of Columbia], [the child] is found to be unable mentally or physically to profit from attendance at school: Provided, however, that if such examination shows that such child may benefit from specialized instruction adapted to his needs, he shall attend upon such instruction.

Failure of a parent to comply with Section 31–201 constitutes a criminal offense. D.C. Code 31–207. The Court need not belabor the fact that requiring parents to see that their children attend school under pain of criminal penalties presupposes that an educational opportunity will be made available to the children. The Board of Education is required to make such opportunity available. It has adopted rules and regulations consonant with the statutory direction. Chapter XIII of the Board Rules contains the following:

1.1— All children of the ages hereinafter prescribed who are bona fide residents of the District of Columbia are entitled to admission and free tuition in the Public Schools of the District of Columbia, subject to the rules, regulations, and orders of the Board of Education and the applicable statutes.

14.1— Every parent, guardian, or other person residing permanently or temporarily in the District of Columbia who has custody or control of a child residing in the District of Columbia between the ages of seven and sixteen years shall cause said child to be regularly instructed in a public school or in a private or parochial school or instructed privately during the period of each year in which the Public Schools of the District of Columbia are in session, provided that instruction given in such private or parochial school, or privately, is deemed reasonably equivalent by the Board of Education to the instruction given in the Public Schools.

14.3— The Board of Education of the District of Columbia may, upon written recommendation of the Superintendent of Schools, issue a certificate excusing from attendance at school a child who, upon examination by the Department of Pupil Appraisal, Study and Attendance or by the Department of Public Health of the District of Columbia, is found to be unable mentally or physically to profit from attendance at school: Provided, however, that if such examination shows that such child may benefit from specialized instruction adapted to his needs, he shall be required to attend such classes.

Thus the Board of Education has an obligation to provide whatever specialized instruction that will benefit the child. By failing to provide plaintiffs and their class the publicly supported specialized education to which they are entitled, the Board of Education violates the above statutes and its own regulations.

The Constitution—Equal Protection and Due Process

The Supreme Court in Brown v. Board of Education, 347 U.S. 483, 493, 74 S.Ct. 686, 691, 98 L.Ed. 873 (1954) stated:

> Today, education is perhaps the most important function of state and local governments. Compulsory school attendance laws and the great expenditures for education both demonstrate our recognition of the importance of education to our democratic society. It is required in the performance of our most basic public responsibilities, even service in the armed forces. It is the very foundation of good citizenship. Today it is a principal instrument in awakening the child to cultural values, in preparing him for later professional training, and in helping him to adjust normally to his environment. In these days, it is doubtful that any child may reasonably be expected to succeed in life if he is denied the opportunity of an education. *Such an opportunity, where the state has undertaken to provide it, is a right which must be made available to all on equal terms.* (emphasis supplied)

Bolling v. Sharpe, 347 U.S. 497, 74 S.Ct. 693, 98 L.Ed. 884, decided the same day as *Brown*, applied the *Brown* rationale to the District of Columbia public schools by finding that:

> Segregation in public education is not reasonably related to any proper governmental objective, and thus it imposes on Negro children of the District of Columbia a burden that constitutes an arbitrary deprivation of their liberty in violation of the Due Process Clause.

In Hobson v. Hansen, 269 F.Supp. 401 (D.D.C.1967) Circuit Judge J. Skelly Wright considered the pronouncements of the Supreme Court in the intervening years and stated that "... the Court has found the due process clause of the Fourteenth Amendment elastic enough to embrace not only the First and Fourth Amendments, but the self-incrimination clause of the Fifth, the speedy trial, confrontation and assistance of counsel clauses of the Sixth, and the cruel and unusual clause of the Eighth." (269 F.Supp. 401 at 493, citations omitted). Judge Wright concluded "(F)rom these considerations the court draws the conclusion that the doctrine of equal educational opportunity—the equal protection clause in its application to public school education—is in its full sweep a component of due process binding on the District under the due process clause of the Fifth Amendment."

In Hobson v. Hansen, *supra*, Judge Wright found that denying poor public school children educational opportunities equal to that available to more affluent public school children was violative of the Due Process Clause of the Fifth Amendment. A *fortiori*, the defendants' conduct here, denying plaintiffs and their class not just an equal publicly supported education but all publicly supported education while providing such education to other children, is violative of the Due Process Clause.

Not only are plaintiffs and their class denied the publicly supported education to which they are entitled many are suspended or expelled from regular schooling or specialized instruction or reassigned without any prior hearing and are given no periodic review thereafter. Due process of law requires a hearing prior to exclusion, termination of classification into a special program. . . .

The defendants are required by the Constitution of the United States, the District of Columbia Code, and their own regulations to provide a publicly-supported education for these "exceptional" children. Their failure to fulfill this clear duty to include and retain these children in the public school system, or otherwise provide them with publicly-supported education, and their failure to afford them due process hearing and periodical review, cannot be excused by the claim that there are insufficient funds. In Goldberg v. Kelly, 397 U.S. 254, 90 S.Ct. 1011, 25 L.Ed.2d 287 (1969) the Supreme Court, in a case that involved the right of a welfare recipient to a hearing before termination of his benefits, held that Constitutional rights must be afforded citizens despite the greater expense involved. The Court stated at page 266, 90 S.Ct. at page 1019, that "the State's interest that his [welfare recipient] payments not be erroneously terminated, clearly outweighs the State's competing concern to prevent any increase in its fiscal and administrative burdens." Similarly the District of Columbia's interest in educating the excluded children clearly must outweigh its interest in preserving its financial resources. If sufficient funds are not available to finance all of the services and programs that are needed and desirable in the system then the available funds must be expended equitably in such a manner that no child is entirely excluded from a publicly supported education consistent with his needs and ability to benefit therefrom. The inadequacies of the District of Columbia Public School System whether occasioned by insufficient funding or administrative inefficiency, certainly cannot be permitted to bear more heavily on the "exceptional" or handicapped child than on the normal child. . . .

1.4. PROGRAMS FOR NEWLY IDENTIFIED CHILDREN: FREDERICK L. V. THOMAS (557 F.2D 374)

OPINION OF THE COURT

ADAMS, Circuit Judge.

In recent years, increasing attention has been focused upon the educational needs of learning disabled children. The lawsuit which has given rise to the present appeal is reflective of this trend. Filed in 1974, the complaint alleges that, in violation of Pennsylvania statutes and the United States Constitution, the School District of Philadelphia (the District) does not provide learning disabled students in its system with a minimally appropriate education.

After certifying the suit as a class action, the trial court declined to abstain, determined that the District had failed to meet its obligations under state law and decided that in order for the District to fulfill its responsibilities it would have to identify all learning disabled students in its educational system.

I. THE BACKGROUND

A.

Since Judge Newcomer's opinion on the merits lucidly sets forth the intricate backdrop for this litigation, we find it necessary to provide only a capsule review of the most salient facts.

Knowledge of the etiology and nature of specific learning disabilities is still in an embryonic state. Thus, it is not surprising that there are many differences of opinion among experts in the field, and that whatever consensus does exist is on a relatively high plane of generality.

Authorities appear to agree that learning disabilities constitute disorders in basic psychological processes that inhibit victims from understanding, assimilating, interpreting or retaining language and other concepts in a normal manner. Though learning disabled students often have the basic capability for normal intelligence, their disabilities ordinarily prevent them from benefiting from regular instruction and from achieving their true potential. As a result, learning disabled students frequently experience substantial frustration, and such reaction is manifested in emotional disturbances and socially disruptive conduct.

While the exact causes of learning disabilities have not, as of yet, been pinpointed, medical testing has led experts to believe that brain injury, either at birth or during early childhood, is a major factor. Also, there is data indicating that the nationwide incidence of learning disability is between one and three per cent of the population.

It appears that experts agree that with the provision of special remedial services, learning disabled students can have a beneficial educational experience. The programs that are necessary to achieve this end depend on the severity of a pupil's disability. Those with the most serious disorders will need separate classes or other forms of special attention. On the other hand, students with less drastic problems can benefit from instruction in regular classrooms so long as supplemental supportive services are available. This latter approach is generally referred to as "mainstreaming."

Instruments for identifying learning disabled students are still in a developmental stage; at this time the basic tools for the task are the administration of standardized achievement tests and subsequent psychological examinations. However, there is little uniformity in the process of selecting those pupils who possibly are learning disabled and should be analyzed by psychologists. Under some programs, tests are administered to an entire school population, and those in the lowest percentiles are then examined by psychologists who ascertain whether they suffer from learning disabilities. Other methods rely upon teacher or parent referrals of particular pupils to school psychologists for ultimate identification of learning disabled students.

B.

It has been estimated that three per cent of the students in the District—approximately 8000 children—suffer from specific learning disabilities. Nonetheless, the record discloses that only 1300 learning disabled students in the District have been identified. The District does not test-screen all pupils in order to identify those who are learning disabled. Rather, it places primary reliance upon teacher referrals to psychologists. Judge Newcomer found, however, that, for a number of reasons, the referral method is not an adequate way for identifying pupils suffering from learning disabilities.

At the present time, the District furnishes several varieties of remedial education for learning disabled students. First, certain special educational services are available to those learning disabled students who, pursuant to Pennsylvania statutes, have been identified as "exceptional." Such services include full and part-time separate instruction for learning disabled students. None of these types of special education, the Board has admitted, are provided to pupils in the seventh grade and above. And only relatively few students in the fifth and sixth grades receive these services.

The District also offers a number of general remedial services to "underachievers," but such services are not specifically directed towards learning disabled students. Indeed, a student does not have to be identified as learning disabled or "exceptional" in order to be eligible for these programs. Moreover, since 40 percent of the students in the system—about 105,000 children—are considered to be underachievers, it is far from clear whether the unidentified learning disabled students who are not in special education programs are receiving general remedial services.

Some efforts have been made by the District to increase the scope of available remedial programs. Then, in 1975, the District submitted a plan to the Pennsylvania Department of Education that would have provided special education for all learning disabled students in the system. A "Special Education Needs Budget" detailing the appropriations required to implement the expanded services that the plan suggested was presented simultaneously. While the Pennsylvania Department of Education approved the special education plan, the Department did not provide sufficient funds to support the proposal. The plan was thus not implemented by the District, and the services available to the learning disabled have not been expanded.

C.

The problem of learning disabled children has been addressed by the Commonwealth through both statutes and regulations. Pennsylvania's Public School Code makes special provision for the education of "exceptional children." "Exceptional children" are those "children of school age who deviate from the average in physical, mental, emotional or social characteristics to such an extent that they require special educational facilities or services."

A series of duties are imposed on various governmental entities by the Code. Local school authorities must "report . . . every exceptional child" within the district. The Commonwealth is required to promulgate "standards and regulations for the proper education and training of all exceptional children." School districts must submit plans for the "proper education" of exceptional children for state approval. And the local districts must "provide and maintain . . . special classes or schools in accordance with the approved plan."

In 1975, the Commonwealth issued regulations to effectuate this statutory framework. These regulations employ the statutory definition of "exceptional children." The term "exceptional children" is then divided into three subcomponents—one of which is "handicapped school-aged persons." And the latter category is defined as including "physically handicapped persons who are . . . learning disabled." The regulations reiterate the obligation of local school districts to prepare plans which provide for the education of exceptional children. They go on to state that "all handicapped and school-aged persons identified shall be provided with an appropriate program of education or training." Finally, the regulations declare that "if a handicapped school-aged person has been reevaluated and is found no longer to have the exceptional characteristics that require special education programs and services," the local district may return him to the regular educational setting.

II. THE PROCEEDINGS BELOW

This suit was filed in January, 1974, and was certified as a class action in May of that year. The class is composed of "all children attending public schools within the City of Philadelphia who have 'specific learning disabilities' and who are deprived of an education appropriate to their specialized needs." In July of 1974, the trial court granted a motion by the Commonwealth to intervene as a defendant.

After extensive discovery had been conducted, trial was scheduled for September, 1975. On September 15, 1975, a week and one-half before the trial was due to commence, the Commonwealth filed a motion requesting that the district court dismiss the action or in the alternative to postpone an adjudication of the controversy pursuant to the abstention doctrine. Judge Newcomer took the motion under advisement and trial proceeded.

In January, 1976, Judge Newcomer denied the Commonwealth's motions. He determined that the constitutional claims asserted by the plaintiffs were not so frivolous as to warrant dismissal and that state law was not sufficiently unclear so as to mandate abstention.

The district court rendered its decision on August 2, 1976. In his opinion, Judge Newcomer did not confront the constitutional claims, since he ruled that the plaintiff class was entitled to relief on its state law theory.

There were several components to the state law holding. First, Judge Newcomer determined that, under Pennsylvania law, learning disabled children are entitled to an "appropriate" or "proper" education. He then ruled that the District had not met this responsibility, and concluded that the District was under an obligation to identify all learning disabled students.

The opinion of the trial court did not provide for immediate relief; instead, after further proceedings were held, Judge Newcomer issued Remedial Order Number 1 on August 13, 1976. This directive is only the first step in the process of crafting a remedy. It provides that a master be appointed to oversee and monitor the implementation of the court-ordered relief. The District was commanded to submit a plan to the Master by October 15, 1976, ". . . which is reasonably calculated to identify all of its learning disabled pupils." This identification arrangement was to be put into effect immediately after its final approval.

Judge Newcomer's order also mandated the eventual submission of interim and final plans for "the appropriate placement of all students identified as learning disabled." In addition, it directed that the final plan go into effect by the beginning of the 1978–79 school year.

Under the Remedial Order the Master has the authority to approve or disapprove any plan submitted by the District. Finally, any unresolved disputes pertaining to the implementation of the court's order or the District's plans is to be submitted to the court. The District has noticed an appeal from the entry of Remedial Order Number 1. . . .

V. IDENTIFICATION OF STUDENTS

We now turn to the remaining issue, namely, whether Judge Newcomer erred in requiring the District to identify all learning disabled students in the system.

The District maintains that such an order goes beyond the Pennsylvania statutory mandate. Under Pennsylvania law, only "exceptional" children are entitled to special educational services. And "exceptional" children are those who are sufficiently abnormal so as to require special services. The District concedes that some learning disabled students fit within the "exceptional" category inasmuch as their disorders are so serious that they cannot benefit from regular education. However, the District continues, not all learning disabled children are necessarily "extraordinary children," since some can benefit from a standard educational program and are consequently not in need of special educational services. Because not all learning disabled students must be given a special education under state law, the District concludes that the state statutes and regulations do not require it to identify all learning disabled students.

In reply, the plaintiffs have put forward a series of contentions to support Judge Newcomer's conclusion. They urge, first, that the state regulations indicate that all learning disabled students are to be considered "exceptional" children. This is so, they assert, since one of the subcategories of "exceptional" children—"handicapped school-aged persons"—is defined as including "learning disabled" children.

The plaintiffs also propose a more functional argument. They note that a large proportion of the learning disabled students in the Philadelphia public school system are presently unidentified. If such students were identified, it might be ascertained that some of them are not in need of special education. However, the plaintiffs add, the only means by which it can be determined which learning disabled children are "exceptional," and thus entitled under state law to special services, is to identify the entire population of learning disabled children, to assess the severity of the disability of each of them, and thereby to determine whether they are in need of special education.

We find this latter proposition to be persuasive. Identification is a means to the end of assuring that those children who are entitled to special educational services receive them. The District's present identification methods, as Judge Newcomer found, are somewhat haphazard and ineffective. As noted above, only 1300 of the estimated 8000 learning disabled students in the system are presently identified. It is possible that, as the District claims, many or most of these unidentified learning disabled students do not need special educational services or are currently receiving adequate remedial services. However, so long as these students are unidentified and the nature and extent of their learning disabilities go unassessed, it will be impossible to know with any certainty whether the District is discharging its statutory obligation regarding these pupils. It would thus appear that the only way to assure that all students who require special educational services receive "appropriate" training pursuant to state law is for the District to adopt procedures calculated to isolate the entire population of learning disabled students and to evaluate the need of these pupils for special educational services. This is what Judge Newcomer ordered, and we cannot say that he misconstrued the mandate of Pennsylvania law in so holding.

It is important to emphasize those matters upon which we express no opinion. We do not rule upon the content of the education that Pennsylvania law requires the District to provide to its "exceptional" children. Nor do we address the problem of precisely which students must be given an "appropriate" education under the relevant statutes and regulations. We hold only that Judge Newcomer did not err in ordering that the District, in order to meet its statutory obligations towards "exceptional" children, must initially identify and evaluate all learning disabled students.

The order of the district court insofar as it mandates the identification of all learning disabled students in the District will be affirmed.

1.5. NOTES

1. 347 U.S. 483 (1954) and extensive discussion cited therein.
2. *Id.* at 493.
3. Pennsylvania Association for Retarded Children v. Commonwealth of Pennsylvania, 334 F. Supp. 1257 (E.D. Pa. 1971) and 343 F. Supp. 279 (E.D. Pa. 1972). The testimony of Dr. I. Ignacy Goldberg detailing the history and requirements of special education programs is especially relevant here.

4. 22 Pennsylvania Code, Chapter 13.
5. 348 F. Supp. 866 (D.D.C. 1972).
6. Catherine D. v. Pittenger, Civil No. 74-2435 (E.D. Pa., Order, June 27, 1975).
7. 419 F. Supp. 960 (E.D. Pa. 1976), aff'd, 557 F.2d 374 (3rd Cir. 1977).
8. Examples of early litigation brought to define and develop the rights of children include Fial-kowski v. Shapp, 405 F. Supp. 946 (E.D. Pa. 1973); Panitch v. Wisconsin, 371 F. Supp. 935 (E.D. Wis. 1974); Harrison v. Michigan, 350 F. Supp. 846 (E.D. Mich. 1972); Lebanks v. Spears, 60 F.R.D. 135 (E.D. La. 1973); Maryland Association for Retarded Children v. Mary-land, Equity No. 100-182-77676 (Cir. Ct. 1974). For additional early cases *see The Right of Handicapped Children to an Education: The Phoenix of Rodriguez*, 59 CORNELL L. REV. 519 (1974).
9. 20 U.S.C. §§ 1401, *et seq.*; 34 C.F.R. Part 300.
10. Section 504 is cited as 20 U.S.C. § 794; for its implementing regulations *see* 34 C.F.R. Part 104 (formerly 45 C.F.R. Part 84). Title IX is 20 U.S.C. §§ 1681 *et seq.*,—for regulations *see* 34 C.F.R. Part 106; Title VI is 42 U.S.C. § 2000(d).
11. 20 U.S.C. §§ 3311 *et seq. See* Central York School District v. Commonwealth of Pennsylvania, 349 A.2d 167 (Pa. Cmwlth. 1979); *see also* Irwin v. McHenry Community Consolidated School District, as cited in *Education Daily*, May 4, 1979.

2

A NATIONAL RIGHT TO EDUCATION
The Education for All Handicapped Children Act

2.1. AN OVERVIEW

As federal and state courts throughout the nation developed the constitutional right of handicapped children to equal treatment in the public school system, Congress considered a uniform national procedure for funding and implementing these educational rights. In the spirit of court decisions in the area, as well as in recognition that vast differences existed among the states in providing services to handicapped children, P.L. 94-142 was passed. It was a critical statutory recognition that, in the famous words of the *PARC* court,

> ... all mentally retarded persons are capable of benefitting from a program of education and training; that the greatest number of retarded persons, given such education and training, are capable of achieving self-sufficiency ... that the earlier such education and training begins, the more thoroughly and the more efficiently a mentally retarded person will benefit from it; and, whether begun early or not, that a mentally retarded person can benefit at any point in his life and development from a program of education and training.[1]

Congress found that of the eight million children it identified as handicapped in the United States, more than half were not receiving appropriate educational programs, and the special needs of the remaining half were not fully met. Fully one million children were entirely excluded from schools, forcing families to obtain their child's education, if at all, at great expense. In response to these findings, the law mandates a free program of education and training "designed to meet the unique needs" of each handicapped child. Although no state is required to accept funding under 94-142, those that do must provide the services and protections mandated.

The keystone of the law is the requirement that every handicapped student be provided with a "free appropriate public education," defined in the law as

19

a program of special education and related services which (a) have been provided at
public expense, under public supervision and direction, and without charge, (b) meet
the standards of the state educational agency, (3) include an appropriate preschool,
elementary, or secondary school education in the state involved, and (d) are provided
in conformity with the individualized education program. . . .[2]

This provision is controversial because of its generality. "Appropriateness," depending on the orientation of the particular school administrator or parent, may
be interpreted in a variety of ways. For some school officials, a program meets the
legal standard if a child is permitted to attend school and is provided with services
a local board of education can afford. Some parents, on the other hand, have
argued that every service that will aid a child should be provided to the fullest
extent possible. Legally speaking, a student need not be offered the best or most
expensive educational techniques, materials, and services available, but public
schools must design and develop an individualized plan for the exceptional
person so that learning can be attained. As the definition indicates, the program
must be provided at no cost to the person's parent or guardian.

Special education is further defined to include "classroom instruction, instruction in physical education, home instruction and instruction in hospitals
and institutions."[3] The specially designed instruction must be offered in the most
normal or least restrictive environment possible. Together with special education, services that will help a child benefit from the program must be provided.
The services described in 94-142 may be transportation, psychological counseling, speech and language or occupational and physical therapy, as well as recreation. This list of services is lengthy but not all-inclusive, so that each child's
needs may be considered. As a result, school officials and parents must allow for
related services that may be somewhat esoteric but that will help a child to learn.

Naturally, disputes arise over the type and nature of the related services to be
offered. One particular bone of contention is the question of therapy. School
administrators have argued that therapy is a medical or treatment service and
need not be provided under an education law. These officials frequently refuse to provide therapy or psychological counseling, instead referring parents to
independent clinics. Others have been known to claim that no related services
need be provided, thus limiting a special education program to classroom instruction. The latter view is contrary to the mandate of 94-142. In all cases a
parent may be called upon to prove, by using the opinions of psychologists,
medical doctors, or other experts, that a certain related service is required.
Although services will undoubtedly help each child, a service is legally mandated
only when a child would otherwise fail to benefit from a program of special
education. Officials are not permitted to deny services merely because they are
not presently provided to any other student or because their provision would
necessitate the hiring of additional personnel. Additionally, a child may not be
placed on a waiting list for a service (or any aspect of a program).

For each student, 94-142 requires school administrators, parents, and teachers to develop an Individualized Education Program (IEP). This is another aspect of the law that teachers and administrators often challenge as a time-consuming and burdensome task. Indeed, the time and paper work involved can be substantial, but a program for each person must be developed. Basically, an IEP includes a statement of the educational goals to be achieved during specific periods and for the entire school year; the educational programs and techniques that will be used to bring about these goals; and the related services, including transportation, for each child. From the standpoint of both parents and educators, it is wise to include all of these aspects so that confusion and misunderstanding will be avoided. Parents are given the opportunity to participate in an IEP meeting, and the proceedings must be made understandable to them. Legal or educational jargon must be avoided, and unless infeasible, the parents' mode of communication or native language should be used during the planning session. That may entail the use of a sign language interpreter if parents are deaf, or a language interpreter for someone whose native language is not English. The IEP must be reviewed at least annually to see if the goals are being met. Everyone involved in this process should realize that the IEP is not a contract, but a guide to follow during the school year. Despite a statement to this effect in the law, teachers and supervisors and professional unions are concerned with the possibility of "educational malpractice lawsuits" for noncompliance with the IEP. These are, in fact, becoming more common and will be discussed in Sections 2.5. and 5.4.

Due process procedures, such as those developed in PARC and similar cases, are set forth in 94-142 for all handicapped children covered by the law. Parents must be notified before an initial evaluation of a child who is thought to be handicapped; similarly, a parent is entitled to request a full and free battery of evaluations performed by a multidisciplinary team when a child is experiencing learning problems. The team consists of the professionals necessary to determine a child's disability, if any, and usually includes a school psychologist. As in PARC's provisions for retarded students, parents must be notified when any change in an educational placement or related services is proposed. A change in the physical location of a particular program may also require notice if it necessitates the addition or modification of related services, as in the case of a handicapped child who would need assistance in gaining physical access to a new program location.

Perhaps the aspect of 94-142 that has provoked the most debate is the provision requiring integration of handicapped students with their nonhandicapped peers. Every educational agency must make certain

(1) that to the maximum extent appropriate, handicapped children, including children in public or private institutions or other care facilities, are educated with children who are not handicapped, and (2) that special classes, separate schooling or other

removal of handicapped children from the regular educational environment occurs
only when the nature or severity of the handicap is such that education in regular
classes with the use of supplementary aids and services cannot be achieved satisfactorily.[4]

For example, a physically handicapped student with academic ability about
the same as students of a similar age must be placed in a regular classroom.
Regular classrooms must be used for all handicapped students who can learn best
in them.

Interestingly, the term "mainstreaming," which is not mentioned once
in the text of 94-142 or its implementing regulations, has evoked fear and
misunderstanding among a number of parents and teachers. Mainstreaming
refers to the placement of handicapped children with nonhandicapped children
in regular classes. Confusion arises from the misconception that mainstreaming
is required in all cases, even if a regular class is not the best placement. Teachers
have expressed concern over the presence of potentially disruptive handicapped
students who present discipline or other educational management problems.
Teachers usually must handle large classes, and these concerns may be very real
in the event a child is misplaced. In some cases parents may oppose mainstreaming for handicapped children with normal intelligence. This concern is especially prevalent in the field of education for hearing-impaired persons. Although
most hearing-impaired students are of normal intelligence, some parents feel that
these children are best placed with other children who have had training in oral,
sign language, or total communication (both oral and sign) programs, before the
effective date in 94-142 of October 1977. Others disagree, and it remains for the
student and parent to advocate their own views about appropriateness.

Parents' and officials' main vehicle for objecting to or obtaining any aspect
of a program is the special education hearing. When a program must be developed and an impasse develops between parents and provider, either side can
request a hearing. An impartial fact-finder presides. Each party may be represented by legal counsel. If it is felt that a student's interests run contrary to the
parent's proposed placement, a separate advocate should be made available to the
student. Any party to the hearing may call experts, as in the PARC procedures,
and a written opinion must be issued by the officer, with a copy to each party.
This decision, based on a transcript of testimony, may be appealed to the chief
state school official and then to an appropriate state or federal district court. In all
contested situations, the student remains in the same class as when the disagreement arose unless an interim placement is mutually agreed upon.

Another major aspect of 94-142 concerns access to a handicapped student's
records. Essentially, the provisions of the Family Educational Rights and Privacy
Act (FERPA),[5] popularly known as the Buckley Amendment, are included in the
special education law. FERPA allows parents (or students who are over 18 or are
attending a postsecondary institution) to obtain access to the educational records.
If a parent or eligible student then determines that any aspect of the records is

incorrect or misleading, a request to delete or "amend" the offending language can be made to the educational authorities. If this request is refused, an informal hearing may be held to resolve the dispute. A hearing officer is mandated, but he need only be an individual not directly involved in the controversy. Written notes of testimony must be kept, and a written opinion issued. Finally, if the amendment is refused after the hearing, a parent has the right to insert in the student's permanent record a statement describing the nature of the dispute and setting forth reasons why the deletion should have been made.

P.L. 94-142 has increasingly been asserted by advocacy groups and individual plaintiffs when they believe the right to special education is violated. Because of its extensive language and specific procedural protections, it is an excellent tool for litigators in the field of disability law who represent clients of school age. Recently a federal district court decided the first case that went to trial under the law, *Armstrong v. Kline.*[6] The main controversy was the definition of the somewhat amorphous term "free appropriate public education." In this action, medical, psychological, and educational experts testified that plaintiffs and a few other seriously impaired students required programs in excess of the normal school year (in this case 180 days) in order to learn to the fullest extent of their individual capabilities. These children would regress so substantially when their programs were interrupted that they would begin each September session without any retention of previous skills.

The court held in favor of the plaintiffs, disallowing the policy of limiting education to 180 days, as applied in this case. According to the court, it is "sometimes still difficult to determine precisely what the state is required to provide"[7] under the Education for All Handicapped Children Act. Educators must first look to the goals of an education program in order to determine the unique needs of a particular handicapped child. These needs, the court held, are similar to those described in *PARC*, because 94-142 was, in large part, based on the holding of that court. The ultimate goal of education is the opportunity to achieve that degree of "self sufficiency"[8] and independence from care-takers which will enable a handicapped person to become a contributing member of society.[9] The court held that in certain cases additional services must be provided to meet the unique needs of handicapped children. This case undoubtedly has significant implications for parents, students, and educational administrators who must plan and obtain funding for students in accordance with the *Armstrong* court's decision. (For the text and a fuller discussion of *Armstrong*, see Section 5.1.)

Mattie T. v. Holladay[10] is another early case that illustrates the sweeping effect of P.L. 94-142 on one state's inadequate special education system. The settlement, approved in February 1979 by a federal judge in Mississippi, was made on behalf of all handicapped children in the state. The plaintiffs included children who were excluded from school, as well as those poorly served and a class of minority children who had been mislabeled as retarded and placed in special classes based on inappropriate testing procedures. The consent decree covers all aspects of the federal law and sets forth the state's specific obligations under P.L. 94-142. It includes the requirements that children be educated in the least restrictive environment; that testing be done in a nondiscriminatory manner; that a complaint procedure be implemented for consumers; that there be a prohibition on suspension of handicapped children in excess of three days; and that procedural safeguards be provided. Unlike many other right-to-education cases, a system of compensatory education was also promulgated.

2.2. Court-Ordered Implementation of P.L. 94-142: Mattie T. v. Holladay No. DC-75-31-S (N.D. Miss. Jan 26, 1979)

The extract that follows is from a Children's Defense Fund memorandum, cited in 3 Mental Disability L. Rep. 98 (March–April 1979):

The major components of the consent decree are:

(i) Least Restrictive Environment (Mainstreaming)

The decree establishes specific criteria for determining when a school district can place handicapped children in classes and buildings separate from the regular education environment. It also requires all state agencies administering institutions to develop specific plans with local school districts for placement of many institutionalized children into local district day programs and provides that placement in these noninstitutional programs be part of the individualized educational plan (IEP) process. The decree also establishes a system of surrogate parents to represent children who are placed in foster homes or institutions and do not have parents.

(ii) Non-Discriminatory Testing

The decree requires the state to hire outside experts to evaluate and revamp the entire state procedure for classifying and placing handicapped children. The experts' report, due this summer, is to be implemented by a change in state policy and a state-wide two-year teacher training program. Because black children are disproportionately placed in classes for the mentally retarded and excluded from classes for the learning disabled, the decree establishes a specific goal for the state to cut this disparity at least in half within three years. Lastly, the decree sets a strict timetable for the individual evaluation-placement process.

(iii) Compensatory Education

Each local school district must identify all children misclassified as mentally retarded and provide them an opportunity for a compensatory educational program. Children under 15 are to receive tutoring and other services to get them on track for a diploma. Older children will have a choice between this academic assistance or a combined GED/vocational education program. This compensatory program is to be provided beyond the Mississippi school age of 21 years, if necessary.

(iv) Suspensions

To insure that handicapped children's problems are addressed programatically and not ignored, school districts are prohibited from removing children from school for longer than three days. Such three-day removals can occur only if the child's behavior represents an immediate physical danger to himself or herself or others or constitutes a clear emergency within the school such that removal is essential. Serial three-day removals are prohibited. A three-day removal triggers a review of the child's educational program and services.

(v) Complaint Procedure

The decree establishes a state-wide mechanism for complaints of systemic problems.

(vi) State Department of Education Monitoring and Enforcement

' The decree strengthens the state system of monitoring local school districts' and other state agencies' compliance with federal law, including a requirement that the state interview parents of children served by the agency being monitored and specific timelines for state remedial action. The decree also requires the state to withhold federal funds from noncomplying districts or agencies.

(vii) Procedural Safeguards and Child Find

The decree improves present state practices by requiring the state and school districts to distribute to parents of all handicapped children in the state an agreed-upon Parents' Rights Booklet, to compile decisions of hearing officers and make them available to the public, and to conduct outreach to community groups (including Headstart programs) in conducting child find.

2.3. FREE APPROPRIATE PUBLIC EDUCATION[11]

Each federal law has its particular concepts that become widely known. One such phrase in P.L. 94-142 is "free appropriate public education," or "FAPE"—a term from which all else flows. Each child reached by this law must be provided with a FAPE, but the term means different things to parents, school administrators, and teachers. FAPE is defined under the law as special education and related services that must be offered to each handicapped child who requires them, at no charge to parents and at the public's expense. Each local school district is responsible for ensuring that all of its resident handicapped children are provided with a free program of education.

From this hopeful beginning, the law informs us that a FAPE must be available to all handicapped children between the ages of three and twenty-one, and no later than September 1, 1980. This age range applies to any agency that receives federal money, unless state law or a court order precludes funding a program to persons who are from three to five or eighteen to twenty-one years old. 94-142 also sets a goal referred to as "full educational opportunity"—services for persons from birth to twenty-one years old, along with the mandate that persons from birth to twenty-one be identified and located. The Department of Education's comments explain this requirement. Locating and identifying hand-icapped persons from birth to twenty-one will assist educational agencies in preparing programs for these persons and in meeting the goal of full educational opportunity. Experts have found (and common sense would indicate) that the earliest possible educational intervention is desirable if a handicapped person is to achieve his potential. If they choose, states may provide services to a person of any age. If state officials do choose to provide services, education must be offered to every handicapped student in the same age category. Similarly, if school services or extracurricular activities are provided to typical children in a particu-lar age group, handicapped children of the same age must be provided with similar services.

These dictates raise an important policy matter. If school officials are pro-viding services and activities to other than exceptional children and advocates demand similar consideration for their clients, it is possible that the benefit granted typical children will be withdrawn. Equal treatment may well be defined as *no* service for every student. This fact underlines the need for parents of all children to work together when making demands of educational authorities. Advocates should note that 94-142 does require that "each agency" take steps to ensure that its handicapped children have available to them the variety of educa-tional programs and services available to nonhandicapped children in the area served—including art, music, industrial arts, consumer and homemaking educa-tion, and vocational education.

A specific and truly special system of instruction must be developed to meet each handicapped child's "unique needs," and must be provided free of charge to parents, guardians, or students. Payment of incidental fees required of regular education students may also be required of handicapped persons. (Most educa-tion advocates feel that *no* fees, whether for special or regular education, may be charged for materials or services that are required components of the educational program.)

The program may include training in the classroom, physical education, and training in hospitals and institutions or at home. Physical education and vocational education are considered special education under the law when they are specially developed as a method of instruction for a particular child.

Physical education is part of the special educational program if it includes the development of physical and motor fitness; fundamental motor skills and patterns; and skills in aquatics, dance, games, and sports. Also included are movement education and motor development techniques. Vocational education includes educational programs that prepare an individual for career training or employment but not for a postsecondary degree.

The definition of special education has confused both parents and educators. HEW's comments to P.L. 94-142's regulations indicate that a child is not handicapped for the purposes of the law unless special education is needed. The question arose: If handicapped children were placed in regular education classes, could they receive special education, even if handicapped? The answer is a simple one: A child may be placed in a regular class under the law, but may also receive special education in that class. On the other hand, a person who is defined as "handicapped" may not necessarily require special education. When a dispute over labels develops, parents or educators would be well advised to initiate the procedures for resolving due process disputes set forth in the law to clarify whether the child is handicapped and the specific special education that is required.

The related services to be developed and offered under the law are another source of confusion. This part of the law may appear fairly simple. Related services, the other aspect of a FAPE, are set forth and include but are not limited to: audiology, speech pathology, psychological services, physical and occupational therapy, recreation, early identification and assessment of disabilities of children, counseling, and the services of a doctor, when required to diagnose a child's exceptionality and needs for special education and related services. The critical question is, What is it that will help a child to benefit from a program of education? The answer must be decided on a case-by-case basis. No one— parent, advocate, or teacher—would disagree that the best possible range of services would help every single child to learn and develop as well as possible. In practice, problems develop when the need for specialized equipment, such as ramps or buses adapted to transport students, are required, or particular physical services such as physical therapy are considered. Transportation itself may raise questions. Some children with severe handicaps or emotional difficulties may require door-to-door service by bus, whereas other, less impaired children may be dropped off at a nearby corner. Some school administrators feel that therapy of any sort is really medical treatment and therefore not the role of the school. Still another common dispute involves the provision of noninstitutional services for physically handicapped students, such as those with spina bifida (a disorder that frequently results in incontinence), and whether the school is required to provide school nursing, diaper service, or similar support.[12] Remember, too, that the list of services described here and set forth at greater length in the law and regulations for 94-142 is not meant to be exclusive, and the needs of children who require particularly creative or unusual services must be met.

Naturally, the question of related services creates a number of very real problems. Virtually all school districts are financially pressed and must seek additional funding to provide the special education and related services. Yet this law and court cases like *Mills*, the District of Columbia case, do not allow lack of money to be offered as an excuse for denying services, nor can waiting lists be used under the guise of waiting for financing. Among others, spina bifida children and those with cerebral palsy who require extensive physical or occupational therapy have immediate needs that must be met by related services.

The standard is admittedly a general one: Does the child need a service to benefit from a program of special education? It is advantageous for advocates that the standard is rather general, so that individual programs may be designed in each case. Again, the refusal to provide a particular service, or the provision of a service insufficient to help a child benefit, may be challenged by school districts or parents through the procedural guarantees of the law.

2.4. HANDICAPPED CHILDREN[13]

Children with a wide range of physical and mental disabilities are protected under the law. They include persons who after being evaluated with appropriate testing tools by certified personnel are classified as mentally retarded, hearing impaired, deaf, speech impaired, visually handicapped, seriously emotionally disturbed, orthopedically impaired, otherwise health impaired, deaf and blind, multihandicapped, or learning disabled. Importantly, they must need special education and related services as a result of these handicaps.

Classifying a child as having a specific handicap is often both legally and educationally difficult. In each case a person must fit into a particular category of disability, or funding will not flow under P.L. 94-142 or state law. It is a well-known fact of special education life that there are children who find learning difficult and, even though they may not be handicapped, are placed in special education programs as the only way they can get adequate instruction. Classification also raises a number of moral issues, including the very real stigma that may attach to a child officially designated retarded or emotionally disturbed.

Regardless of their performance on psychological or educational tests, virtually all children are sensitive to being labeled by their peers. They may feel uncomfortable in separate special classes or even when receiving special instruction in regular classes, knowing that they are singled out. Parents have been known to shrink from requests to permit evaluations when they think their child will be identified as having something wrong. In other cases, educators may refuse to classify children as handicapped because of funding difficulties. Teachers may feel that they cannot obtain a special class for a particularly disruptive student because they receive no help from parents or administrators in the classification process.

Additionally, classifications present problems for students who may be "borderline" in their test scores. Scores and performance levels may fall in a grey area not easily classifiable as one disability. For example, learning-disabled or retarded children can often be classified as being in either group. Traditionally, parents have seemed to prefer the label of learning disability, because of the long history of stigma attached to retardation in our society, however unfair that stigma may be. However, with increasing public attention to these issues, funding for community education programs, and greater understanding of the problems of handicapped children in general, these parental fears and societal snubs will, it is hoped, be on the wane. Some propose a system such as that used in Massachusetts, where children do not receive traditional disability labels but are instead designated as children with special needs.

Finally, another classification problem involves certain severely handicapped children who are unable to participate in public programs. These children must be placed in private special education schools at public expense. However, many states set a funding cap on private programs that is based on the number of handicaps a student has. For example, a child with one handicap will be funded for a certain amount of money, but that amount may not cover all aspects of the program a seriously handicapped person requires. In these cases, funding officials claim only one handicap is "primary" and requires private programming. A dispute then arises as to whether there are other "primary" and distinctive handicaps so that additional funding may be obtained. These laws are probably illegal under 94-142, but the problem does exist and those working in the field should be aware of it.

2.5. Individualized Education Program[14]

The Individualized Education Program or IEP is a term peculiar to 94-142, but the concept has been used by special educators for years. As defined by the law, it means "a written statement for a handicapped child that is developed and implemented" by the following procedures.

First, the State Department of Education or other primary state educational agency is required to ensure that local educational entities providing services for handicapped children design, develop, and implement an IEP for each child. IEPs must also be provided for those persons placed or referred to private schools by the public school district or a related agency, and for those in parochial school receiving services from a public agency. HEW stresses in its comments that any public agency providing special education in any form to a handicapped child, including state welfare departments, is within the coverage of the IEP mandate.

An IEP must be in effect at the beginning of each school year for every special education child. The law stresses that IEPs must be developed before the provision of special education or related services. Although neither the law nor 94-142's regulations set a specific time for implementing a program after it is developed by parents and educators, it must be in effect "as soon as possible" following the required meetings. Some states or local school districts have their own policies relating to time, and these should be examined and followed.

An IEP conference must be held to develop a program, and its participants must include, at the very least, a representative of the school district, intermediate unit, or other agency who is qualified to provide or supervise the provision of special education; the child's special education teacher (or regular teacher if the child is not currently receiving special education); the child's parents; the child, if that would be appropriate; and other individuals at the discretion of the parent or agency. It is always a good idea for parents to bring their own experts, such as the child's psychologist, psychiatrist, or pediatrician, and/or an advocate who is familiar with the IEP process. In many areas trained parent advocates, members of disability advocacy groups, or other parent activists are willing to attend meetings. Having a person knowledgeable in special education, legal requirements, or psychological testing benefits both the school administration and the child. Time is saved and a better IEP is written when knowledgeable people attend the IEP conferences. In addition, a person who works for the public agency and who knows the particular evaluation procedures to be used is required to attend when a handicapped child is evaluated for special education services for the first time. HEW has ruled that for purposes of confidentiality, which will be discussed later, persons not having a "legitimate educational interest" in the child, such as teachers union or administrative union personnel, may not attend.

In accordance with one of the major aspects of due process and with the spirit in which 94-142 was developed, the agency responsible for developing the IEP must make certain efforts to ensure the attendance of one or both of the child's parents, including:

1. The parents must be notified early enough so that they can prepare and make plans to attend. This notice must tell them the purpose, time, and location of the conference, as well as who will be there.

2. The meeting must be scheduled at an initially agreed-upon time and place.

3. If no parent can attend, telephone calls or other methods may be used to obtain parental input and participation. Meetings can be held without parents present only if the agency is unable to convince the parents to attend. In such a

case the agency is required to record its attempts to arrange a meeting, including an indication of the telephone calls attempted, copies of the letters sent to parents, and records of personal visits made to a parent's home or workplace.

4. At the meeting, agency officials responsible for the development of the IEP must make certain that parents understand what is going on. This requirement includes finding an interpreter for parents who are hearing impaired and whose primary language is not English.

The IEP itself is a written statement of (1) a handicapped child's present level of educational performance and function; (2) the specific annual goals, including shorter-term goals, that educators hope to achieve for the child; (3) the special education and related services to be provided the child; and (4) the specific times and classes in which the child will be able to participate in regular programs. Note here that transportation, physical and occupational therapy, counseling, and other related services should and must be included in the statement. The IEP must also set out specific times when parents and teachers can meet to determine whether the goals are being met.

The IEP should be reviewed at least annually, but more frequent meetings may be held if revisions are appropriate. Conferences for special education purposes should be initiated by the agency or parent when revisions are necessary; in any event the yearly meeting should not be the only time educators and parents get together to discuss a child's special education requirements. Parents who are uncertain whether a proposed IEP will succeed should include a specific review date in the IEP in order to discover if any progress is being made or if revisions are necessary. Since meetings can be requested to discuss the program in this manner, parents should not be fearful that a proposed educational technique or service cannot at any time be eliminated if not successful. For those children not receiving special education when the law became effective in October 1977, a meeting was to be held within thirty calendar days from the time it was determined that a child required special education and services. Remember, too, that parents are entitled to have a copy of the IEP. It is a good idea for parents to have a knowledgeable and concerned expert examine an IEP to see if educators are offering the program a child requires, and if all legal protections have been provided.

When an agency places or refers a handicapped child in a private school or other facility, agency officials must participate in an IEP meeting similar to those described for public school students. It cannot be stressed enough that every public agency retains responsibility for children under its jurisdiction whom it chooses to place in or refer to a private facility. A representative of the private school must also attend the meeting, and most of the state-approved private schools for exceptional children have designated specific representatives for this purpose. Again, conferences or telephone calls can be used to ensure the participation of any individual, including the private school representative, who cannot personally attend this meeting. Although a private school or other facility may initiate the meeting, parents and a representative from the public agency must be notified about their right to participate and must agree before the implementation of any proposed changes. These requirements apply equally to children in parochial or any other private schools who are receiving services from public agencies.

In an increasingly litigious society, fear of being sued has even entered into the individualized education procedure. As a result, P.L. 94-142 provides that "the act does not require that any agency, teacher, or other person be held accountable if a child does not achieve the growth projected in the annual goals and objectives."[15] Of course, this provision does not mean that the written statement of goals should be ignored, but instead that a good-faith effort must be made to reach these goals. The comments to the regulations emphasize that although an IEP is not a legally binding contract, the fact that a teacher or administrator cannot be held accountable for reaching a specific goal does not mean that any aspect of the IEP cannot be challenged at any time by parents, or that school officials and teachers can never be sued pursuant to 94-142 or other laws. ("Special Education Malpractice" is discussed at length in Section 5.4.)

2.6. DUE PROCESS PROCEDURES[16]

The procedural safeguards, or due process procedures, set out in the Education for All Handicapped Children Act are the law's cornerstone for protecting the rights of handicapped children. They provide students or parents the right to challenge any aspect of a child's special education program, including the very question of whether the child is handicapped; whether evaluations should be performed; how the child should be classified, if at all; the particular programs or services to be received; and the specific location of the program of special education and related services. Either parents or school officials may raise these questions about the education program.

Before any change or proposal to initiate change in the education services takes place, an educational agency is required to provide, in writing, notification to the parents of an exceptional person a "reasonable time" before the activity is supposed to take place. If a parent requests a particular change, and the school district refuses to comply with a parental request, parents must receive notice of this refusal.

The notice is required to include a detailed explanation of the steps available under the law the parent may use to challenge the agency's actions. Additionally, it must include a description of why a change is proposed or why the agency refuses to undertake a particular suggested change and a description of any options school officials considered and why those options were rejected, a requirement that is frequently ignored. The notice must contain a description of all the evaluations and testing procedures, records and reports that were used that served as the reasons for the action taken, and a discussion of any other relevant reasons on which the actions were based.

Reflecting a growing understanding that average people do not understand many legal or educational terms, the law requires that the notice must be in language the average citizen can understand. Too frequently in the past, the notice offered was skeletal in its form and included citations from antiquated or ill-drafted education laws that were not understandable even to the average lawyer. The right to be informed of something that a governmental agency is going to do is at the very heart of due process; the intelligible notice required in this section of the law, will enable parents to cope with actions that are often confusing and are too frequently undertaken in an emotional atmosphere. Thus parents can participate fully in the decision-making process when their child's education is under scrutiny.

Equally as important is a provision that notice must be written in the native language of the parent or guardian, and must be in any other mode of communication used by the parent, unless it would not be feasible. Moreover, if this mode of communication is not a written language, the state or the local educational agency must make certain that the notice is translated orally or is communicated properly to the parent, and that a record of this communication is kept. Thus the rights of minority students whose parents speak a language other than English— and there are many languages in large school districts, including Spanish, Portuguese, and, increasingly, Vietnamese—will be protected. For some groups of native Americans who do not have a written language, these protections would apply equally.

In addition to notice, specific parental consent must be obtained before an agency undertakes an evaluation prior to placement and before initially placing a handicapped child in a special education situation. However, consent may not be required in other than first-evaluation situations. If a parent refuses this consent before the initial placement or preplacement evaluation, the educational agency must undertake the appropriate state legal procedures to obtain authority for evaluating a child against parental wishes; if no state procedure exists, the same due process procedures and hearing triggered in the event of other special education disagreements will be applicable.

When parents and school districts disagree, either may initiate a hearing on any aspect of the special education dispute. Before undertaking a hearing, it is always meaningful and worthwhile to meet in a prehearing conference or negotiation session to thrash out disputed issues. Frequently, disputes are the result of misunderstandings that can be resolved in this informal manner, and in practice very few full-blown due process hearings need be requested. Although hearings can be emotionally draining, contentious, and time-consuming, parents should not be deterred from advocating on behalf of their children if they have evidence with which to justify their position and requests.

The State Department of Education or other state agency or governmental unit responsible for the child's education must inform parents of any free or low-cost legal and advocacy services, including evaluation services, available when either party initiates a hearing or when the parents request such information. Legal Services programs exist in virtually every area where hearings take place. There are also a growing number of parent advocacy organizations and other legal groups and public interest firms that have expertise in the area. Increasingly, private lawyers are developing knowledge of these procedures. At the very least, it is often possible to find someone who has some familiarity with the due process hearing procedure. Of course, parents are free to represent themselves.

Hearing officers are generally appointed by the state educational agency and are usually college professors or special educators. They must not be employed by the agency involved in the child's education or by any other person having a private interest conflicting with the neutrality required of hearing officers. Often, the question of who may be a hearing officer is disputed between some advocacy groups and state education officials. Advocates feel that because the hearing officer is invariably paid by the state and is in essence a representative of the state education secretary, a conflict of interest exists as a matter of course. Similarly, parents feel compromised in presenting their cases to individuals who may hold the same position in another school district as the person they are challenging. That person, they feel, may very well have too much sympathy for the financial burdens, personnel and union disputes, or other distasteful occurrences a compatriot may have to undergo if required to do what the parents wish. As a matter of constitutional law, however, it would not appear that the hearing officer is necessarily partial if paid and selected by the state, and only obvious conflicts of interest will preclude an appointment of a particular individual to serve as a special education hearing officer.

If parents and educators do not resolve their difficulties at a prehearing conference or negotiation session, a hearing is requested and scheduled. Under 94-142, a hearing officer must make a final decision and a copy of this decision must be mailed to all of the parties "not later than 45 days after the receipt of the request for a hearing." Since a number of states have other time limitations, when parents request hearings they should check the state's time limitations against 94-142 and its implementing regulations to see if they are in compliance with federal requirements.

Any party to a due process hearing has certain rights:

1. The right to have a lawyer or other advocate or experts in special education.

2. The right to present evidence and to cross-examine witnesses, whose attendance can be compelled.

3. The right to exclude any evidence the other party has not disclosed at least five days before the hearing (if evidence introduced at a hearing is helpful, it is obviously not a good idea to seek its prohibition even though it may not have been disclosed at least five days before the hearing—a situation that does come up).

4. The right to obtain a written or electronic verbatim record of the hearing.

5. The right to obtain written findings of fact and an opinion.

6. The right of a parent to request that the public be admitted or denied access to the hearing.

7. The right to have the child who is the subject of the hearing present.

Some points are worth underlining. It is not always necessary that a lawyer participate in the proceeding, even if the opposing party is represented by an attorney. Although hearing officers are required to be trained in the hearing procedures, they are more interested in listening to the special education evidence rather than in worrying about the types of procedural wrangling that may occur in a courtroom situation. Indeed, court rules of evidence are not applicable in special education administrative hearings, so hearing officers can be somewhat more flexible than they would be if they felt constrained by such rules. On the other hand, it is important for each party to have spoken with somebody familiar with the procedures. In all cases it is wise for the parents to have a parent advocate of some sort. Although the hearings are more flexible than court proceedings, legal rights are being exercised and handicapped persons are in a very real sense personally affected by the decisions made by hearing officers. Thus all parties and their representatives must not forget the true purpose of these hearings: to determine an exceptional person's educational needs.

2.7. APPEALS[17]

After the due process hearing has been held and all evidence has been presented, the hearing officer is required to weigh the evidence and arrive at a written decision detailing an appropriate program of services. If under state law or policy the hearing is not considered the final determination of an administrative agency, any party who is unhappy with the hearing officer's findings may appeal to the chief state educational officer. In conducting the review, this official is required to examine the record of the hearing as a whole (the written or recorded transcript). For this reason it is usually good practice to ask for a written transcript, which is easier to review. Having a transcript in writing may also be convenient for any potential appeal to the courts. The proceedings must be examined to see if due process was met and if facts were properly considered during the conduct of the hearing. Parties may submit additional arguments in writing or orally at the discretion of the final reviewing authority. State policy, if any, should be examined to determine the time deadline for submitting such arguments. Finally, the reviewing official makes an independent decision and then sends a copy of this document to each of the parties. The final administrative decision must be reached not later than thirty days after a party's request for review is received, although a hearing or final reviewing official may grant continuations beyond these deadlines when either party requests one. When this decision is made, it becomes a final determination of a state administrative agency and may be appealed to an appropriate state or federal court.

In each case it is important to follow the mandate that hearings and oral arguments on review must be conducted "at a time and place which is reasonably convenient for the parents and child involved." Some states require the hearings to be held in the local district where the child attends school. Parents or their representatives must therefore guard against any attempt by state educational personnel to hold hearings in the state capital or some other place convenient only to state officials or hearing officers.

While all of these procedures, including prehearing conferences, hearings, or appeals to court, are taking place, the child who is the subject of all of this controversy must remain in the current educational placement—unless parents or the public agency agree otherwise. Importantly, parents or school districts may in any instance agree to a trial or "interim" placement at any time during the course of the procedures without violating any legal provisions.

2.8. SURROGATE PARENTS[18]

Whenever the law requires that a parent be notified in accordance with the due process procedures, the law provides for the use of a new concept known as the surrogate parent. This person is not a legal guardian, but someone who will undertake in special education matters the protection of a child's rights. The surrogate parent is utilized if the parents or guardians cannot be located after a reasonable effort is made to find them, or when the child is a ward of the state. Public agencies must have procedures for appointing surrogates, and many states now have detailed written procedures for such appointments. For example, in some states the intermediate education unit—which is frequently a special education backup center—is responsible for appointing the surrogate within the area of their jurisdiction. Basically, the surrogate is a person aware of special education legal procedures and rights, and whose personal interests would not conflict with those of the child. A surrogate cannot be an employee of the agency making the appointment. Finally, surrogates can represent the child in every aspect of due process or in more general matters relating to the provision of special education. Although they may be appointed in each case, the handicapped child, when possible, should determine whether the surrogate has a different interest than he does; in that case, another representative should be located and assigned. In some cases handicapped persons covered by the law seek out and obtain legal assistance at a public interest law firm or some other legal services or advocacy agency.

2.9. EVALUATIONS[19]

Before any placement decisions are made, a full battery of tests by a team of experts must be administered and the appropriate diagnoses and evaluations made. No placement can be accomplished without the benefit of these tests. Evaluations must not be racially or culturally discriminatory, and must be administered in the child's native language or mode of communication, unless it is not feasible. For example, children have been known to be misclassified because they spoke Spanish best, but were given the tests in English; in such cases, testing results may imply a much lower level of functioning than a child actually has. All the testing must be administered by qualified personnel, who must make certain that tests have been validated for exactly the matter they are trying to measure. No single intelligence quotient may be relied on; instead a wide variety of tests must be used to assess specific areas of educational need. When a child's impairment can depress testing scores, this factor must be taken into consideration. This is especially important in the case of certain learning-disabled children who may function in the retarded range on testing when, in fact, their scores and other performances have been impaired by frustration, hyperactivity, lack of interest, or other manifestation of their specific learning disability. Finally, testing must measure all areas that relate to the disability being tested, and should include health and psychological evaluations when necessary. Comments by HEW emphasize that children whose obvious primary handicap is a speech impairment may require a speech and language expert to make a determination about the tests to be administered.

Parents of handicapped children have the right to purchase independent educational evaluations at any time. In other cases, however, school districts and other agencies are required to provide information describing where independent educational evaluations can be obtained. These are usually available at state mental health/mental retardation centers on a sliding scale dependent on the parent's income. In certain cases, parents do have the right to evaluations at the expense of the public agency. In this somewhat limited situation, parents may disagree with the results of an evaluation performed by the agency in question. Usually, a parent disagrees with the classification or the services recommended by a psychologist employed by the school district or other educational agency and desires a second opinion. The school district may request a due process hearing to show that an independent evaluation is not necessary. Even if the hearing is decided in favor of the school district, an independent evaluation the parent wishes to pay for is not precluded. When any outside evaluation is presented to a public agency, its determinations must be taken into consideration. It can also be used as evidence at the due process hearing. When a hearing officer demands an independent evaluation, parents are not required to bear the cost of this request.

Evaluations and placement decisions must be made by a group of experts rather than by a single individual. The group or "multidisciplinary team" must ensure that evaluations, teacher comments, and other social, emotional, or cultural matters are all taken into consideration. Parents certainly may be included in the meeting, and an invitation to them may be required by local school district procedures. Reevaluations must be provided pursuant to 94-142 once every three years or more often if necessary, but many states require reevaluations to be performed more frequently. A wise policy for state education departments is to allow parents to request an evaluation annually, but to require one perhaps every two years as a matter of course. In this manner, students experiencing difficulties could be retested more frequently than federal law requires.

2.10. LEAST RESTRICTIVE ENVIRONMENT[20]

It is by now a well-established principle of law that whenever the state acts to institutionalize, place, or otherwise impinge on the liberties of an individual, the person involved must be confined in the least restrictive environment possible. This is particularly true for handicapped children, who are being placed in a particular environment by the state through no fault of their own. Due process requires nothing less. This requirement, which has been described in numerous cases involving disabled children, has been incorporated into the statutory language of P.L. 94-142. Placing children in the most normal environment possible is also considered sound educational policy.

Under the supervision of the state educational agency, which is responsible for monitoring least restrictive placements, children, regardless of whether they are placed in public or private facilities, must be educated with their nonhandicapped peers—or, in the "most normal setting." Special classes or segregated education must occur only when "the nature or severity of the handicap is such that education in regular classes with the use of supplementary aids and services cannot be achieved satisfactorily." It must be noted that every effort be made to place children in the most normal setting for them and that this provi-

~itting exclusion in certain cases must be used only in extreme cases truly cannot benefit from a less restrictive setting. It cannot be used to set up a dumping ground for children an educational agency does not wish to assist with supplemental aid or to fund sufficiently.

To ensure that this requirement is met, the law provides for a "continuum of alternative placements" to meet the special education needs of handicapped children. The so-called continuum must include alternative placements in regular classes, special classes, special schools, home-bound instruction, and educational instruction in hospitals or other institutions. When children are placed in regular classes, additional services must be considered including: resource rooms to which children can go for a percentage of their instruction, or itinerant instruction by teachers who may meet with students for particular services in school or other environments. Placements, like IEPs, must be examined at least annually; they must be based on the individualized education program, and must be as close as possible to the person's home. This requirement is particularly important for students with severe handicaps who must be placed in potentially distant intermediate education units, private schools, or residential facilities. Such matters as the amount of time a child must spend on a bus going to and from the more restrictive environment are also to be considered in developing the IEP.

In all cases the regular neighborhood school a child may attend with his nonhandicapped peers is preferred, even if special classes are needed to some degree. This principle is especially important in the case of children who have traditionally been segregated in either special classes or centers for physically handicapped individuals. Educators feel that integration of students, both exceptional and typical, must take place in order to provide the highest quality of educational experience for each child. In fact, there have been recent attempts at "reverse special education integration" where nonhandicapped children are educated in classes previously set aside for their disabled peers. In essence, there must be a compelling reason for removing a handicapped child from a regular classroom. Integration must also take place in extracurricular activities, lunch, recess, and the like whenever it will benefit a handicapped child. This provision is consistent with and parallels similar provisions in Section 504 of the Rehabilitation Act of 1973, to be discussed more fully. The statute also requires personnel training to inform teacher and administrators of the least restrictive imperative, and requires the state and local boards of education to aid in training efforts by offering appropriate technical assistance to these teachers and administrators.

2.11. Least Restrictive Environment and the Courts: The Willowbrook Case (466 F. Supp. 479)

> ... The principal action of *New York State Ass'n for Retarded Children, Inc. v. Carey* was brought under 42 U.S.C. § 1983 on behalf of a class of

mentally retarded residents of Willowbrook Developmental Center (now Staten Island Developmental Center). The major points of contention were settled by a Consent Judgment, the thrust of which is to require the defendants to place the class members in the community in the least restrictive environment and arrange programs for them in the community so that they develop their potential and live as normal a life as possible.

In furtherance of this mandate, the defendants, under the primary supervision of Commissioner Coughlin, have placed a number of children in family homes and community residences and have arranged for them to attend special education programs in the public schools under the jurisdiction of the Board of Education.

Under circumstances which will appear below, the Board of Education identified fifty pupils in its Track IV (severely and profoundly mentally retarded) special education programs who happened to be carriers of hepatitis B. The Board of Education, on September 7, 1978, suddenly ordered these carriers to be excluded from the public schools, planning to arrange for their education in developmental center schools under the jurisdiction of the New York State Office of Mental Retardation and Developmental Disabilities. Forty-two of these carriers are members of the Willowbrook class. Commissioner Coughlin, who is obligated by the Consent Judgment to place and maintain these class members in the least restrictive environment possible, commenced this ancillary proceeding on behalf of these forty-two carriers in order to gain their readmission to the public schools. . . .

The epidemiology of hepatitis B was discussed at length during the hearing. Unlike hepatitis A, which is highly contagious, hepatitis B is of limited communicability. It is generally communicated solely by the parenteral, or blood-to-blood route, by means of transfusions of infected blood, or by use of a contaminated needle. Long believed to be found only in the blood, or in body fluids where blood is present, recent studies indicate that hepatitis B antigen may also be present, on occasion, in saliva. Dr. Bakal testified with respect to one study he had read where the disease was experimentally transmitted by placing infected saliva into the mouth of a recipient. However, according to a Center for Disease Control study issued in May 1976,

> [a]lthough [hepatitis B antigen] has been detected in many human biological fluids during acute infection, transmission of disease by saliva or other body fluids containing antigen has not yet been convincingly demonstrated. . . .

As a result of concerns which surfaced last school year when a special education teacher became infected not with hepatitis B but with hepatitis A, the New York City Department of Health sent observers to the special education classes in the affected school. There sufficient unhygienic personal behavior was observed to warrant a further study by a Department of Health task force of nine hepatitis B experts. Accordingly, under the coordination of Dr. Bakal, all of the children in the Track IV programs where a known hepatitis B carrier was present for most or all of the school day were slated for study. (Forty-four children were already known to be carriers because they had come from Willowbrook, where they had undergone testing.) The total sample numbered approximately 450 children. Of these, approximately 120 had come from institutions where they had been previously tested, and Dr. Bakal did not subject these children to further testing, even though he was able to obtain blood records for only 70 to 80 of these. Of the remaining children, approximately 270 were tested, giving a total of approximately 340 test results out of the original 450 sample. The results indicated that in addition to the forty-four known carriers, there were five additional carriers. It is not known, nor does it appear that it could ever be discovered, exactly how these five persons contracted the disease. Suspicion, however, then focussed on the forty-four known carriers, but there was no direct proof that the five new carriers contracted the disease as a result of contact with the known carriers. . . .

It appears to the Court that the Board of Education has overreacted to the problem of hepatitis B contagion in its special education classes, and that this overreaction has caused and will continue to cause irreparable harm to the children involved. In testimony to which this Court must accord great weight, the Commissioner and other witnesses in his behalf stressed the deleterious effect that the Board's exclusionary policy has on the children affected. These children have long been prepared for their entry into more normal community activities and placements and have been told that this is a very important step. The traumatic effect of being told at the last minute that they can no longer participate in the schools where many of them have already spent two or three years is extremely great. To this must be added that due to the timing of the Board's action no interim programs could be developed, and many of the excluded children are simply remaining home while their peers and co-residents go to school. However, the most serious consequences of the Board's plan would be felt if the pupils were sent to school in developmental centers. The Court is convinced that this would have a severely retrogressive effect on the development of these children, and would be an enormous setback to the process of normalization of these children. The Board's policy would also be a serious setback to implementation of the Willowbrook Consent Judgment. . . .

We also believe that the Board of Education has violated the Education for All Handicapped Children Act. . . .

For years the needs of these hepatitis B carrier children were satisfied without objection in special education classes. The needs are the same, but the children are now excluded for reasons which the hearing has shown to be unjustified and which are in direct opposition to the children's needs. The Board's overreaction to the hepatitis B problem is not countenanced by the law. We also believe that the Board's action violates the provisions of the Consent Judgment and the constitutional rights of the children to equal protection and due process of the law.

In sum, we find that upon taking simple prophylactic and classroom management measures which it is in the Board of Education's power to take, there is no substantial risk of communication of hepatitis B from carrier pupils in the Track IV special education programs that justifies their discriminatory exclusion from the benefits of a public school education, particularly in view of the unavoidable and irreparable harm such exclusion would work on the students involved.

2.12. CONFIDENTIALITY OF RECORDS[21]

Until 1974 parental access to educational records was, from a legal standpoint, not uniformly permitted across the country. Local school boards had differing policies, and in many cases parents and guardians could not obtain access to many of their child's records on file. As a result parents were unable to determine how an educational decision was made, or even if the material contained in records was accurate. In some school districts records were contained in a number of different places, which made access difficult even when permitted, and records were kept for unreasonable amounts of time. Moreover, a variety of people had potential access to records, regardless of their professional interest. These same files could, in the absence of a confidentiality policy, be distributed to outside persons without permission.

In 1974 Congress passed the Family Educational Rights and Privacy Act, also known as the Buckley Amendment or FERPA, the purpose of which is to solve the problems relating to the collection, dissemination, and confidentiality of personal information contained in school records. The basic provisions of FERPA are incorporated in 94-142, and the two laws essentially parallel each other. The major provisions relating to records are the following.

First, a state education agency is required in its 94-142 State Plan to notify parents about their method of collecting records in its jurisdiction, including a description of all rights parents and children have regarding access to and confidentiality of information. The notice must also include a description of the degree to which this notice is given in languages spoken by minorities within the state. The state must tell parents when it is collecting information, exactly the type of personally identifiable information needed and the source of the information, as well as the use to which it will be put. The policies that agencies involved in educational programs have relating to the collection, storage, and disclosure of this information must also be included. When a major statewide identification or evaluation activity is proposed, this notice must be published in media having a circulation large enough to notify parents that the state is going to undertake a major evaluation activity.

Each individual educational agency must give notice personally to parents or guardians describing its own records policies, including the requirements of the Buckley Amendment, and a list of the types of education records kept and their location. Records are sometimes kept not only in educational agencies, but also in hospitals or centers where evaluations take place. They may also be kept on file in several places within the local school district. All of these places must be identified. As part of its records policy, the educational agency is required to allow parents to review in person any and all education records relating to their children that the agency uses in any way. This request to review records must be honored no later than forty-five days after it has been made. In no case should there be unnecessary and unreasonable delay between the time a request is made and access granted. In each case, review must be permitted before any IEP meeting or hearing relating to the child's placement is held. There are school districts that have policies requiring access in a shorter period than 94-142 permits, but none can have a procedure allowing for more than the time specified in the law. Much as school officials are required to explain proposed special education evaluations, officials responsible for records must answer questions about interpretations of these records at a parent's request. Parents can have representatives of their own choosing inspect and review records, and may receive copies "if failure to provide those copies would effectively prevent the parent from exercising the right to inspect and review the records." In other words, if the parent cannot personally go to the records center to examine material, or if substantial time for review is necessary, copies would be in order. A list must be kept of anyone, including school personnel, who looks at a particular child's records. Although fees may be charged for copies of records, a fee cannot be so high as to prevent parents from exercising their right to inspect or review the records. Thus if a person cannot afford the records charge, or if it is unreasonable, free copies would have to be provided.

An interesting and key provision of Buckley and 94-142 is the amendment process. It goes into effect when a parent believes after examination that material in the records is "inaccurate or misleading, or violates the privacy or other rights of the child." A request for deletion of the information, known as an amendment, can be made. Within a reasonable period after the request is made, agency officials must decide if they wish to delete the information in accordance with the parental request. If the request is rejected, a parent has the right under law to an informal meeting chaired by a school official not directly involved in the dispute. A written summary of the parent's reasons and evidence supporting the amendment request must be kept, and an opinion issued. Unlike a due process hearing, there is no specific time limitation when a decision should be made, but a reasonable deadline should be set. Parents can have counsel present, and may call witnesses or present any evidence they feel is relevant to the amendment process. If the agency decides that the information should in fact be deleted or modified, the amendment is effected and the process ends. If the hearing officer decides that the information is not inaccurate, misleading, or violative of privacy, the student or parents must be told of the right to place a statement describing and detailing why the information should have been removed. This statement must be placed in the permanent record file. Whenever the records or the portion in dispute is disclosed to anyone, the explanation why this material should have been amended must also be disclosed.

To resolve problems resulting from having records in many locations, each agency must designate a custodian responsible for maintaining and assuring the confidentiality of information on file. These persons must be trained in laws and policies concerning confidentiality, and their names must be published. Before a custodian may disclose any personally identifiable information to third parties (those who are not officials of the agency), parental consent is required. Third parties are usually, hospitals or clinics who will evaulate an exceptional child, other schools that the child will attend during the next year, or private schools to which the child is referred for placement. According to the Buckley Amendment, no person or agency without any "legitimate educational interest" can gain access to the personally identifiable information. In fact, to underline this requirement in the special education field, HEW ruled, through its FERPA office, that union officials may not participate in IEP conferences or due process hearings without a parent's permission. In certain cases, teacher union representatives sat in on special education meetings when they felt the decisions reached would result in teacher obligations not part of a collective bargaining agreement. However, the FERPA office—to which confidentiality complaints concerning records may be brought—ruled that the information discussed in special education meetings is confidential, and falls within the compass of this law.

When the personally identifiable information used to provide a special education is no longer required, an agency is obligated to inform parents of this fact, and parents may request that the information be destroyed. "Directory" information relating to the student's name, address, grades, or telephone number may be kept on file without regard to a time limitation.

2.13. Excluding Persons without a Legitimate Educational Interest: The Government Requirements

DEPARTMENT OF HEALTH, EDUCATION AND WELFARE

Office of the Secretary
Washington, D.C. 20201

January 8, 1979

Ms. Caryl M. Kline
Secretary of Education
Commonwealth of Pennsylvania
Department of Education
Harrisburg, Pennsylvania 17126

Dear Ms. Kline:

This is in further response to the questions you raised regarding a practice by the Philadelphia School District of allowing representatives of teachers to attend meetings between parents, teachers, and other school officials to discuss development of an individualized education program (IEP) for a handicapped child. The representatives of the teachers include union officials and attorneys. You raised the question of whether this was in conflict with the parental prior consent provisions of the so-called Buckley Amendment, the Family Educational Rights and Privacy Act of 1974 (FERPA), section 438 of the General Education Provisions Act.

I subsequently received a complaint about this practice from the Education Law Center at Philadelphia. That complaint indicated, further, that the Philadelphia School District may be planning to permit these representatives of teachers to be present at due process hearings regarding issues relating to free appropriate public education for handicapped children.

I cannot comment on the propriety of permitting union representatives to participate in conferences at which student records are not discussed. However, in those parent-teacher conferences in which information from student records is disclosed, it is improper to include parties whose participation is intended to protect the interests of teachers rather than the interests of the student, without obtaining the consent of the student's parent. To do so violates both the protective provisions of the Family Educational Rights and Privacy Act and the confidentiality and procedural safeguards requirements of Part B of the Education of the Handicapped Act (a formula grant program providing assistance to States in educating handicapped children on the condition that the State assures various protections and rights to each handicapped child).

As you know, the FERPA Regulations published in the June 17, 1976 issue of the Federal Register, require each educational agency receiving funds from the U.S. Office of Education to adopt policies to protect the confidentiality of its students' education records. There are specific statutory requirements that the educational agency have a policy of not disclosing personally identifiable information from student education records without the consent of the student's parents except to specified parties under specified conditions (45 CFR Section 99.5(a)(3)). The Department does not interpret any of the exceptions to the prior consent provisions to apply to teachers' union representatives or attorneys. Even if these persons were employed by the school district and might be, by the district's definition in its FERPA policy, other school officials, the district's specification (in the FERPA policy) of a "legitimate educational interest" would preclude the district from making disclosures from student education records to them without parental consent. The Department interprets a "legitimate educational interest," within the history and intent of the Section 438(b)(1)(A) exception found in the Family Educational Rights and Privacy Act, to mean an interest in students and their parents.

In addition to the requirements of FERPA, there is the requirement in Part B of the Education of the Handicapped Act (EHA) that the States adopt policies and procedures to protect the confidentiality of information about the child (45 CFR Section 121a.129, published at 42 FR 42476; August 23, 1977). I would assume, then, that a State's policy under EHA would provide that teacher representatives are not proper parties at an IEP meeting or, for that matter, at a due process hearing.*

Beyond all of the above, I feel that union involvement in IEP meetings would not "square" with Congressional intent regarding such meetings. The legislative history makes it clear: (1) that the overarching purpose of IEP meetings

---

* Note that Section 300.344 of EHA Regulations provides that either the parents or the agency may, at their discretion, allow other than specified parties to be present at the IEP meeting, and Section 300.508 allows any party (the school district or parent/child) to present witnesses. In both situations, it is implicit that the additional parties are to be present only if they will contribute to a determination of what is most appropriate for the child.

is to insure active and open involvement of parents in all major decisions
affecting their child's education, and (2) that IEP meetings should be confined to those persons who have an intense interest in a particular child.

                                        Sincerely yours,

                                        Thomas S. McFee
                                        Deputy Assistant Secretary for Management

2.14. NOTES

1. 334 F. Supp. 1257, 1259.
2. 20 U.S.C. § 1401(18); 34 C.F.R. § 300.4.
3. 20 U.S.C. § 1401(16); 34 C.F.R. § 300.14.
4. 20 U.S.C. §§ 1412, 1414; 34 C.F.R. §§ 300.550–556.
5. 20 U.S.C. § 1232g; 34 C.F.R. Part 99.
6. 476 F. Supp. 583 (E.D. Pa. 1979), aff'd, 629 F.2d 269 (3rd. Cir. 1980).
7. Id. at 603.
8. Id.
9. Id. at 604.
10. Mattie T. v. Holladay, C.A. No. DC-75-31-S (N.D. Miss., Feb. 22, 1979).
11. See note 2. See also Rowley v. Board of Education of Hendrick Hudson Central School District,
    483 F. Supp. 528 (S.D.N.Y. 1980).
12. 46 Fed. Reg. 4912 (1981), citing Tatro v. State of Texas, 625 F.2d 557 (5th Cir. 1980); Tokarcik
    v. Forest Hills School District, No. 79-338 (W.D. Pa., Oct. 31, 1980); Hairston v. Drosick, 423
    F. Supp. 180 (S.D. W.Va. 1976).
13. 20 U.S.C. § 1401(1),(15); 34 C.F.R. § 300.5.
14. 20 U.S.C. § 1401(19); 34 C.F.R. §§ 300.340 et seq.
15. 34 C.F.R. § 300.349.
16. 20 U.S.C. § 1415; 34 C.F.R. §§ 300.500 et seq.
17. 34 C.F.R. §§ 300.510–513.
18. 34 C.F.R. § 300.514.
19. 34 C.F.R. §§ 300.530–534, 540–543.
20. 34 C.F.R. §§ 300.550–556.
21. 34 C.F.R. §§ 300.560–576; 20 U.S.C. 1232g. See note 5.

3

Prohibiting Discrimination against Handicapped Students

3.1. Section 504 of the Rehabilitation Act of 1973[1]

Section 504 is a civil rights law passed by Congress in order to eliminate discrimination against handicapped persons in any program receiving federal financial assistance. Unlike the Education for All Handicapped Children Act, which is a grant-in-aid program for funding special education programs, 504 covers discrimination in a wide range of national activities, including employment, transportation, and education. The basic purpose of this law is to eliminate traditional societal bias toward disabled persons and to assist them in becoming integrated with others who are not handicapped. It allows for equal access to jobs and educational programs when a person who can otherwise participate in the activity is qualified to do so. In short, it is illegal to refuse a benefit to a handicapped person who is qualified by reason of training, education, and other factors solely because of the person's disability.

When dealing with discrimination in education, 504 and 94-142 must be read together. The goals of these two laws are essentially the same in elementary and secondary programs: they both require the provision of a free appropriate public education. Likewise, 504 prohibits discrimination in higher and post-secondary education.

Section 504 is one of the most succinct statements of equal rights available under federal or state law. It provides that "no otherwise qualified handicapped individual in the United States... shall solely by reason of his handicap, be excluded from the participation in, be denied the benefits of, or be subjected to discrimination under any program or activity receiving federal financial assistance." In 1977 the Department of Health, Education and Welfare promulgated implementing regulations that cover discrimination in all education programs receiving federal aid, as well as in a number of other areas.

For the purpose of vindicating the rights of handicapped persons, those

47

persons included in the protection of this law are much more broadly defined than they might be under P.L. 94-142. To be covered an individual must fall within the definition of a "qualified, handicapped person," that is, "any person who (i) has a physical or mental impairment which substantially limits one or more major life activities, (ii) has a record of such an impairment, or (iii) is regarded as having such an impairment."[2] It is easy to see how this definition goes beyond the one given in the Education for All Handicapped Children Act. To be covered by P.L. 94-142, a handicapped person must also require special education and related services. As a result of 504's definition, the impairment must limit a major life activity, there must be a history of the impairment, and, interestingly, an individual may be defined as handicapped if he is regarded as having an impairment. Therefore a situation can and sometimes does arise where a handicapped person may not require special education and related services, but could receive an education not because he is covered by the protections of 94-142 but because he is covered by 504. For example, in certain cases, particularly where a student has been misclassified or is thought to have a particular disability, that person could not be discriminated against under 504 even though he might not, in fact, have such a disability. This distinction is very important, and helpful for handicapped persons wishing to participate in all aspects of federally funded education program. Thus both laws must be examined carefully to see if the benefits not covered by one may in any event be obtained from the other.

The law defines a physical or mental impairment in a manner that may go beyond 94-142's coverage:

(A) [A]ny physiological disorder or condition, cosmetic disfigurement, or anatomical loss affecting one or more of the following body systems: neurological; musculoskeletal, special sense organs, respiratory, including speech organs; cardiovascular, reproductive; digestive, genito-urinary, hemic and lymphatic; skin; and endocrine; or

(B) [A]ny mental or psychological disorder, such as mental retardation, organic brain syndrome, emotional or mental illness, and specific learning disabilities.[3]

It is apparent that virtually any physical or mental impairment is covered by law. Again, note that exceptional children classified as gifted are, as in the case of 94-142, not covered by this law.

The major life activities that must be limited include "functions such as caring for one's self, performing manual tasks, walking, seeing, hearing, speaking, breathing, learning and working."

Central to the law's functioning is the requirement that school officials, among others, must take affirmative action to remedy discriminatory policies existing before the law was passed and that may still exist, and to provide such things as program access for handicapped persons when not currently available. Schools at all levels must build ramps and provide other aids and services that will allow handicapped persons full participation. In addition, school districts may not discriminate against qualified handicapped persons who wish to be teachers, administrators, or other employees in an educational agency solely based on handicap. Discrimination in hiring does in fact still exist. In one case involving a blind high school English teacher,[4] employment was denied despite the fact that the teacher's credentials were acceptable and qualified her for the position. Officials apparently thought that because she was blind she could not properly control the classroom. A federal court case was brought under Section 504 alleging that she was discriminated against solely on the basis of her handicap, and the court agreed. She was ordered reinstated as a teacher with back pay. Thus 504 does cover all aspects of education, including the hiring of teachers.

Note also that a recipient of federal financial assistance may include not only a local school district, but also the State Department of Education or any of its subdivisions, including intermediate education units. Other public agencies are also included, so that in order to vindicate the rights of disabled persons under this law, not only education funds but any federal money accepted would trigger the nondiscrimination procedures. The type of discrimination prohibited cover the following:[5]

1. A handicapped person cannot be denied the opportunity to participate in or benefit from a particular aid, benefit, or service.

2. The person must have been afforded an opportunity to participate in the benefit, aid, or service that is equal to that offered others.

3. Recipients cannot provide a qualified handicapped person with a benefit, aid, or service that is not as effective as that provided others.

4. A recipient cannot provide different or separate benefits or services to handicapped persons unless doing so is necessary to ensure that they receive services as effective as those provided to others.

5. A recipient cannot provide aid to a person or organization that discriminates on the basis of handicap.

3.2. PRESCHOOL, ELEMENTARY, AND SECONDARY EDUCATION

Every recipient of federal funds operating a public elementary or secondary education program must on an annual basis identify and locate all handicapped persons covered under 504 who are not receiving a public education. In doing so, they must provide notice to the persons and their parents that it is the responsibility of the education agency to provide an appropriate program. As in 94-142, the education provided must be free as well as appropriate, and it must be offered to every person regardless of the nature or severity of the handicap in question. The definition of free appropriate public education[6] is similar to the one given in 94-142, and includes the provision of regular or special education and related aids and services that (1) are designed to meet the needs of handicapped persons as adequately as the needs of nonhandicapped persons are met, and (2) are based on adherence to the requirements of a least restrictive environment, appropriate evaluation and placement procedures, and due process procedures.

Developing and implementing an IEP in accordance with 94-142 is specifically set forth as one way to meet the free appropriate public education mandate, but no great attempt is made to define related services. Transportation is treated as one service that must be provided regardless of whether the handicapped person is placed in public education or is referred by the school district of residence to a private facility. When a child is placed in a residential program, the school district or other recipient must make sure that a free appropriate public education is undertaken. All the costs of the program must be provided free of charge to the parent, including nonmedical care, and room and board, as well as psychological and medical services necessary for diagnostic purposes. Moreover, this care must include custodial and supervisory care.

These requirements have created a good deal of controversy when school districts and state boards of education do place students in state-approved private facilities. Officials of these agencies claim that all noneducational costs are in fact treatment and need not be funded by educational funds. The requirements of 504 and HEW's own explanatory comments clearly contradict this viewpoint. As always, parents are certainly free, as they are in the case of 94-142, to place a handicapped person in a school of their own choosing. In this case, a public agency would not have to pay for the schooling. Again, any disputes in this area are to be resolved by appropriate due process procedures.

3.3. The Integration Requirement[7]

The integration requirement provides for placement of children in the most normal setting, to the maximum extent possible in order to meet the needs of the handicapped child. Students must be placed in a regular educational setting, unless a school district can show that the student would best be served in another setting. For such activities as extracurricular events and the like, integration must also be achieved as far as possible. In addition, a handicapped person should be placed as close to home as possible. When placed in residential settings, children should be integrated with other children when possible.

3.4. Court-Ordered Integration: Hairston v. Drosick (423 F. Supp. 120)

K. K. HALL, District Judge.

This is a civil proceeding challenging the refusal of the defendants to admit the plaintiff child, Trina Evet Hairston to the regular public classroom at Gary Grade School and her exclusion therefrom as being contrary to 29 U.S.C. § 794, a section of what is commonly known as "The Rehabilitation Act of 1973," and her exclusion without procedural safeguards as being contrary to the Fourteenth Amendment to the United States Constitution.

The plaintiffs, Larry Hairston and Sheila Hairston, on behalf of their child, Trina Evet Hairston, are seeking the right of their child, Trina Evet Hairston, to attend Gary Grade School, a regular public school. The complaint alleges that the plaintiff child has a physical condition known as spina bifida and that on account of this condition her right to attend the regular public school classroom has been infringed upon; that on or about September 1, 1975, the plaintiff Sheila Hairston received a telephone call from the teacher of the class in which the plaintiff Trina Hairston was to be enrolled indicating that the plaintiff child would not be accepted into her classroom. The complaint further alleges that upon going to the school after extensive discussion it was determined by the school authorities that the plaintiff child's right to attend public school was conditioned upon the mother's attendance at such school which was an impossibility. The plaintiffs further allege that none of them had received written notice or following such written notice an opportunity to be heard and accompanying procedural safeguards to contest the exclusion or limitations upon the attendance of plaintiff Trina Evet Hairston at Gary Grade School. The plaintiffs further allege that the Board of Education of McDowell County and the schools therein are recipients of federal funds.

The plaintiffs contend that such exclusion or placement constitutes a discrimination against the named plaintiff Trina Evet Hairston on account of her handicap in violation of Title V of the "Rehabilitation Act of 1973," 29 U.S.C. § 794, which prohibits discrimination against and denial of benefits to handicapped persons in any program or activity receiving federal financial assistance. Secondly, the plaintiffs assert that the exclusion or conditional exclusion of the plaintiff child from the regular public classroom at Gary Grade School without written notice and accompanying procedural safeguards is contrary to the mandate of due process of law afforded to them by the Fourteenth Amendment to the United States Constitution. . . .

The Court, after careful review of the facts and applicable law, concludes that:

1. The exclusion of a minimally handicapped child from a regular public classroom situation without a bona fide educational reason is in violation of Title V of Public Law 93-112, "The Rehabilitation Act of 1973," 29 U.S.C. § 794. The federal statute proscribes discrimination against handicapped individuals in any program receiving federal financial assistance. To deny to a handicapped child access to a regular public school classroom in receipt of federal financial assistance without compelling educational justification constitutes discrimination and a denial of the benefits of such program in violation of the statute. School officials must make every effort to include such children within the regular public classroom situation, even at great expense to the school system.

2. The exclusion of a child from the regular public classroom situation

and placement in special education situation or otherwise without prior written notice and accompanying procedural safeguards including opportunity to be heard is contrary to the due process clause of the Fourteenth Amendment to the United States Constitution. The mandate of due process of law is satisfied by the procedural safeguards set out in West Virginia regulations, which provide:

(a) Written notice, describing in detail the proposed or requested action and a reason why such action is deemed appropriate or inappropriate for the child; specifying any tests or reports upon which the proposed or requested action is based; stating that the school files, records and other reports pertaining to the child will be available for inspection and copying at reasonable costs; giving the reasons why alternative placements are not appropriate for the child when the proposed or requested action involves placement or denial of placement; indicating the opportunity to obtain an independent evaluation of the child and including the names and addresses and telephone numbers of appropriate agencies where such services can be obtained; encouraging the parent to contact the county director of special education for a conference to discuss the matter; indicating the right to obtain a hearing if there are any objections to the proposed or requested action; listing those agencies in the community from which legal counsel may be obtained for those unable to pay for counsel; stating that the child will remain in the present educational placement until such time as there is a decision following a hearing or until a proposed educational placement is accepted by the parties.

(b) Providing for a hearing in the event that the conference with the parents does not result in an agreement as to the placement of the children including: a fifteen day written notice; assurances that the child will remain in the present educational placement until a decision is entered following the hearing; granting the parents the opportunity to obtain evaluation of the child's educational needs and giving the parents access to school reports, files and records pertaining to the child for inspection and copying at reasonable cost; the right to request the attendance at the hearing of any employee or agent of the county educational agency who might have testimony or evidence relative to the needs, abilities, or status of the child; the scheduling of the hearing within five days of the request and that the county board of education supply to the parents written notice of the time and place within at least fifteen days prior to the hearing; a verbatim record or tape recording of the proceedings to be provided by the county.

(c) That the hearing be presided over by an impartial hearing officer; that the parties have an opportunity to present their evidence and testimony; that the hearing shall be closed to the public unless the parents request an open hearing; that the parents and other persons have an opportunity to confront and question all witnesses at the hearing; that the child have the right to determine whether or not the child will attend the hearing; that the burden of proof as to the appropriateness of any proposed placement be upon the school personnel recommending the placement; that a decision be issued within thirty days of the decision in writing and forwarded by certified mail to the parents; that the decision include findings of fact, conclusions and reasons for these findings and conclusions; that such decision be based solely upon the evidence and testimony presented at the hearing; and that the parents be afforded a mechanism for administrative appeal. . . .

3.5. EVALUATION PROCEDURES[8]

Funding recipients must develop policies for the evaluation and placement of handicapped persons who require special education or related services. As in the case of 94-142, tests must be valid for the particular purposes for which they are used, and they must be administered by personnel who know what they are doing in the testing field. The tests must be tailored to discover each specific area of educational need rather than one single IQ. School administrators must also ensure that testing accurately reflects the student's achievement and ability, and that impairments that mask academic potential are taken into account. As in 94-142, teachers and other experts evaluating data are required to take into account many factors in evaluating a handicapped child, not solely testing. These factors include teacher recommendations, the child's social background, physical ability, and degree of adaptive behavior. Placement decisions must be made by a multidisciplinary team consisting of persons familiar with the performance and evaluation techniques used for the child as well as the various programs available. Reevaluation is required, and procedures set forth in 94-142 may be followed to meet 504 requirements. In 94-142, reevaluations must be performed at least once every three years. Opportunity to contest any placement must be given through appropriate due process procedures; those protections described under 94-142 may be implemented to meet the purposes and intent of this law.

3.6. NONACADEMIC SERVICES[9]

When academic services are provided to handicapped persons, nonacademic and extracurricular services must also be provided. Additional aids, if necessary, must be offered so that equal educational opportunity is afforded to handicapped persons. The additional aids and services must be provided in such areas as counseling, physical recreation and athletics, health services, clubs, groups, and other organizations sponsored by the recipient of federal money, including assistance to students in employment and placement services. HEW has commented that handicapped students must be allowed the opportunity to compete for team sports and participate in regular activities provided for nonhandicapped peers.

When possible, then, students who have a disability that does not substantially interfere with their participation must be allowed to participate. Section 504 also extends nondiscrimination against handicapped persons to preschool education, day-care programs, and adult or compensatory education programs; in addition, the needs of participants in these nontraditional programs must be taken into account, including provision of additional aids or services that would allow participation in these programs. Such programs would in many cases not be included within the coverage of 94-142.

3.7. Postsecondary Education

This area is another in which 504 differs from 94-142 in its educational coverage. The former covers each postsecondary education program, including vocational education, every college that receives federal financial assistance, and other higher-education programs and activities. Beginning with the admissions process, handicapped persons who are otherwise qualified to attend a certain institution cannot be denied admission or be subject to discriminatory practices in the admissions process if they are qualified to attend the institution. Testing that has a disproportionate impact on handicapped persons may not generally be used in admissions. As in the case of younger students, testing cannot be used if the disability masks an applicant's skills or level of achievement. Moreover, the testing must be performed in places physically accessible to handicapped persons. Although agencies may not discriminate against handicapped persons in this admissions process, they may request information relating to a handicapping condition if school administrators are in the process of taking voluntary affirmative action to remediate previous discrimination. The school must indicate that information regarding the extent of the handicap is intended for affirmative action purposes, and that supplying the information is voluntary and will be kept confidential.

When attending a postsecondary program, no handicapped student covered by the law will, solely on the basis of handicap, be excluded from programs or in any other way be discriminated against in training, housing, health programs, insurance, counseling or financial aid, physical education, athletics, recreation, transportation, extracurricular, or other programs. As in the case of the elementary and secondary programs, handicapped students must be integrated to the fullest extent possible with their nonhandicapped peers. In the area of academic services, schools must make modifications in their academic requirements if necessary to ensure that current policies do not have a discriminatory effect on a handicapped student otherwise qualified to participate in the program. Modifications include changes in the length of time permitted for the completion of degree requirements, substitution of specific courses required for the completion of degree requirements, and adaptation of the manner in which specific courses are conducted. If schools can demonstrate that specific academic requirements are essential to the program of instruction or to any directly related licensing requirement, these programs will not be regarded as discriminatory.

This requirement has been the subject of a substantial amount of litigation in the area of postsecondary programs. Students have, for example, brought legal action against schools to demand that they provide sign language interpreters for them in their courses. In one such case, *Camenisch v. University of Texas*,[10] a hearing-impaired graduate student who worked in the area of deaf education was denied a sign language interpreter, although he was qualified by background and credentials to otherwise participate in the class. The student brought suit, and a federal judge required the university to pay for an interpreter. Similar cases have been brought in North and South Carolina, thereby focusing public attention on the import of the law and its financial burdens. These cases have reinforced administrators' claims that Congress essentially passed a civil rights law without providing funding to implement the statute. There is no question, of course, that additional funding would be most helpful, but civil rights of disabled persons must initially take precedence.

Agencies serving handicapped students may not impose unfair and discriminatory regulations, such as prohibiting guide dogs or tape recorders on campus if these policies hinder student participation in school matters. In examinations, course requirements, and other areas in which the academic progress of a student might be tested, students who have handicaps that would impair their sensory, manual, or speaking skills must be tested in a manner that would best represent their actual level of achievement.

3.8. AUXILIARY AIDS[11]

Another source of litigation in the 504 regulations is the requirement for auxiliary aid. In full the law reads as follows:

> (1) A recipient to which this subpart applies shall take such steps as are necessary to insure that no handicapped student is denied the benefits of, excluded from participation in, or otherwise subjected to discrimination under the education program or activity operated by the recipient because of the absence of educational auxiliary aids for students with impaired sensory, manual, or speaking skills.
>
> (2) Auxiliary aids may include taped texts, interpreters, or other effective methods of making orally delivered materials available to students with hearing impairments, readers in libraries for students with visual impairments, classroom equipment adapted for use by students with manual impairments, and other similar services and actions. Recipients need not provide attendants, individually prescribed devices, readers for personal use or study, and other devices or services of a personal nature.[12]

This legal requirement has provoked litigation responsible for the first 504 case to reach the Supreme Court of the United States, *Southeastern Community College v. Davis.* [13] The essential question the case raises is: To what degree must auxiliary aids be provided? As some college administrators may ask, how much must be provided and how much accommodation must be made in a particular course of study or other postsecondary program? In *Davis*, a woman working as a practical nurse had a serious hearing disability and wished to be trained as a registered nurse. In seeking training for her potential occupation, she applied to the community college and was denied admission based on the college's view that she was not "otherwise qualified." Because Southeastern is run by the state and is a recipient of federal funds, 504 and its nondiscrimination provisions apply. The problem in *Davis* was that she was, according to an evaluation done by an audiologist, so severely hearing impaired that she could only understand the speech of others by reading their lips; hence the college rejected her application. It determined that as a result of the handicap she could not participate safely in the program or care appropriately and safely for patients as a registered nurse. She therefore sued in the U.S. District Court, asserting that she was discriminated against because of her disability in violation of 504. The court disagreed and found for the community college, agreeing that she could not safely participate either in the profession or in the initial training program offered by the school. The court decided that she was not an "otherwise qualified" handicapped person, and could not be granted admission on the basis of a 504 violation.

This holding was reversed by the federal court on the next level, the Court of Appeals for the Fourth Circuit, and the U.S. Supreme Court decided to hear the case. The Court was asked to consider the middle court's holdings that HEW, in promulgating its implementing regulations, meant that persons who were academically qualified should be able to participate in a program such as that offered by the community college.

The Supreme Court unanimously held that no violation of 504 had occurred. The judges found that Davis did not meet the requirement of being physically able to participate in the program, which the judges felt was a reasonable requirement considering the nature of the training program in question. The Court held that Davis would not reasonably benefit from the requirement of affirmative action incorporated in the regulations, and that she could not reasonably be a "qualified" individual even with the provision of the auxiliary aids required under this subsection. There was no need, according to the Court, to make what they considered to be major adjustments in the nursing program in order to accommodate the prospective nursing applicant.

This decision caused a storm of protest from advocacy organizations, who felt that the very purpose of the affirmative action and auxiliary aids provision in 504 is to remedy the type of discrimination they felt Davis faced. In their view the decision was a major setback and ran contrary to the spirit and intent of 504 law. The petitioner here, Davis, was certainly otherwise qualified to participate in the program, but could not because of her disability, resulting in what these groups saw as discrimination.

Although the final impact of the *Davis* decision will not be known until it is cited as precedent or distinguished in other court decisions, it would appear that it should be severely limited based on the facts of the case. The question of participation in postsecondary programs such as in the one in *Davis* would have to be decided on a case-by-case basis. In the interim, however, it would appear that *Davis* is strictly limited to highly technical, postsecondary training programs.

3.9. ACCESS TO POSTSECONDARY PROGRAMS: SOUTHEASTERN COMMUNITY COLLEGE v. DAVIS 442 U.S. 397 (1979)

MR. JUSTICE POWELL delivered the opinion of the Court.

This case presents a matter of first impression for this Court: Whether § 504 of the Rehabilitation Act of 1973, which prohibits discrimination against an "otherwise qualified handicapped individual" in federally funded programs "solely by reason of his handicap," forbids professional schools from imposing physical qualifications for admission to their clinical training programs.

I

Respondent, who suffers from a serious hearing disability, seeks to be trained as a registered nurse. During the 1973–1974 academic year she was enrolled in the College Parallel program of Southeastern Community College, a state institution that receives federal funds. Respondent hoped to progress to Southeastern's Associate Degree Nursing program, completion of which would make her eligible for state certification as a registered nurse. In the course of her application to the nursing program, she was interviewed by a member of the nursing faculty. It became apparent that respondent had difficulty understanding questions asked, and on inquiry she acknowledged a history of hearing problems and dependence on a hearing aid. She was advised to consult an audiologist.

On the basis of an examination at Duke University Medical Center, respondent was diagnosed as having a "bilateral, sensori-neural hearing loss." App. 127a. A change in her hearing aid was recommended, as a result of which it was expected that she would be able to detect sounds "almost as well as a person would who has normal hearing." App. 127a–128a. But this improvement would not mean that she could discriminate among sounds sufficiently to understand normal spoken speech. Her lipreading skills would remain necessary for effective communication: "While wearing the hearing aid, she is well aware of gross sounds occurring in the listening environment. However, she can only be responsible for speech spoken to her, when the talker gets her attention and allows her to look directly at the talker." App. 128a.

Southeastern next consulted Mary McRee, Executive Director of the North Carolina Board of Nursing. On the basis of the audiologist's report, McRee recommended that respondent not be admitted to the nursing program. In McRee's view, respondent's hearing disability made it unsafe for her to practice as a nurse. In addition, it would be impossible for respondent to participate safely in the normal clinical training program, and those modifications that would be necessary to enable safe participation would prevent her from realizing the benefits of the program: "To adjust patient learning experiences in keeping with [respondent's] hearing limitations could, in fact, be the same as denying her full learning to meet the objectives of your nursing programs."

. . . [T]he District Court concluded that respondent was not an "otherwise qualified handicapped individual" protected against discrimination by § 504. In its view, "[o]therwise qualified, can only be read to mean otherwise able to function sufficiently in the position sought in spite of the handicap, if proper training and facilities are suitable and available." Because respondent's disability would prevent her from functioning "sufficiently" in Southeastern's nursing program, the Court held that the decision to exclude her was not discriminatory within the meaning of § 504. . . .

On appeal, the Court of Appeals for the Fourth Circuit reversed. 574 F. 2d 1158 (1978). It did not dispute the District Court's findings of fact, but held that the Court had misconstrued § 504. In light of administrative regulations that had been promulgated while the appeal was pending, see 42 Fed. Reg. 22676 (May 4, 1977), . . . the appellate court believed that § 504 required Southeastern to "reconsider plaintiff's application for admission to the nursing program without regard to her hearing ability." Id., at 1160. It concluded that the District Court had erred in taking respondent's handicap into account in determining whether she was "otherwise qualified" for the program, rather than confining its inquiry to her "academic and technical qualification." . . .

. . . Section 504 by its terms does not compel educational institutions to disregard the disabilities of handicapped individuals or to make substantial modifications in their programs to allow disabled persons to participate. Instead, it requires only that an "otherwise qualified handicapped individual" not be excluded from participation in a federally funded program "solely by reason of his handicap," indicating only that mere possession of a handicap is not a permissible ground for assuming an inability to function in a particular context.

The court below, however, believed that the "otherwise qualified" persons protected by § 504 include those who would be able to meet the requirements of a particular program in every respect except as to limitations imposed by their handicap. See 574 F. 2d, at 1160. Taken literally, this holding would prevent an institution from taking into account any limitation resulting from the handicap, however disabling. It assumes, in effect, that a person need not meet legitimate physical requirements in order to be "otherwise qualified." We think the understanding of the District Court is closer to the plain meaning of the statutory language. An otherwise qualified person is one who is able to meet all of a program's requirements in spite of his handicap. . . .

Moreover, an interpretation of the regulations that required the extensive modifications necessary to include respondent in the nursing program would raise grave doubts about their validity. If these regulations were to require substantial adjustments in existing programs beyond those necessary to eliminate discrimination against otherwise qualified individuals, they would do more than clarify the meaning of § 504. Instead, they would constitute an unauthorized extension of the obligations imposed by that statute. . . .

We do not suggest that the line between a lawful refusal to extend affirmative action and illegal discrimination against handicapped persons always will be clear. It is possible to envision situations where an insistence on continuing past requirements and practices might arbitrarily deprive genuinely qualified handicapped persons of the opportunity to participate in a covered program. Technological advances can be expected to enhance opportunities to rehabilitate the handicapped or otherwise to qualify them for some useful employment. Such advances also may enable attainment of these goals without imposing undue financial and administrative burdens upon a State. Thus situations may arise where a refusal to modify an existing program might become unreasonable and discriminatory. Identification of those instances where a refusal to accommodate the needs of a disabled person amounts to discrimination against the handicapped continues to be an important responsibility of HEW.

In this case, however, it is clear that Southeastern's unwillingness to make major adjustments in its nursing program does not constitute such discrimination. The uncontroverted testimony of several members of Southeastern's staff and faculty established that the purpose of its program was to train persons who could serve the nursing profession in all customary ways. See, *e.g.*, App. 35a, 52a, 53a, 71a, 74a. This type of purpose, far from reflecting any animus against handicapped individuals, is shared by many if not most of the institutions that train persons to render professional service. It is undisputed that respondent could not participate in Southeastern's nursing program unless the standards were substantially lowered. Section 504 imposes no requirement upon an educational insitution to lower or to effect substantial modifications of standards to accommodate a handicapped person.

One may admire respondent's desire and determination to overcome her handicap, and there well may be various other types of service for which she can qualify. In this case, however, we hold that there was no violation of

§ 504 when Southeastern concluded that respondent did not qualify for admission to its program. Nothing in the language or history of § 504 reflects an intention to limit the freedom of an educational institution to require reasonable physical qualifications for admission to a clinical training program. Nor has there been any showing in this case that any action short of a substantial change in Southeastern's program would render unreasonable the qualifications it imposed. . . .

3.10. OTHER SECTION 504 PROVISIONS

Other provisions of the law cover housing for handicapped students in post-secondary institutions, financial assistance, and other nonacademic services. When a school provides housing for students, it must be available in "sufficient quantity and variety" so that handicapped students have similar options to participate in accommodations as would their nonhandicapped peers. When outside housing is arranged by a school that receives money from the federal government, the school must make certain that this housing is provided to handicapped students in a nondiscriminatory manner.[14] In the matter of financial assistance, an equal amount of assistance should be provided to handicapped as is to nonhandicapped students; nor can discriminatory measures be taken to limit financial aid for disabled students.[15]

A critical and frequently misunderstood requirement of 504 concerns accessibility for all handicapped persons to programs or activities maintained by recipients of federal funds, including schools.[16] Although each program run by these recipients must be made readily accessible to handicapped persons, not every part of every facility need be usable by handicapped persons. The key is allowing equal opportunity for participation in a class, laboratory, library, or other aspect of a school. Common sense can save school officials a good deal of money and consternation. For example, classes can be scheduled to take place in accessible buildings. Massive structural changes in currently existing buildings and other facilities are not required where less cumbersome and costly means are available. In determining how to make existing buildings comply with 504, schools must ensure that the method chosen allows the greatest amount of integration with nonhandicapped students. When there is no other feasible way to obtain accessibility to programs, HEW mandated structural changes as a last resort.

Even in the case of access to elective classes in universities, common sense prevails: only a "reasonable selection of elective courses in accessible facilities"[17] is sufficient for compliance. On the other hand, a university would not be permitted to bar a disabled student from a course specially required or requested by that student solely for the reason that it is not available in a suitably accessible building. Schools need not make every section of that course accessible. Specifically prohibited, however, is a consortium of universities in a specific geographic location designating one school in the group to be program accessible. [18] This action would restrict the choice of these students and, contrary to the law, would only be applicable to handicapped individuals. Any consortium arranged for the benefit of every student is accessible.

By now, buildings that were in existence at the time the 504 regulations were issued in May 1977 should have made all the required structural changes. The three-year grace period established at that time is now over. All new buildings must be constructed such that disabled students would have immediate access without structural changes. [19]

3.11. NOTES

1. 29 U.S.C. § 794. Regulations at 34 C.F.R. Part 104. Education sections at § 34 C.F.R. §§ 104.31 et seq. See generally Cherry v. Mathews, 419 F. Supp. 922 (D.D.C. 1976).
2. 34 C.F.R. § 104.3(k).
3. 34 C.F.R. § 104.3(i).
4. Gurmankin v. Costanzo, 411 F. Supp. 982 (E.D. Pa. 1976), aff'd, 556 F.2d 184 (3rd Cir. 1977).
5. 34 C.F.R. § 104.11.
6. 34 C.F.R. § 104.33; see Kruse v. Campbell, 431 F. Supp. 180 (E.D. Va. 1977), vacated and remanded, 98 S. Ct. 38 (1977) (E.D. Va., Jan. 5, 1978); Howard S. v. Friendswood Independent School District, 454 F. Supp. 634 (S.D. Texas 1978); cf. Halderman v. Pittenger, 391 F. Supp. 872; Scavella v. School Board of Dade County, 363 So.2d 1095 (S.Ct. Fla. 1978); and Cuyahova County Association for Retarded Adults v. Essex, 411 F. Supp. 46 (N.D. Ohio 1976); Levy v. City of New York, 345 N.E.2d 556 (Ct. App. N.Y. 1976).
7. 34 C.F.R. § 104.34; Hairston v. Drosick, 423 F. Supp. 120 (S.D. W.Va. 1976) (court ordered admission of spina bifida child to regular classroom); see also Pecunas v. Kline, Civil No. 78-3133 (E.D. Pa., filed Sep. 19, 1978) (resulted in admission of quadriplegic child with cerebral palsy to regular classroom).
8. 34 C.F.R. § 104.35.
9. 34 C.F.R. § 104.37. See, e.g., Kampmeier v. Nyquist, 553 F.2d 296 (2nd Cir. 1977).
10. No. A-78-CA-061 (S.D. Texas 1978), aff'd, 616 F.2d 127 (5th Cir. 1980). See also Barnes v. Converse College, 436 F. Supp. 635 (D.S.C. 1977); Crawford v. University of North Carolina, 440 F. Supp. 1047 (M.D.N.C. 1977).
11. 34 C.F.R. § 104.44(d).
12. Id.
13. 442 U.S. 397 (1979).
14. 34 C.F.R. §§ 104.43; 104.45.
15. 34 C.F.R. §§ 104.43; 104.46.
16. 34 C.F.R. §§ 104.43; 104.44.
17. 34 C.F.R. § 104.22 and comments to Part 104 at 45 C.F.R. p. 268.
18. Id.
19. 34 C.F.R. § 104.23.

4

THE SPECIAL EDUCATION HEARING
Preparation and Litigation

4.1. THE PURPOSE OF A HEARING

Federal right-to-education law provides for special education hearings in the event an impasse develops between parents and school officials relating to any aspect of an exceptional person's evaluation procedures, program, or placement.[1] The hearing right is assured, but the guidelines are brief and somewhat amorphous, so parties and their advocates must ascertain for themselves a good deal of information that affects their hearing but is not set forth in the 94–142 or 504 statutes and regulations.

It is important that whenever a hearing is considered, a prehearing conference or negotiation session, not specifically mandated by law, be held.[2] Some state laws provide for these conferences, and if at all possible, settlements avoiding hearings should be attempted. Hearings are frequently emotional, invariably time-consuming, and deplete funds and school personnel time that may, in some instances, be better spent educating the exceptional children who are the subject of the hearings. These factors should not dissuade parents or authorities who have a valid and supportable issue, but must be considered by either side when requesting hearings for purposes other than the best interests of the child. For example, it has not been unknown that school officials will seek a hearing to dissuade other parents from requesting similar and potentially costly related services, or that parents will do so in order to prove a point or "take the school to court." In practice, most controversies in special education can be resolved through the negotiation process.

A dispute having arisen, a hearing may be requested and scheduled. As mandated by P.L. 94–142's regulations, we know only that a final decision must be reached "not later than 45 days after the receipt of a request for a hearing";[3] still, several other deadlines need to be ascertained. When a request is made by a concerned party, does the local school district have a certain period in which to submit the request to the state education agency? Some states provide for a particular time when this request must be forwarded; in others no such time limit is set forth in state regulations or policy. It is possible that a request must initially be directed to the state agency. In any event, the name of the specific individual responsible for scheduling hearings should be determined to learn if and when the request has been received; when the hearing will be scheduled; and to have an appropriate contact from whom to obtain correct information or to direct complaints about procedural violations. In all circumstances it is wise and appropriate to check the information received from this source against both existing state and federal law, as well as with persons familiar with the special education system in the state. The hearing must be conducted by the state educational or other agency responsible for the child's education "as determined under state statute, state regulation, or a written policy of the State educational agency,"[4] according to 94–142 regulations. As such, a copy of the law, policy, or regulations must be obtained by any party requesting a hearing.

The agency is further required to inform parents of any free or low-cost legal assistance available.[5] Yet obtaining knowledgeable counsel for special education representation can be difficult. Public interest firms frequently concentrate on "law-reform" or "impact" cases, and their small staffs are usually not available for substantial numbers of individual cases. Legal aid or offices funded by the federal Legal Services Corporation often have other priorities or limited expertise in the field; private attorneys may be similarly untrained or economically unable to provide advocacy services. However, although these lawyers may not be available for total representation, they may be able to provide consultations on techniques and strategy. In any event, all of these sources should be contacted.

Lawyers are permitted to represent parents at hearings, and a school district will usually carry a staff lawyer or local attorney or retainer for hearing purposes. However, hearings are somewhat "informal" in the legal sense, and parents and educators frequently represent themselves.[6]

4.2. PREPARATION FOR THE HEARING

Laws and regulations often give little information about the specifics of organizing and preparing for a hearing. Any party can bring persons with "special knowledge or training with respect to the problems of handicapped children,"[7] and can "compel"[8] the attendance of other witnesses. Moreover, they can prohibit the introduction of "any evidence" not disclosed at least five days before the hearing is held.[9]

Ostensibly, the sole reason for holding a hearing is to consider a free and appropriate program of special education and related services for an individual exceptional child. Usually, however, the dispute is not quite so general. Instead only one aspect of the program such as the type and amount of a particular service to be provided is at issue; however, specific placements or a classification may also be under dispute. It must always be kept in mind that, legally, a hearing officer is entitled to change an entire program based on the evidence presented; any party initiating a hearing should be cautioned to consider this fact when challenging specific aspects of a large program.

After determining the several issues to be litigated, next comes the question of finding evidence for a party's viewpoint. A party convinced of the rightness of a certain principle may find little or no documentary support for that stand. At this critical juncture, parents especially must decide whether to seek additional independent experts. School districts, on the other hand, usually have reports, documentation, and experts readily available, and have based their educational decisions on that evidence. The cost of expert analysis is an important concern for most parents; high expenses are associated with retaining psychological and medical authorities who are also familiar with special education. In certain circumstances, experts with a special interest in an area may well wish to testify at limited cost or for expenses incurred. Other evaluations may be available on a sliding-scale basis from local mental health/mental retardation centers, but parents, through previous experience or for fear of the stigma of "welfare" evaluations, sometimes prefer not to consider these centers for assistance. Thus the cost, inconvenience, and time lost in securing independent evaluations have to be weighed against the benefit sought from the hearing.

If a parent's own experts are needed and available, they should be instructed in special education legal procedures and about the purpose of their evaluation. Any potential conflicts of interest should be determined. For instance, many experts in a particular geographic location are consulted by educational agencies. Another problem with well-known experts is whether they will be available for the hearing date, since lectures, teaching, consultations, and other obligations are often scheduled far in advance.

After independent evaluations are administered, it is mandatory from the standpoint of the child's advocate that the evaluator, parent, representative, and the child, when possible, meet together to discuss the testing results. All other educational, medical, and psychological records must be obtained pursuant to P.L. 94–142 before this time, and relevant documents made available to the expert. This meeting is a prerequisite for determining whether a hearing should occur. All aspects of the testing procedures should be discussed, and a well-organized presentation of the examiner's conclusions and recommendations for the child's program must be given. It is this latter section of any evaluation that is crucial for determining if parents should proceed with hearings, and that will be used as evidence in the event testimony is eventually presented. This expert must also be called upon to distinguish differences among various existing reports, if any, and to explain how these disagreements arose.

If the hearing is to continue after consultation with independent experts, further and substantial preparation remains. After determining all issues to be litigated and gathering all expert reports, a decision is made concerning expert witnesses to be presented. At times the number of witnesses willing to testify is overwhelming. In the course of an exceptional person's academic career, a great number of professionals, including teachers, therapists, physicians, and psychologists have played some role, and there can be many volunteers to serve as witnesses at a hearing. It cannot be too greatly emphasized that the list of witnesses must be strictly limited to those individuals who not only have a specific knowledge of the child, but who can also contribute to an understanding of the issues at hand. Although noted experts can be marshaled for a cause (many experts in this field are also experienced witnesses), their use when they have not directly tested a child should be limited to explaining a technical point or program. Such witnesses should at least examine extant reports on the exceptional person. In general, though, persons of renown who have no specific knowledge of the child's requirements contribute little, take up time, and obfuscate the unique and specific programs the need for which a party seeks to prove. In all cases, a curriculum vitae or résumé must be obtained for use at the hearing that includes experience, degrees, and publications.

The preparation of experts is time-consuming but unavoidable in building a hearing. After documents are examined and the issues have been distilled, a party must draft a list of specific questions that will develop a witness's purpose before the hearing officer and on the record. The initial requirements include a display of who the witness is and his qualifications, including name and business address as well as current title and employment. Involvement with the child and a description of tests performed, if any, as well as conclusions and recommendations are detailed. When an initial draft of queries has been concluded, the potential witness must again be contacted and the questions read to him as if at a hearing. It is not unknown that a distinguished practitioner may be nervous. Moreover, this step is necessary to develop additional questions and to ascertain if those proposed accurately describe the exceptionalities, tests performed, and conclusions an expert believes are applicable. Unless it is absolutely not feasible, these meetings should be in person, not by telephone. In this way accurate meanings can be determined, and witnesses become somewhat more used to being personally confronted with the specific questions to be asked.

All persons to be questioned at a hearing must be similarly prepared, whether scientific experts, teachers, administrators, or, especially, parents. It is rare when a hearing is not trying and burdensome to the parents of an exceptional person. The very act of requesting a hearing means that specific demands have been made and have been refused by officials acting in what they invariably believe to be an appropriate manner. A hearing is thus a last resort to obtain a related service, placement, or other program aspect parents have been seeking for some extended period. These same parents are now required to bring a legal action and to confront the same administrator with whom they have a conflict. To further complicate matters, this very same school authority will, if a parent is successful, be legally mandated to implement a program previously rejected as unsound. Finally, the exceptional person frequently will be enrolled in the same school district for years to come.

It is therefore apparent that parents are in a difficult and emotionally trying position by the time a hearing date arrives. In some cases years of frustrating attempts to secure the best educational program available for an exceptional person must be painstakingly documented.

That is not to imply, on the other hand, that at a hearing parents should be deprived of the opportunity to explain their reasons for seeking a particular program. A history of the person's exceptionality and the attendant difficulties encountered in school must be presented, and the tasks the person performs out of school must be described. The point is that the hearing is not an appropriate forum for presenting a generalized petition of grievances to a readily available designee of the chief state education authority, the hearing officer. As in the case of all witnesses, questions must be focused so that the record will reflect a child's capabilities and needs, as seen by the individuals who have had significant contact with the child. This stipulation holds for professionals, parents, and teachers who may be called upon to relate their observations of particular academic needs and skills.

The question-drafting and interrogation process must, of course, be repeated individually for each witness—several times if possible or necessary. When this stage is complete, it is extremely worthwhile to gather favorable witnesses together so that a "mock" hearing can be conducted. The purposes of this technique are to give witnesses the opportunity to learn how their testimony fits into a coherent whole, to ensure that they will maintain their positions under hearing conditions, and, most importantly, to allow other participants the opportunity to suggest additional critical testimony that had not previously been discussed.

The rules and policies regarding hearings and hearing officers should be examined in detail. Generally, materials have been developed by school officials for the purpose of training hearing officers, and this information should be obtained. Little-known hearing officer's handbooks are available to the public and may be studied to discover exactly which evidence the hearing officer is trained to consider. State and federal regulations and statutes must be learned so that their relation to the particular case can be analyzed. Different states also have distinct rules for administrative-agency hearings (which may or may not be in conformity with state and federally mandated special education procedures). Included in these local procedures are requirements regarding which party has the burden of proof concerning particular special education issues. As a rule of thumb, the party proposing the change has the burden of proving an issue, but the degree of proof may vary in the different states. For example, one jurisdiction may require that matters in administrative proceedings be proved by "substantial evidence on the record." Another may require a case to be proved by a "preponderance" of the evidence.

The U.S. Supreme Court long ago defined substantial evidence as evidence "affording a substantial basis of fact from which the fact in issue can be reasonably inferred".[10] A "preponderance" is a somewhat more difficult burden to meet, requiring the hearing officer to weigh evidence to ascertain which party is more believable. A third and higher standard is "clear and convincing" evidence, which requires an extremely convincing case virtually unchallenged by an adversary's evidence. Whichever standard a state requires, it may be helpful to examine previous due process hearing decisions and court appeals to learn how cases are handled by the state's system.

4.3. AT THE HEARING

There will be some preliminary housekeeping to be resolved upon arriving at the actual hearing. Of primary importance for witnesses is the need to meet with them briefly as they arrive and repeat the basic caveats concerning their presentations. They should be advised to answer only the questions asked them, and new and surprising information should not be volunteered. In addition, they should be advised to ask that the attorney or advocate repeat or explain a question if they do not understand it. They should remember to be firm in their views, but not contentious with an adversary or opposing advocate. The attorney should make clear to the hearing officer and court stenographer, if one is there, the names of the representatives and of the witnesses, so that the reporter's job will be easier and the hearing will go more smoothly. In addition, special education hearings often involve technical terms including medical, legal, and educational jargon, or esoteric school policies or forms. Copies of prepared documents containing these terms are helpful for the hearing officer and reporter and should be supplied to them.

Although some state policies have predetermined which parties will open or present evidence second, these rules are not inflexible and a representative should make certain at the outset in what order the parties will present their case. Frequently, parents have spent a good deal of time, effort, and their own funds in arranging for witnesses to be present; thus, in the interest of obtaining all relevant testimony quickly and efficiently, it may be advisable to allow parents to present their case first. School officials who will testify on the opposite side are present and available because hearings invariably take place in school buildings or administrative offices. Furthermore, a statement concerning whether the hearing will be open or closed to parties not directly involved in the hearing process should be made to the hearing officer and placed on the record. Persons who arrive for a closed hearing to observe the proceedings should be excluded by the hearing officer.

4.4. The Hearing Officer[11]

The hearing officer has been selected by the state secretary of education and should be totally unfamiliar with the specifics of the case at hand. Most likely, officers will be from a different intermediate education unit, and in all cases they may not be an employee of the school district involved in the hearing. They are present to hear testimony regarding the person whose program is in dispute, and not to hear a general list of grievances either from parents or school district officials relating to the unfairness of the system, or problems with special education in the state. It should be underlined that in every hearing the purpose is to place testimony on a record, and the personality or background of the hearing officer is not in dispute. At least one court that frequently hears appeals of special education decisions has recently held that objections to the fairness of a hearing officer should be placed on the record of the hearing or they will be deemed to be waived.[12] This decision is a strategic one on the part of the representative, involving whether a hearing officer should be immediately antagonized before a multihour (or potentially multiday) hearing involving his client. Unless the hearing officer has a blatant conflict of interest, appeals courts will generally not reverse decisions on this basis alone, so it might be best not to challenge the officer's objectivity merely because his stipend is paid by the administrative agency. Quite often the hearing officer may also hold the same administrative post as the person the parents are challenging, but this situation would not appear to be a conflict of interest so egregious as to lead to reversible error on appeal. Nevertheless, the possibility of challenging a hearing officer's fairness is available and should at least be considered.

As in all legal hearings, the hearing officer should not be unnecessarily harassed. The purpose of the hearing is to determine a program for an exceptional child and not to become involved in self-serving histrionics. Objections should be made respectfully, and a basis for each objection should be set forth. A key objection is to limit a witness to testifying on the subject in which he is qualified. When a hearing officer rules on an objection, a ruling has been made and the hearing should continue. Although it is not necessary to take a formal "exception" to the hearing officer's ruling, the objection should be clearly stated and made known for purposes of appeal.

4.5. The Opening Statement

The hearing officer will call on representatives of both parties to see if they wish to present an opening statement. These statements are not legally required, but they are an integral part of the organization of a hearing. At least a brief presentation should be made at the outset. It should include a succinct statement of the exceptional person's legal rights detailed by state law and regulations, as well as school district or other agency guidelines. The law cited should specifically relate to the present hearing. The second aspect to be covered is a description of the child's exceptionality and a brief procedural history leading to the present hearing. The third major aspect is a brief description of the testimony to be presented and references to the individuals who will be testifying. Basically, the opening statement relates how the story will be told and develops for the record and the hearing officer how and by whom the case will be related.

The following is a model opening statement.

The Hearing Officer: It has been determined that this will be a hearing closed to the public. As such, the transcripts and hearing opinions will exclude personally identifiable information and parties who are not testifying or representing either side will be excluded from the hearing room. Does the attorney for the parents have an opening statement?

Mr. Goldberg: Yes, I do. The State Department of Education's regulations, known as 22 Pa. Code Chapter 171, provide that an exceptional person's school district of residence has the sole responsibility for providing to that person a free, appropriate program of special education and related services that must meet the child's unique needs. If the local district is not able to provide the program "effectively and efficiently," it must seek the services of an intermediate education unit. If both of these local educational agencies cannot offer such a program, the law requires that a program be funded in a private special education school or other more restrictive institution.

Before supporting the need for a nonpublic placement, a school district superintendent, as well as the intermediate unit's special education director, must certify to the chief state school officer, in this case the secretary of education, that all lesser restrictive placements have been examined and found inappropriate. This continuum of educational placements consists of a combination of programs, from the placement of an exceptional child in a regular class with regular programs to special schools, to private schools. When private school is determined appropriate by local officials, these local districts must, according to law, file an application for this purpose with the State Department of Education responsible for funding the program. The application describes why the lesser restrictive program is necessary to meet the child's needs in a particular case.

In this special case, John is a severely and multiply handicapped person who is mentally, as well as physically, handicapped. He suffers from emotional disturbance, learning disabilities, and is a paraplegic. His local school district has been unable to provide a program for his needs and as a result filed the appropriate supporting documents with the intermediate education unit and the Department of Education. The intermediate education unit also certified that it could not provide a program that would be appropriate for John's needs. Because both local education agencies could not meet John's educational requirements, the school district recommended the Johnson School, a state-approved private school for children who are learning disabled and also emotionally disturbed. It is also physically accessible for children who have wheelchairs. The school district's own psychologist, who has evaluated John, as well as his child neurologist have supported this recommendation.

As John's representative, I intend to present three kinds of witnesses. The first are school district officials who will describe the existing programs in their agencies. They will show that the process by which John's placement application was completed is accurate and in conformity with the law and John's needs. The second group of witnesses will be the school's own psychologist, Mr. X., the pediatric neurologist, Dr. Y., and an independent evaluator and psychologist, Dr. Z., who are experienced with the problems of persons with John's requirements. They will describe the evaluations they have performed, results of these evaluations, and their recommendations for an educational program. Finally, John's mother will testify as to his skills and difficulties in the learning and developmental process.

As a result of this testimony, the record will completely support the assertion that the Johnson School is the only appropriate program that can reasonably meet John's needs. We do not, of course, claim that all programs supported by parents or school districts should be approved in all cases or that every exceptional person is by law entitled to receive the most expensive or convenient placement available. We do claim, however, that John's placement at the school recommended for him, or at a similar placement, is in accordance with the minimum requirements of state and federal law that a free appropriate program be made available to serve an exceptional child's unique educational needs.

4.6. The Presentation of Witnesses

Virtually everyone who has ever presented a special education hearing has a separate and distinct theory regarding the presentation of expert and lay witnesses. Some claim that parents should make an opening statement and should also testify first, thereby creating an immediate and emotional impression concerning the child's requirements. Others would exclude parents from opening and closing statements, and would allow school officials and experts to testify first. From a standpoint of creating an effective case, the attorney should direct the order of witnesses and should be the sole person to make the opening statement. Repetition and unnecessary emotion should be avoided in all instances. The hearing "foundation" should be developed by presenting witnesses in the natural order they have affected the issues in the case at hand. In particular instances, the order may need to be changed in order to obtain the testimony of an expert who must leave early, or because a particular witness may not be able to arrive until substantially after the hearing begins.

Once the opening statement is made and the child's needs are set out, as well as the issues that will be presented and proved, the particular order of expert witnesses is probably not of overwhelming importance. It is worthwhile to present those whose official actions have formed the basis for the resulting hearing, so that experts such as medical and psychological witnesses can then relate the child's needs. In some cases school district superintendents or special education officials should be presented first to describe the procedural matters that led to their policy, decisions, and determinations for placement and programming. Then come the medical and psychological witnesses, who describe the particular child's needs and program recommendations. Finally, the parent, as the person who has responded to the placement decisions and recommendations of the school district and independent evaluators, should be presented. In this fashion the parent can summarize why a particular program is appropriate in light of the child's perceived needs, skills, and accomplishments. The parents have requested the hearing, and it is their thoughts that constitute an effective and worthwhile summary to conclude a hearing.

4.7. The Testimony of School District Officials

The initial witnesses, such as school district administrators, are used to lay a foundation for the more substantive witnesses. Basically, they should be required to state their name and place of employment, as well as their particular position in the school district. They should describe their duties and responsibilities in their position as well as those in connection with the administrative special education responsibilities in general. They should then be asked to relate their responsibility in the specific case and to state the information they relied on in making the particular placement determination. Aside from the school district superintendent, who may not be a necessary witness in all cases, there is usually a director of special education. Questions for these officials involve more specific information. Depending on their responsibilities, it may be necessary to ascertain their prior positions with the particular school district and their previous experience; whether and to what degree they are acquainted with the particular student; the process by which the local district prepares its placement recommendations; the procedures that were followed in this particular case; and the involvement this person had in preparing the placement recommendation. In addition, they should be asked to describe the recommended educational program and the information relied on in formulating this recommendation.

These officials are also used to identify school district documents for later use in the hearing. They should be required to explain why particular classes, placements, or programs were not considered, and should describe the rejected alternatives in detail. In the case of a more restrictive placement, officials should be asked why less restrictive alternatives were not considered, and why programs outside the local school district may be the only ones appropriate. They may also be called upon to describe their familiarity with the program and services that have been recommended. After the documents have been described, usually at the end of the testimony, they should be entered into evidence. Questions should cover such relevant matters as

- Class size
- Ages of the children
- Characteristics of children in the class
- IQ range
- Teacher–pupil ratio
- Supportive and related services

The use and presentation of this material at a hearing depends on the ultimate litigation strategy, but these questions and suggested materials are basic and should at least be considered.[13]

4.8. MEDICAL TESTIMONY

Generally speaking, medical testimony is not central to the development of a special education program, but must always be considered when the needs of a handicapped child are in dispute. Especially in the case of physical or occupational therapy, physicians are called upon to certify certain conditions and prescribe services to be provided by therapists and other personnel. In the case of an emotionally disturbed exceptional person, psychiatric (or psychological) evaluations are frequently required for placement, and the testimony of the school district and independent psychiatrist (or psychologist) is of substantially more importance than it would be in other types of cases.

Like other experts, physicians must be qualified as such. Their name and profession should be stated, and a summary of their educational background, training, and work experience be provided. Their résumés should be entered into the record. The physicians should then be asked if they have ever medically evaluated the student, when the evaluation took place, and for what purpose. They should also be asked to describe (1) the tests and procedures used and the purpose for each test; (2) the physical or relevant mental impairment the person has; (3) the diagnosis arrived at as a result of that evaluation, setting forth the reasons why the diagnosis was established; and (4) other medical evaluations, and the tests used.

The physician should be requested to read the diagnostic impressions and recommendations into the record, explaining the particular medical terminology employed. The main problems should be summarized and the programs and services, based solely on the physician's expertise and personal involvement, should be described. Again, the particular documents related to the physician, his résumé and medical evaluations, should be entered into the record at the appropriate times during the course of the testimony.

4.9. THE PSYCHOLOGICAL TESTIMONY[14]

The most critical kind of testimony is that of the educational psychologist. It is this person who has tested and evaluated the person's current level of achievement, potential for the future, and social and emotional development. A psychological expert is trained to perform the testing and is familiar with such matters as teaching techniques, psychological counseling, and services available and under development. If the school district's psychologist is the individual whose recommendations are disputed by parents at a hearing, it is critical that a competent and independent psychologist be obtained by parents to test and evaluate the child. This expert is also particularly helpful in comparing the child's needs to the school district evaluation, and is in a position to spend substantially more time conducting an evaluation than are harried and overburdened school district psychologists. Private "psychologicals" are, in large part because of the time available, usually more thorough in every aspect: the observations recorded; tests administered; results of the testing; diagnostic impressions; and the recommendations for programs and services.

In most areas there are known experts available who have knowledge of and training with children of various exceptionalities. One of the the best methods for finding an expert is to contact the various advocacy groups for exceptional children, including the Association for Retarded Citizens, the Association for Children with Learning Disabilities, the Society for Autistic Children, and the various mental health groups. Failing that, medical schools and large hospitals will have such experts on the staff or at least persons who can recommend an expert.

As previously described, the psychologist should meet with the advocate, and the due process procedures and purpose of the testimony should be gone over. The psychologist's background must be ascertained and a schedule established for evaluating the child and issuing a report. In each case an advocate should determine the qualifications required by the state school code for certified school psychologists and an independent evaluator should, unless it is not feasible, be state certified/licensed in all respects.

Like other witnesses, psychological witnesses should be qualified as experts in their field. Their name, professional and educational background, training and experience should be described briefly but in enough detail to establish their status as an expert. Such things as clinical experiences, teaching, and some publications might be noted. Training in the specific needs of children such as the one whose program is in question should also be detailed. A résumé should be obtained and entered into the record.

The witness should be shown a psychological evaluation of the child and asked to identify it for the purpose of the record. At that point the following questions are relevant:

- How long did it take to complete the evaluation?
- How long does it usually take to complete a comparable battery of tests? (This question is relevant in cases where the hyperactivity or distractibility of a child is relevant in terms of making test scores or in setting a foundation for the unique services that may be required.)
- Describe the particular techniques used to deal with the testing difficulties the child may have.

The major part of psychological testimony concerns the testing performed and a description of the type of tests used and the purposes to which they will be put. Although a description of all the tests used and the results may be somewhat lengthy and detailed, it must be included to give an appropriate picture of the student. Each procedure must be separately described, and their relationship to the expert's diagnostic impressions must be detailed. At the conclusion of the evidence relating to testing, educational recommendations and services should be detailed in light of the psychologist's impressions. When appropriate, the conflicting testimony of others should be distinguished, and the appropriateness of a particular program should be either supported or rejected with suitable data.

4.10. The Parent as a Witness

As described in the section on preparation, the parent is invariably an important witness, not as a psychological or medical expert but to detail everyday observations of the child's progress and function. Many parents have in the course of their dealing with a child's exceptionality become quite versed in the current professional literature of the field, but they usually are not professional experts and their testimony should be limited to parental observation. Questions should center around experiences in school, extracurricular activities, and the household as they relate to the programs and services that must be addressed by the hearing officer. A brief educational history should be included; the following information may also be relevant: (1) the types of extracurricular activities in which the child has participated; (2) the organized activities in which the child has participated outside of school; (3) current daily activities, such as participation in religious or social groups; (4) the child's responsibilities around the home; (5) the types of children the child plays with and the games in which he participates; and (6) the ability to make independent decisions.

In light of these descriptions, a parent may be asked for his thoughts regarding the level of the exceptional person's abilities and the type of program in which he would best function.

4.11. CROSS-EXAMINATION[15]

There are numerous materials available on the art of cross-examination, but a few brief points should be noted as they relate to due process hearings. Each witness, including parents, can be cross-examined by an adversary. Although it is not always possible to make assumptions about the types of questions an adversary may ask after cross-examination has begun, any perceived weaknesses in a witness's testimony should be fully exposed during the preparation period. In this way inconsistencies and uncertain testimony during the hearing will be avoided. The issues are known to each party, and testimony is based on evidence made available to the opposing party at least five days before the hearing. Thus questions for cross-examination can be prepared and discussed beforehand. Witnesses should in all cases attempt to avoid appearing defensive on cross-examination. The classic admonition for lawyers is that they should never ask questions (even at due process hearings) when they are not absolutely certain of the answer.

4.12. CLOSING STATEMENT

Much like an opening statement, a closing statement is neither legally required nor procedurally mandated. It does serve to summarize the testimony presented to a hearing officer after what is generally a fairly lengthy proceeding. The testimony of each key witness should be summarized in a few sentences and, most importantly, a reasonably detailed summary should be given of an exceptional child's programmatic needs. Finally, the particular placement deemed appropriate by the parent's experts should be noted.

After the cases are presented the hearing is concluded, but some additional material may be recorded, including requests for free, written transcripts or for extensions of time. In a particularly lengthy hearing the officer may ask for some time greater to issue a report than that provided for in the state or federal regulations, and it is usually advisable not to protest this request unless it is patently unreasonable. Representatives should submit briefs to the hearing officer, including suggested findings of fact, conclusions of law, and recommended programs and services. It is at this point that such requests should be made and a time set for submitting briefs.

4.13. APPEALS[16]

After the hearing officer's opinion is received, a decision has to be made as to whether an appeal should be taken to a higher authority, either the state secretary of education or a court. Although the hearing officer may not have decided all factors in a parent's favor, the opinion may still be favorable. It may detail a larger number of services than anticipated, or the specific placement described may differ from the one sought but still be appropriate. In considering the options available, a representative, the parent, as well as the person, if possible, should discuss an appeal in light of the fact that everything gained may be lost by an appeal. The entire opinion, or any part of it, can be altered if the ultimate administrative authority sees the record in a different manner than the hearing officer. Because the child remains in the same placement throughout the course of all administrative and judicial proceedings, time may be of the essence and no appeal may be warranted. A parent may not wish to delay further the educational program, although certain aspects may not be exactly the ones that were sought. Moreover, if the opinion is generally favorable, minor programmatic aspects could conceivably be changed when the individualized education program is developed or revised. All these factors carry weight, and an appeal is not and should not automatically be taken in every case.

If the decision to appeal is made, it must be done in consideration of the time guidelines and other policies set forth under 94-142, state regulations and guidelines. For example, 94-142 provides that a final appeal by the chief state school officer must be rendered no later than thirty days after a request for review is received by the state,[17] but state policy may be limited by other time constraints. In all circumstances copies should be submitted to the opposing party, who may wish to respond. This opportunity to respond is sometimes delineated by state procedures.

When the state education secretary issues a final opinion on appeal, it is considered the final decision of the state administrative agency. As such, it may be appealed to the appropriate state court or, under 94-142, it may be appealed by either party to state or to federal court.[18] At this point the parties may attempt to avoid court proceedings by filing a request for the administrative agency to review its final decision. State administrative codes usually provide for such reconsideration of administrative-agency decisions, and these codes should be studied for the procedures that would be involved. Although the chance of an official reconsidering a recently issued decision may be slim, this strategy may be implemented to underline particularly glaring aspects of testimony that were not covered, and its use may avoid lengthy and expensive litigation in court.

4.14. MODEL EXCEPTIONS

IN RE: X

EXCEPTIONS TO DECISION OF THE HEARING EXAMINER

AND NOW COMES "A," the father of "X," and assigns the following exceptions to the decision issued by "Z," Hearing Officer. The Officer's decision recommended placement of "X" in a regular classroom in the _____ School of the _____ School District, with resource room services to be provided to "X." Appellant believes that the Officer's decision is in error and submits the following in support of this belief:

  1. The Hearing Officer's decision is not supported by
     substantial evidence.

The hearing officer's function is to weigh the evidence presented by both the parent and the school district/intermediate unit in order to determine the educational needs of an exceptional child. The officer is bound to uphold a school district's proposed educational assignment if there is substantial evidence in the record of a due process hearing to support each element of the proposed assignment. The officer must explain why the school district's proposal will meet the child's needs in light of the evidence presented at the hearing; if his findings are not supported by substantial evidence, the officer's recommendation will be rejected if appealed. (Right to Education Hearing Officer's Handbook, Pennsylvania Department of Education, 1975, at pp. 2, 11.)

It is clear to all parties in this case that "X" needs a special educational program because he suffers from a specific learning disability. Unfortunately, the school's facilities fail to meet his needs. He has been
attending a state-approved private school where he has been making excellent
progress. Testimony at the hearing shows that his self-esteem and his
confidence have markedly improved in his present placement there.

There is a great deal of discussion in the testimony regarding the
resource room services in "X's" school district of residence, which is
a very small district. There is a critical lack of testimony, however,
which shows any positive relationship between the services available and
"X's" individual needs--a relationship which, under the Department of Education's own instructions, a hearing officer must find in order to uphold
a school's proposed placement. (Right to Education Hearing Officer's
Handbook, supra p. 11.)

In stark contrast to the demonstrated success of the private school
program, there is no evidence that the school district service approved by
the hearing officer for "X" will continue to meet his individual needs. The
hearing officer's opinion relies heavily on the testimony of "C," Coordinator
of Disabilities Programs for the district. Yet "C" testified that he had
never observed "X" in a classroom situation; he did not prepare a prescriptive program for "X" at the conclusion of his testing, and he did not
know how much daily support was necessary to keep "X" functioning with school
skills commensurate with his age. (Transcript, pp. **-**.)

The hearing officer also relied on the testimony of "D," the resource
room teacher. But "D" is not certified to teach learning-disabled children.
Moreover, although she testified that a special educational program should be
individually designed to meet each student's needs, no such prescriptive program tailored to "X's" specific educational needs has been presented in this
case. In fact, "D" testified that she did not even consider whether a resource room placement would exacerbate "X's" emotional problems. (Trans-
script, pp. **-**.)

Individualized education programs for handicapped children are legally

required under the holdings of <u>Frederick L. v. Thomas</u>, 408 F. Supp. 832
(E.D. Pa. 1976) and <u>Fialkowski v. Shapp</u>, 405 F. Supp. 946 (E.D. Pa. 1975)
and by federal law, including the Education for All Handicapped Children
Act, 20 U.S.C. §§ 1401, <u>et</u> seq. and Section 504 of the Rehabilitation
Act of 1973, 29 U.S.C. § 794, as well as their implementing regulations.
34 C.F.R. Part 300 and §§ 104.1, <u>et</u> seq., respectively. Thus, in this
regard, the hearing officer's decision is not only without substantial
evidentiary support, but is also contrary to law.

This failure to consider "X's" emotional situation is critical with
regard to the need to continue his program in the school he has been
attending. "X" has a well-documented history of emotional disorientation
in his previous school district placement.

When "X" first began to experience difficulty with reading, the
school district's solution was to transfer him to a class for lower-
achieving students. The district's own expert witness, Dr. "Y," concluded
that "'X' does have considerable anxiety and will need to learn to relax."
(Transcript, p. *** School Dist. Exhibit*, p. *.) Dr. "G," a certified
school psychologist and his personal tutor, testified that

> he was feeling stress and strain--he was
> not in a good state emotionally...he was
> extremely unhappy and lacked self-esteem....

He continued that "X"

> was feeling an incredible amount of stress...
> no improvement of his emotional condition seems
> likely in his present placement.... (Transcript,
> p. ***.)

"X's" father also testified that his child would become emotionally
distressed with being put into a lower-achieving group. (Transcript, p.***.)
These problems, directly related to a previous school district placement,
were not even considered by the hearing officer in this matter.

For the above-described reasons, the hearing officer has failed to
follow his mandate to uphold a school district's proposed placement only
if such placement meets a child's individual needs, and his decision is
unsupported by substantial evidence and contrary to law. It must therefore be reversed.

   2. **The Hearing Officer's decision was issued in violation of**
      special education due process procedures.

The hearing officer is bound by Pennsylvania Special Education regu-

lations, 22 Pa. Code § 13.61(c)(21), to issue a written decision no later

than 20 days after the hearing, and to send such decision by registered

mail to the parents and their representative.

   In this case, the hearing was held on July 3, 1976. The Decision

was received by Mr. and Mrs. "A" on October 2, 1976. A passage of this

amount of time is not only a prima facie violation of due process, but

also ensures that "X's" placement in a public school will be disrupted for

yet another year. The time spent in determining a program for "X" could

cause serious educational and emotional harm and might well impede his fur-

ther progress. A timely decision might have avoided such disruption and

allowed for a full resolution of this case before the commencement of yet

another school year. Instead, the procedural violations affect "X's" sub-

stantive rights, and are in themselves grounds for reversal.

   Conclusion

   The hearing office is charged with the responsibility for approving a

school's proposed plan for an exceptional child only if it can be shown by

substantial evidence that the plan meets a child's individual needs.

This burden has not been met.

   Recent federal law and cases also emphasize the need to provide an

individual eduation program suited to a child's specific needs. Although

these needs may possibly be met by trial and error in a school district

placement, they are currently being met in the private school placement--

a placement sought by the parents only after the school district had

failed to consider this student's emotional and learning needs.

   Furthermore, the hearing officer's decision was issued in violation of

due process regulations.

   Thus the hearing officer's recommendations should be rejected, and

"X" should remain in his current placement, which has proved suitable to

his learning needs and emotional well-being. It should be continued.

THE SPECIAL EDUCATION HEARING

```
     WHEREFORE, the Appellant respectfully submits that in light of the

error and defects in this record, that:

     a.   the hearing officer's decision be reversed;

     b.   "X" be maintained in a proper placement that offers a program of

special education and related services appropriate to his individual needs.



                                        Respectfully submitted,



                                        STEVEN S. GOLDBERG, ESQUIRE
```

4.15. Appeal to Court[19]

After all the administrative proceedings have ended, an appeal can be taken by either party to state or federal court. Time deadlines for filing appeals should be considered, and the drawbacks and benefits of seeking court relief should be studied. Remember again that the child is to remain in the current placement unless other suitable arrangements are agreed to between the parent and the school district. Importantly, this is one stage in which an attorney must in every case be retained (although there is no legal prohibition against parents representing themselves in court at any time). Expenses, including filing fees, reproduction of records, legal time for drafting pleadings, filing papers, the cost of printing and distributing these briefs, and argument time in appeals court are critical factors an attorney must discuss with the client. Finally, the time consumed in judicial appeal will most certainly involve substantial delay. Years may pass from the initial hearing request to a court's final order.

4.16. Notes

1. 34 C.F.R. § 300.506.
2. The comments to 34 C.F.R. § 300.506 suggest but do not require mediation between the parties to a special education dispute.
3. 34 C.F.R. § 300.512(a).
4. 34 C.F.R. § 300.506(b).
5. 34 C.F.R. § 300.506(c). This information must be provided pursuant to this section if "(1) The parent requests the information; or (2) The parent initiates a hearing under this section."
6. Parents have an absolute right to be represented by counsel, but they may of course represent themselves. 34 C.F.R. § 300.508(a).
7. 34 C.F.R. § 300.508(a)(1).
8. 34 C.F.R. § 300.508(a)(2).
9. 34 C.F.R. § 300.508(a)(3).

10. National Labor Relations Board v. Columbian Enameling and Stamping Company, 306 U.S. 292 (1939).
11. 34 C.F.R. § 300.507.
12. Savka v. Commonwealth of Pennsylvania, Department of Education, 403 A.2d 142, 145 (Pa. Commw. 1979).
13. State administrative practice codes and special education hearing officer manuals, if any, should be consulted to determine the type of information that is stressed in a particular jurisdiction, in terms of both how a case should be presented and what a hearing officer will examine in making a determination in a particular case.
14. There are numerous materials available relating to the use of psychologists as expert witnesses in legal cases, as well as to the use of their data in the courtroom. *See, e.g.*, R. L. SCHWITZGEBEL & R. K. SCHWITZGEBEL, LAW AND PSYCHOLOGICAL PRACTICE (1980).
15. Law libraries are the best source of information on cross-examination matters. Some of the more popular volumes in this field include H. BODEN, PRINCIPLES OF CROSS-EXAMINATION (1967); I. GOLDSTEIN, GOLDSTEIN TRIAL TECHNIQUE (1969–present); and I. YOUNGER, THE ART OF CROSS-EXAMINATION (1976).
16. 34 C.F.R. § 300.510.
17. 34 C.F.R. § 300.512(b).
18. 20 U.S.C. § 1415; 34 C.F.R. § 300.511.
19. *Id.*

5

Major Issues in Special Education Law

5.1. Continuous Special Education

The free appropriate public education mandates of P.L. 94–142 and Section 504 on their face require an individualized program of education and related services to meet the unique and individual needs of each handicapped child. Based on expert evaluations, parents have requested and hearing officers have ordered programs that may, in terms of days to be spent on a program, exceed the usual limit of days set by state school codes for the normal school year. In this case an obvious conflict arises, and parents in the past have been faced with the choice of accepting the program and services offered or taking legal steps to ensure individualized education.

In *Armstrong v. Kline*,[1] a case that has become the legal landmark in this area, parents challenged the refusal of certain local Pennsylvania school districts and the State Department of Education to provide programs in excess of the state's "normal" school year of 180 days. The handicapped persons and their parents who commenced *Armstrong* claimed that an "appropriate" program for certain seriously impaired children, including those who are severely and profoundly retarded and others who are emotionally disturbed, cannot be restricted to an arbitrary 180-day limit. They did not argue that all handicapped students need such special education or even that programs must last twelve months. For this group of children, however, substantial breaks in programming led to regression during summers, resulting in a deprivation of skills developed during the previous school year. They had to start from scratch each September. Although plaintiffs admitted that most children regress to some extent, they claimed that their total loss of skills during summer program breaks made educational programming leading to progress impossible. Moreover, the case raised serious questions regarding the definition of an appropriate education for severely impaired children.

Armstrong was certified by the court as a class action, allowing this case to be brought on behalf of all handicapped children in the state who need or may require an educational program in excess of the state-limited 180-day period. Two policies were challenged: the refusal of state or local education agencies to provide programs in excess of 180 days, and a state policy barring parents from the opportunity to prove the need for such programs at special education hearings.

Trial was held in federal district court in Philadelphia, and Judge Newcomer rendered his opinion on June 21, 1979. In ruling for the plaintiffs, the judge agreed that the particular class of impaired children is subjected to regression attributable to programming breaks. Additionally, for certain of these children who regress, there is a limited ability to recover skills lost during these breaks. Included in this group are certain severely and profoundly impaired, autistic, and socially and emotionally disturbed children.

According to the court, the plaintiffs were legally correct in asserting that not all children who are classified within these groups are entitled to programming beyond the regular school year. Instead, in accordance with the requirements of P.L. 94–142 law, each program and the need for education without substantial break periods must be determined as part of an individualized education program. If a dispute about a continuous program arises, hearing officers must accept evidence regarding the handicapped child's individual needs and, if applicable, must order programming in excess of 180 days.

The court agreed that even with 94–142's definition of appropriate education, "it is still sometimes difficult to determine precisely what the state is required to provide." At the very least, however, the legislative history of the federal law shows that Congress intended to adopt the PARC standard describing the educational needs of retarded persons, who are all

> . . . capable of benefitting from a program of education and training; that the greatest number of retarded persons, given such education and training, are capable of achieving self-sufficiency, and the remaining few, with such education and training, are capable of achieving some degree of self-care.[2]

In applying this standard to the *Armstrong* case, the court found that

> the defendants' 180 day rule precludes plaintiffs and those similarly situated from receiving an education that is likely to allow them to reach their reasonably set educational goals with respect to self-sufficiency, whether that be merely avoiding institutionalization or living in a community living arrangement and working in a sheltered workshop.[3]

The 180-day rule is therefore in violation of P.L. 94–142. *Armstrong* was appealed, and the United States Third Circuit Court of Appeals issued its decision on July 15, 1980. Although the three judges filed separate opinions, there is no question that they agreed with plaintiffs contentions that special education cannot legally be limited to a "normal" school year if certain students require additional programming.

The impact of *Armstrong* is difficult to assess at this early date, although it seems apparent to advocates that its implications are at least initially limited to the class of children delineated by this court. At least one court, in Oregon, has followed *Armstrong* in approving a year-round special education program, and a similar case has been filed in South Carolina. Claims that *Armstrong* will result in twelve-month programs for all the handicapped students—and eventually for all students—are on the face of the *Armstrong* opinion unwarranted.

5.1.1. *Special Education beyond the "Normal" School Year: Armstrong v. Kline (629 F.2d 269)*

HUNTER, *Circuit Judge.*

1. The Education for All Handicapped Children Act, 20 U.S.C. §§ 1401–1420 (1976), requires that every state which elects to receive federal assistance under the Act provide all handicapped children with the right to a "free appropriate public education," *id.* § 1412, and establishes detailed procedures for implementing that right. *Id.* § 1415. The Commonwealth of Pennsylvania, a recipient of aid under the Act, has established an administrative policy which sets a limit of 180 days of instruction per year for all children, handicapped or not. We are called upon, in this case of first impression, to examine the scope and purpose of this recent act and to decide whether Pennsylvania's policy and the statute may coexist. We conclude that they may not. . . .

5. The Education for All Handicapped Children Act, 20 U.S.C. §§ 1401–1420 (1976), represents an attempt by Congress to assist the states in meeting the burdens imposed upon them by the widespread judicial recognition . . . of the right of handicapped children to a free public education appropriate to their needs. . . .

The Act establishes a program of cooperative federalism which sets requirements which must be complied with in order for states to be eligible to receive financial assistance. A number of these requirements are relevant to the instant case. First, each state seeking assistance must have "in effect a policy that assures all handicapped children the right to a free appropriate public education," 20 U.S.C. § 1412(1) (1976), and must develop a plan which details the policies and procedures which insure the provision of that right. *Id.* § 1412(2). Each state must also establish the requisite procedural safeguards, *id.* § 1412(5), and must insure that local educational agencies in the state will establish the individualized educational programs required by the Act, *id.* § 1412(4). Compliance is enforced by the requirement that the state plan must be submitted to and approved by the Commissioner of Education before the state is entitled to assistance. *Id.* § 1413.

6. At the center of the controversy in this case is the definition of "free appropriate public education." According to the Act, "free appropriate public education" means

special education and related services which (A) have been provided at public expense, under public supervision and direction, and without charge, (B) meet the standards of the state educational agency, (C) include an appropriate pre-school, elementary, or secondary school education in the state involved, and (D) are provided in conformity with the individualized education program required under section 1414(a)(5) of this title.

Id. § 1401(18). "Special education" is defined as "specially designed instruction, at no cost to parents or guardians, to meet the unique needs of a handicapped child, including classroom instruction, instruction in physical education, home instruction, and instruction in hospitals and institutions." *Id.* at § 1401(16). "Related services" are those services which "may be required to assist a handicapped child to benefit from special education. . . ." *Id.* § 1401(17). These include transportation and developmental, corrective, and supportive services such as speech pathology, audiology, recreation, psychological services, certain medical services, . . . physical therapy, occupational therapy, and counseling services. *Id.*

7. The individualized educational program (IEP) provides the vehicle for giving content to the required "free appropriate public education." The IEP is a

> written statement for each handicapped child developed in any meeting by a representative of the local educational agency or an intermediate educational unit who shall be qualified to provide, or supervise the provision of, specially designed instruction to meet the unique needs of handicapped children, the teacher, the parents or guardian of such child, and, whenever appropriate, such child, which statement shall include (A) a statement of the present levels of educational performance of such child, (B) a statement of annual goals, including short-term instructional objectives, (C) statements of the specific educational services to be provided to such child, and the extent to which such child will be able to participate in regular educational programs, (D) the projected date for initiation and anticipated duration of such services, and (E) appropriate objective criteria and evaluation procedures and schedules for determining, on at least an annual basis, whether instructional objectives are being achieved.

Id. § 1401(19). The IEP must be reviewed and revised by the local educational agency at least annually. *Id.* § 1414(a)(5).

8. In order to assure that the IEP is properly formulated to provide a free appropriate public education, the Act prescribes several procedural safeguards. Whenever the local agency proposes to change or refuses to change the identification or evaluation of a child, or the provision of a free appropriate public education to a child, the child's parents or guardian must be notified, and the parents or guardian must be given the opportunity to present complaints about any such matter. *Id.* § 1415(b)(1). When a complaint is made, the parents or guardian are entitled to an impartial due process hearing, conducted by a hearing examiner unrelated to the local agency involved in the care of the child, or by the state educational agency. *Id.* § 1415(b)(2). If the hearing is conducted by a hearing examiner, any

aggrieved party may appeal to the state educational agency. *Id.* §
1415(c). . . . The hearing examiner is appointed by the DOE and may not be
an employee of the district or intermediate unit . . . from which the case
originates. It is, however, the policy and practice of the DOE to refuse to
provide or to fund the provision of education in excess of 180 days per year
for any child, handicapped or nonhandicapped. . . . In keeping with this
policy, the DOE has instructed hearing examiners that they are "without
authority to, and may not, order a special education program which is in
excess of 180 days per year." *Id.* at 587.

B. The Plaintiff Class

12. Although the plaintiff class has been broadly defined, the district
court classified the handicapped children involved into two general groups:
the severely and profoundly impaired by mental retardation alone or, as is
frequently the case, combined with other impediments; and the severely
emotionally disturbed. These conditions vary greatly from child to child and
generalization is difficult and may suggest seductively simple solutions. . . .

18. The district court, faced with the difficult question of the validity of
the 180 day rule, perceived the issue as defining the parameters of a "free
appropriate public education." This analysis began with the definition of
special education be designed "to meet the unique needs" of the handicapped child. The court, however, recognized that

> "[n]eeds arise in [the] context of achieving certain ends, and surely there are
> certain ends, and not others, that are the concern of this legislation." *Id.*
> From this perceptive conclusion, the court sought to discern the educational
> goals intended by the statute to be attained by the plaintiff class. Finding no
> guidance in the Act itself, the court turned to the legislative history. There,
> the district court found language to support its conclusion that

"[t]he congressional intent was to provide for that education which would
leave these children, upon school's completion, as independent as possible
from dependency on others, including the state, within the limits of the
handicapping condition." *Id.* at 604. Based on this legal conclusion, and its
finding that the 180 day rule precluded these children from attaining that
degree of self-sufficiency which they could otherwise (i.e., with the 180 day
rule) reach, the district court invalidated the 180 day rule.

IV.

19. The core of this case is the conflict between the 180 day rule and
the statutory mandate of "free appropriate public education." The district
court concluded that the Act provides a specific educational goal for members of the plaintiff class. We believe that by focusing on the Act as providing
a particular educational goal, the district court erred. Rather, the Act contemplates that in the first instance each state shall have the responsibility of
setting individual educational goals and reasonable means to attain those

goals. The Act, however, imposes strict procedural requirements to insure the proper formulation of a free appropriate public education. We conclude that the 180 day rule precludes the proper determination of the content of a free appropriate public education, and, accordingly, that it violates the Act.

20. To reach this conclusion, we must necessarily interpret the Act's requirement of a free appropriate public education. Unfortunately, the Act provides only limited guidance. First, free appropriate public education must meet the standards of the state educational agency. 20 U.S.C. § 1401(18)(B) (1976). Second, it must be provided in conformity with an individualized education program. *Id.* § 1401(18)(D). Finally, the Act requires that special education, which is a component of "free appropriate public education," meet the unique needs of the handicapped child. *Id.* § 1401(16). We find nothing in the Act or regulations promulgated thereunder which further amplifies these provisions so as to provide a clear solution to the conflict in this case. *See generally Rowley v. Board of Educ.*, No. 79-2139, slip op. at 11–12 (S.D.N.Y. Jan. 17, 1980).

21. The requirement that a free appropriate public education meet the unique needs of the child raises the most difficult question. As the district court properly recognized, needs are necessarily determined in reference to goals. 476 F. Supp. at 603. The only reason a child needs certain programming is to accomplish certain educational objectives. If those objectives are removed, these needs cease to exist. We must, therefore, decide how the Act contemplates that appropriate educational goals are to be determined.

22. The first possibility, of course, is that the Act itself mandates specific educational goals. Here, again, however, we find little assistance. In requiring that education programs for handicapped children meet the child's unique needs, the Act appears to focus on those needs which derive from the difference between the handicapped child and a normal child. Thus, the Act probably anticipates that, where possible, educational objectives for the handicapped should be set with reference to those objectives established for the nonhandicapped. . . . So, for example, a blind or deaf child may be expected to attain educational achievements commensurate with normal children upon the provision of special services, such as braille books or a sign language interpreter. . . .

31. Having concluded that the states are responsible in the first instance for setting reasonable educational objectives and reasonable means to achieve those objectives, it falls upon us to determine if the Act restricts the states in these determinations. We believe that it does. First, the Act provides for pervasive federal oversight by the Commissioner of Education. Second, the Act sets forth explicitly detailed procedures to assure that the states will properly exercise their responsibility to provide "free appropriate public education." We now consider whether by imposing the 180 day rule the Commonwealth of Pennsylvania comes into conflict with these provisions of the Act.

32. At the core of the Act is a detailed procedure for determining the

contours of the free appropriate public education to be delivered to each child. 20 U.S.C. § 1415. . . .

We believe that these procedural safeguards require individual attention to the needs of each handicapped child. *See Lora v. Board of Educ.*, 456 F. Supp. at 1226 (clear national commitment to meet each child's special needs in a complete and integrated way). . . .

The strongest statement of this requirement is the statutory mandate of individualized educational programs. The IEP is the statutory vehicle for formulating the educational objectives and the educational program for each child. We consider it most persuasive that at this fundamental point in the educational decision making process, the statute requires consideration of each individual child. Nor do the later procedures required by the Act depart from this emphasis. The appeal prescribed by the Act is an appeal from the decisions reflected in IEP. *See* 20 U.S.C. § 1415(b)(2) (1976). Moreover, as difficult as it is to define the scope of the "unique needs" which must be met by special education, *see id.* § 1401(16), there can be little doubt that by requiring attention to "unique needs," the Act demands that special education be tailored to the individual.

33. This emphasis on the individual is necessary in light of the wide variety of the handicapping conditions covered by the Act. The Act explicitly includes the following children within the meaning of "handicapped children":

> mentally retarded, hard of hearing, deaf, speech impaired, visually handicapped, seriously emotionally disturbed, orthopedically impaired, or other health impaired children, or children with specific learning disabilities, who by reason thereof require special education and related services.

Id. § 1401(1). Indeed, even within the limited conditions which characterize the plaintiff class there is a wide divergence of educational characteristics. This divergence is reflected in the findings of the district court which note the variance among members of the plaintiff class in their degree of impairment, 476 F. Supp. at 588–90, their recovery time from regression, *id.* at 596–97, and the ability of their parents to provide programming, *id.* at 594–95.

34. We believe the inflexibility of the defendants' policy of refusing to provide more than 180 days of education to be incompatible with the Act's emphasis on the individual. Rather than ascertaining the reasonable educational needs of each child in light of reasonable educational goals, and establishing a reasonable program to attain those goals, the 180 day rule imposes with rigid certainty a program restriction which may be wholly inappropriate to the child's educational objectives. This, the Act will not permit.

35. To be sure, the Act contemplates that reasonable educational standards may be set by the states. *See* 20 U.S.C. § 1401(18)(B) (1976) (definition of "free appropriate public education"); *id.* § 1412(2)(B) (development

of state plan detailing policies and procedures). We believe, however, that these standards must allow for individual consideration of each handicapped child. . . .

5.2. DISCIPLINE AND SPECIAL EDUCATION

Excluding students for behavior that teachers find disruptive is a traditional punishment in American schools. Although suspensions and expulsions may well remain a legally acceptable administrative practice, the U.S. Supreme Court held in the famous 1975 case, *Goss v. Lopez*,[4] that the ability to suspend is not unlimited. According to the Court, a student's education is a constitutionally protected liberty interest on which the government cannot infringe without benefit of due process of law. Thus, in *Goss*, where students were excluded for periods up to ten days without the protections of notice and a hearing, the Court called for appropriate procedures holding that the "total exclusion from the educational process for more than a trivial period . . . is a serious event in the life of a suspended child."[5] Suspensions may not be "imposed by any procedure the school chooses, no matter how arbitrary."[6] The damage to a student's reputation, both in school and for potential employment, may be permanent, and the student must be protected.

As a result of *Goss*, state and local boards of education were required to develop a suitable hearing procedure, including notice to a suspended student and the opportunity to respond to the proposed exclusion, in school statutes, statewide regulations, or other guidelines. Statutes or policies allowing suspensions or expulsions for unlimited periods were thus constrained, at least so far as they involved exclusions up to ten days without the notice and hearing requirement.

For exceptional children entitled to a right to education, exclusions create a separate concern. Although all students are protected by *Goss* and the U.S. Constitution, these children—in particular, the mentally handicapped—have been subject to inconsistent treatment in the disciplinary exclusion process. Before the *PARC* case, for example, retarded children were subject to arbitrary exclusions when their conduct was thought to be disruptive. The *PARC* Consent Decree and resulting State Board of Education regulations resulted in the legal requirement that any suspension or expulsion of a retarded child is deemed "a change in educational assignment which would . . . require notice and a due process hearing" to determine an appropriate special education placement. When a disciplinary matter involving a retarded student is "so immediate or severe" as to require "summary action" an exclusion can take place, but a special education hearing must be held "promptly," as this removal is an "interim change" in an educational setting.[7]

Section 504 and P.L. 94–142 and their implementing regulations do not address exclusions of handicapped children as specifically as does *PARC*. No time limitations are set for suspensions or expulsions, nor is an exclusion included as an absolute change of educational assignment. In a comment to one section of 94–142's regulations (34 C.F.R. § 300.552), HEW analysts wrote that a handicapped child may be removed from a placement when the program of other class members is "significantly impaired." A similar statement may be discovered in comments to a 504 regulation provision (34 C.F.R. § 104.34). These comments strongly imply that a parent–school meeting, or possibly a hearing, must be held to determine an appropriate placement, but no such mandate is specifically included in the law. This concern was settled by several cases brought on behalf of mentally handicapped children faced with expulsion.

In *Stuart v. Nappi*,[8] a Connecticut case, a learning-disabled and emotionally disturbed high school student was threatened with expulsion as a result of several school incidents. She requested an evaluation and a hearing to determine her special education needs, but was threatened with permanent expulsion before this program could be resolved. A federal court enjoined the expulsion hearing, holding that 94–142 requires all handicapped students to remain in their current educational placements when special education procedures to resolve placements are ongoing. To remove a student from a current placement would otherwise not be in conformity with the Education for All Handicapped Children Act.

Donnie R. v. Wood,[9] with similar facts, was brought primarily under Section 504. After a South Carolina school district expelled this student, who was emotionally disturbed, for fighting, he was removed without benefit of notice and only received a hearing following the passage of several weeks. The hearing resulted in permanent exclusion despite his disability. As a result of a court-approved consent decree, evaluations and an educational placement were eventually agreed upon. In still another case involving a consent decree for all exceptional children protected by 94–142 in Mississippi, plaintiffs and school officials agreed that any exclusion of a handicapped child in excess of three days triggers an IEP review, and continuous or "serial" three-day suspensions are prohibited.[10] (For other implications of this important case, see Section 2.2.)

5.2.1. A Federal Court Opinion: Stuart v. Nappi (443 F. Supp. 1235)

DALY, District Judge.

Plaintiff, Kathy Stuart, is in her third year at Danbury High School. The records kept by the Danbury School System concerning plaintiff tell of a student with serious academic and emotional difficulties. They describe her as having deficient academic skills caused by a complex of learning disabilities and limited intelligence. Not surprising, her record also reflects a history of behavioral problems. It was precisely for handicapped children such as plaintiff that Congress enacted the Education of the Handicapped Act (Handicapped Act), 20 U.S.C. § 1401 *et seq. See* 20 U.S.C. § 1401(1).

Plaintiff seeks a preliminary injunction of an expulsion hearing to be held by the Danbury Board of Education. She claims that she has been denied rights afforded her by the Handicapped Act. Her claims raise novel issues concerning the impact of recent regulations to the Handicapped Act on the disciplinary process of local schools. . . . As a handicapped student in a recipient state, plaintiff is entitled to a special education program that is responsive to her needs and may insist on compliance with the procedural safeguards contained in the Handicapped Act. After scrutinizing the recent regulations to the Handicapped Act and reviewing both plaintiff's involved school record and the evidence introduced at the preliminary injunction hearing, this Court is persuaded that a preliminary injunction should issue. . . .

On September 14, 1977 plaintiff was involved in school-wide disturbances which erupted at Danbury High School. As a result of her complicity in these disturbances, she received a ten-day disciplinary suspension and was scheduled to appear at a disciplinary hearing on November 30, 1977. The Superintendent of Danbury Schools recommended to the Danbury Board of Education that plaintiff be expelled for the remainder of the 1977–1978 school year at this hearing. . . .

. . . The Handicapped Act and the regulations thereunder detail specific rights to which handicapped children are entitled. Among these rights are: (1) the right to an "appropriate public education"; (2) the right to remain in her present placement until the resolution of her special education complaint; (3) the right to an education in the "least restrictive environment"; and (4) the right to have all changes of placement effectuated in accordance with prescribed procedures. Plaintiff claims she has been or will be denied these rights.

Plaintiff argues with no little force that she has been denied her right to an "appropriate public education." The meaning of this term is clarified in the definitional section of the Handicapped Act. Essentially, it is defined so as to require Danbury High School to provide plaintiff with an educational program specially designed to meet her learning disabilities. *See* 20 U.S.C. § 1401(1), (15)–(19). The record before this Court suggests that plaintiff has not been provided with an appropriate education. Evidence has been introduced which shows that Danbury High School not only failed to provide plaintiff with the special education program recommended by the PPT in March of 1977, but that the high school neglected to respond adequately when it learned plaintiff was no longer participating in the special education program it had provided. . . .

Plaintiff also claims that her expulsion prior to the resolution of her special education complaint would be in violation of 20 U.S.C. § 14-15(e)(3). . . . This subsection of the Handicapped Act states: "During the pendency of any proceedings conducted pursuant to this section, unless the state or local educational agency and the parents or guardian otherwise agree, the child shall remain in the then current educational placement of such child... until all such proceedings have been completed." Plaintiff qualifies for the protection that this subsection provides. . . .

It is important that the parameters of this decision are clear. This Court is cognizant of the need for school officials to be vested with ample authority and discretion. It is, therefore, with great reluctance that the Court has intervened in the disciplinary process of Danbury High School. However, this intervention is of a limited nature. Handicapped children are neither immune from a school's disciplinary process nor are they entitled to participate in programs when their behavior impairs the education of other children in the program. First, school authorities can take swift disciplinary measures, such as suspension, against disruptive handicapped children. Secondly, a [change may be requested] in the placement of handicapped children who have demonstrated that their present placement is inappropriate by disrupting the education of other children. The Handicapped Act thereby affords schools with both short-term and long-term methods of dealing with handicapped children who are behavioral problems. . . .

5.2.2. The Legal Arguments: Kenneth J. v. Kline

(Set forth by the Education Law Center in its motion on behalf of the plaintiff for a Temporary Restraining Order, June 28, 1977.)

The legal arguments asserted in *Kenneth J. v. Kline*[11] cover the entire range of law that preserves and protects the rights of exceptional children to obtain an appropriate placement, when threatened with exclusion. In this case, a fifteen-year-old emotionally disturbed student was involved in several school conflicts, but an expulsion decision was prompted by a particular alleged incident involving a teacher. Attorneys for Kenneth asserted violations of 504 and 94–142. Moreover, since the case originated in Pennsylvania, the state where *PARC* regulations are in effect, his representatives claimed that state law allowing protection of mentally retarded but not learning-disabled or emotionally disturbed students violated the U.S. Constitution's guarantees to due process and equal protection under the law. The legal claims in this case are supported by statutes and court decisions that describe and document the right of exceptional students to a hearing, as opposed to exclusion.

If one is faced with a similar situation, the following arguments and authorities set forth by the plaintiffs in their pleadings should be considered. Remember that the legal arguments made in *Kenneth J.* are especially interesting for those concerned with the special education/discipline interface, because Pennsylvania law protected mentally retarded but not other exceptional children. The following is a summary of the legal arguments presented.

1. *Excluding exceptional students denies them due process of law.*
   a. *Introduction.*

"Where certain 'fundamental rights' are involved, the [Supreme] Court has held that regulations limiting those rights may be justified only by a 'compelling state interest,' and that legislative enactments must be narrowly drawn to express only the legitimate state interests at stake."

Not only fundamental rights are protected by the due process clause. Once a right falls within the due process clause guarantee of liberty, the inquiry is whether a legitimate state interest is served, and if so, if the legitimate state interest reasonably requires such intrusion on individual liberty.

Plaintiffs asserted that Section 1318 (allowing exclusions of any student) as enforced against nonretarded, mentally handicapped, school age children deprives those children of their protected rights and, under either of the above tests, must be held to violate the due process clause.

   b. *Excluding mentally handicapped students violates the due process clause of the Fourteenth Amendment.*

The importance of a public education has been consistently reaffirmed by the Supreme Court. It held in *Meyer v. Nebraska* that "[t]he American people have always regarded education and acquisition of knowledge as matters of supreme importance which should be diligently promoted."

At least some of the plaintiffs in this case, including the named plaintiff, were excluded from all educational opportunity as a result of defendants' action. In addition, since the named plaintiff is a handicapped child, this deprivation will be even more egregious than a similar deprivation would be for a normal child who is less in need of supportive services in order to learn and to function adequately in society.

But regardless of whether education is considered a fundamental right, it is clearly a state-created right of vital importance protected by the due process clause:

> While this court has not attempted to define with exactness the liberty thus guaranteed [by the due process clause], the term has received much consideration and some of the included things have been definitely stated. Without doubt, it denotes not merely freedom from bodily restraint but also the right of the individual to contract, to engage in any of the common occupations of life, to acquire useful knowledge, to marry, establish a home and bring up children, to worship God according to the dictates of his own conscience, and generally to enjoy those privileges long recognized at common law as essential to the orderly pursuit of happiness by free men.

A second protected right, in fact a fundamental right, is abridged by defendants' indiscriminate use of Section 1318. In *St. Ann v. Palisi*, the court held that the due process clause protects an individual's right to be punished only on the basis of personal guilt. In *St. Ann*, the school board involuntarily transferred two children because their mother was disruptive. Finding that this action was a violation of the above-described fundamental right, and that the violation was not justified by a compelling state interest, the court overruled the school board's transfer.

That the State Board of Education (the defendants) recognizes that the suspension or expulsion of a mentally handicapped child may be punishing him because his handicap is causing him to act out, rather than for voluntary misconduct, is clear from the language of 22 Pa. Code Section 13.62, the regulation that protects mentally retarded children faced with disciplinary action:

> Section 1318 (24 P.S. Section 13-1318) means that the suspension of a mentally retarded child under the same circumstances as a typical child might amount to punishment for a ramification of the very disability which a public school program of education is attempting to remedy. To avoid such a result, it shall first be concluded that a suspension or expulsion pursuant to Section 1318 is a change in educational assignment which would, except as provided in this section, require notice and a due process hearing.

The exception referred to in Section 13.62(2) is set out in Section 13.62(3), which states:

> Acknowledging, however, that a disciplinary problem with a mentally retarded child may be so immediate or severe as to require summary action, the parties in Pennsylvania Association for Retarded Children v. Commonwealth of Pennsylvania, 334 F. Supp. 1257 (E.D. Pa. 1971) agreed to Amended Stipulation 3(V). Thus, in those cases which warrant immediate action, and after the approval of the State Director of Special Education, an interim change in the educational assignment of a mentally retarded child, in the form of suspension, expulsion or other placement, may be made so long as there is a due process hearing as promptly as possible after that interim change.

The second interest, the exclusion of disruptive children so that others may learn, is a legitimate state interest. However, the indiscriminate application of Section 1318 to mentally handicapped children without regard to their handicap is entirely unnecessary to achieve this goal.

As Pennsylvania law recognizes with regard to mentally retarded children, special education hearing procedures must be commenced to determine an appropriate educational placement for the child. The law provides a mechanism for dealing with an emergency situation, namely, an interim change in placement subject to a prompt hearing.

An identical procedure could be established for nonretarded mentally handicapped children without any additional cost or disadvantage to any of the defendants, and there can be no rational basis for not establishing such a procedure.

The failure of the state defendants to provide this protection for plaintiff and plaintiffs' class violates the due process clause of the Fourteenth Amendment, as does the continued expulsion and suspension of nonretarded mentally handicapped children without regard to their handicap by the school board defendants and the continued failure of the school board, school district, and intermediate-unit defendants to provide such children with appropriate programs of education or training.

2. *Excluding nonretarded mentally handicapped children from school without regard to their disability denies them equal protection of the laws.*

There are two equal protection violations in this case. The first violation is the distinction drawn between the nonretarded mentally handicapped and the mentally retarded children by the operation of 22 Pa. Code Section 13.62. The second violation is the disparity in treatment between nonretarded mentally handicapped children and normal children. This disparity is attributable to Section 1318, which allows defendant school boards to expel or suspend both normal children and nonretarded mentally handicapped children without regard to the latter group's handicap.

3. *A hearing that fails to take account of the handicaps or educational needs of the plaintiff violates the Fourteenth Amendment's guarantees of procedural due process.*

That a public education is a property and liberty interest protected by the due process clause of the Fourteenth Amendment is beyond dispute. However, "[o]nce it is determined that due process applies, the question remains what process is due." The basic requirement, in any case, is that "at a minimum... deprivation of life, liberty or property... be preceded by notice and opportunity for hearing appropriate to the nature of the case."

Plaintiff and members of plaintiff class, threatened with suspensions or permanent expulsions, are granted the right to a hearing in Section 1318. That hearing, however, is only concerned with whether misconduct alleged was actually committed and whether that misconduct warrants an exclusion. The plaintiffs contended that the only type of hearing that would be "appropriate to the nature of [their] case" must take into account the relation of a handicap to that conduct and to their educational needs as mentally handicapped children. It is this kind of hearing that Section 13.62 guarantees to mentally retarded children when it provides that a proposed suspension or expulsion of a retarded child must be treated as a proposed change in educational placement. Such a proposed change triggers a due process hearing under 22 Pa. Code Sections 13.1 *et seq.,* the object of which is to determine what educational program is appropriate to meet that mentally retarded child's needs.

No such protection, however, is afforded to nonretarded mentally handicapped children, such as learning-disabled or emotionally disturbed children, who are at least as likely as retarded children to misbehave as a consequence of their disability. The above-described Section 1318 hearing currently available to plaintiff and the plaintiff class takes no cognizance of this fact, and thus does not comply with the requirements of procedural due process.

4. *Defendants' conduct violates plaintiff's civil rights under Section 504 of the Rehabilitation Act of 1973.*

The Rehabilitation Act of 1973, 29 U.S.C. Section 701 *et seq.*, provides as follows at Section 504 (29 U.S.C. Section 794):

> No otherwise qualified handicapped individual in the United States, as defined in Section 7(6), shall solely by reason of his handicap, be excluded from the participation in, be denied the benefits of, or be subjected to discrimination under any program or activity receiving federal financial assistance.

"Handicapped individual" is defined in 29 U.S.C. Section 706(6) as:

> . . . any person who (A) has a physical or mental impairment which substantially limits one or more of such person's major life activities, (B) has a record of such impairment, or (C) is regarded as having such an impairment.

The plaintiff, an emotionally disturbed child, is clearly a "handicapped individual" under the above definition. He was acknowledged by the school district as suffering from a disability for many years, and has been receiving special services for that disability since 1974.

The plaintiff is therefore entitled to the protection of Section 504. It is also clear that the defendants, or the governmental units for which they are responsible, receive "federal financial assistance," including but not limited to funding under the Education of the Handicapped Act, 20 U.S.C. Section 1401 *et seq.*

The regulations of the Department of Health, Education and Welfare applying Section 504 to elementary and secondary education programs—45 C.F.R. Section 84.31 *et seq.*—prohibit discrimination against handicapped students as practiced by the defendants herein. Section 84.33(a) provides:

> A recipient that operates a public elementary or secondary education program shall provide a free appropriate public education to each qualified handicapped person who is in the recipient's jurisdiction, regardless of the nature or severity of the person's handicap.

Those children "who, because of handicap, need or are believed to need special instruction or related services" must receive, under Section 504, a special education due process hearing when it becomes clear that they can no longer benefit or are not adapting to their present placement (45 C.F.R. Section 84.36).

The Department of Health, Education and Welfare's analysis of the education regulations makes it clear that the Section 504 education regulations

> are designed to insure that no handicapped child is excluded from school on the basis of handicap and if a recipient demonstrates that placement in a regular educational setting cannot be achieved satisfactorily, that the student is provided with adequate alternative services suited to the student's needs.

Thus the defendants herein are doing exactly what Section 504 prohibits—excluding plaintiff and members of his class from a publicly supported education by expelling or suspending them on the basis of their handicaps and such handicaps' behavioral manifestations. Such acts and practices expressly contravene the language of Section 504 by excluding children from participation in and the benefits of a federally funded program "solely by reason of [their] handicap."

5. *The Education for All Handicapped Children Act is also violated.*

Pursuant to the provisions of the Education of the Handicapped Act (now the Education for All Handicapped Children Act of 1975), 20 U.S.C. Section 1401 *et seq.*, assistance in the form of federal grants is made to states for "initiation, expansion and improvement of programs for the education of handicapped children. . . ." (20 U.S.C. Section 1411.)

Section 1413 of the law provides, in pertinent part, that:

> (a) Any State which is entitled to receive payments under this subchapter shall submit to the Commissioner through its State educational agency a State plan (not part of any other plan) in such detail as the Commissioner deems necessary. Such State plan shall—. . . . (13) provide procedures for insuring that handicapped children and their parents or guardians are guaranteed procedural safeguards in decisions regarding identification, evaluation and educational placement of handicapped children including, but not limited to (A) (1) prior notice to parents or guardians of the child when the local or State educational agency proposes to change the educational placement of the child, (ii) an opportunity for the parents or guardians to obtain an impartial due process hearing, examine all relevant records with respect to the classification or educational placement of the child, and obtain an independent educational evaluation of the child. . . . (iv) provision to insure that the decisions rendered in the impartial due process hearing required by this paragraph shall be binding on all parties subject only to appropriate administrative or judicial appeal; . . .

However, the state defendants have failed to take effective action to provide such hearings to plaintiffs. School boards are presently free to change the educational placement, and indeed to preclude placement altogether, of nonretarded mentally handicapped school-age children whose behavior has been deemed disruptive by suspending or expelling such children without limitation, pursuant to the inadequate procedures of Section 1318. Accordingly, the state defendants herein are in violation of the rights guaranteed to plaintiffs under 20 U.S.C. 1413 and the state plan submitted pursuant thereto.

No court opinion resulted from *Kenneth J.*, but the State Board of Education issued the following regulations prohibiting permanent exclusions of learning-disabled and emotionally disturbed students. When an exclusion in excess of ten days is proposed, a special education hearing is mandated. This limitation is still unequal to the protections afforded retarded students, for whom only emergency exclusions are permitted. Still, handicapped students are covered by laws applicable to all students relating to suspensions in this or any other state, and those require due process (although not a special education hearing) for suspensions involving lesser time periods.

5.2.3. *Kenneth J. v. Kline Regulations (22 Pa. Code § 341.90)*

Section 341.90 Disciplinary exclusions of certain handicapped students from special education placement.

(a) Definitions.

When used in this section, the following words and phrases shall have, unless the context indicates otherwise, the following meanings:

Educational agency—A school district, an intermediate unit, or an approved private school.

Exclusion—A suspension, expulsion, disenrollment, or transfer of a student by an educational agency from the school in which the student is in attendance for a violation of established school rules and law dealing with student conduct, as outlined in Chapter 12 of this title (relating to students).

(b) Due process hearing required.

(1) Change in educational placement. If an educational agency excludes a student who is either socially and emotionally disturbed or learning disabled from a program of special education and if this exclusion exceeds or has been proposed to exceed ten days, then this exclusion constitutes a change in educational placement or status. Such an exclusion may not, therefore, occur if the due process procedures of this subsection have not been complied with.

(2) School district initiated due process procedures. Before an educational agency can exclude or propose to exclude—for more than ten days—a student who either is socially and emotionally disturbed or is learning disabled from a program of special education, the educational agency must follow the procedures set forth in § 13.32 of this title (relating to school district initiated due process procedures). This means, among other things, that the district must provide the student's parents with notice, the opportunity for a special education due process hearing, and such other rights as are outlined in this section.

(3) Parent initiated due process procedures. If an educational agency either excludes or proposes to exclude a socially and emotionally disturbed or learning disabled student from a program of special education for a period exceeding ten days, the parents of the student shall have the right to request a due process hearing, pursuant to § 13.31 of this title (relating to the opportunity for due process procedure), in order to contest such exclusion or proposed exclusion.

(4) Exclusions of ten days or less. Nothing in this section shall be interpreted to mean that existing due process or hearing procedures, under other sections of this title, dealing with exclusions of ten days or less are in any way superseded by this section.

(c) Approved private schools.

(1) An approved private school which proposes to exclude a student in the circumstances stated in subsection (b) of this section shall inform both the parents of the student and school district of the proposal.

(2) Upon receipt of a notice from an approved private school that it proposes to exclude—for more than ten days—a student who either is socially and emotionally disturbed or is learning disabled, the school district of residence shall initiate the procedures outlined in § 13.32 of this title (relating to school district initiated due process procedures).

(3) Nothing in this section shall be interpreted to mean that any other section of this title dealing with the disenrollment, suspension, or expulsion of a handicapped student from an approved private school is hereby superseded by this section.

5.3. LANGUAGE AND RACIAL MINORITIES

Special education law now reflects the view that psychological testing and other evaluations should be done in a manner that is not racially or culturally discriminatory. This concept gained legal support from a series of court challenges alleging that minorities are frequently misclassified as requiring special services because of biased testing. The law also specifies that all notices sent to a parent or student must be in the recipient's native language. This provision reflects the realization that there are now a large number of parents and students involved in the special education process whose native language is other than English.

Hobson v. Hansen, [12] a widespread attack on economic and racial discrimination in District of Columbia schools, underlined the invidious use of intelligence tests to misclassify and misplace minority students. Although a number of other conditions, including segregation and the poor physical state of the schools, were held to violate the U.S. Constitution, the court also found that racial minorities were overwhelmingly "tracked" in slower or retarded classes. Because IQ tests were inherently biased against poor persons with limited cultural backgrounds or with different levels of communication skills, the testing and consequent tracking into slower classes was deemed unacceptable.

Children will be handicapped in their performance on standardized achievement tests because of their inability to use standard English; in addition, such children must be given intensive remedial instruction in all of the basic skills, and their verbal abilities must be stimulated. [13] Furthermore, using standardized tests to score the intellectual capacity of what the court called disadvantaged children is inherently biased. Because the background of poor children differs from that of the people who wrote the test, and because of other environmental and psychological barriers, the tests are, according to this court, practically meaningless. A track system that relies on these IQ levels is imprecise and discriminatory.

Larry P. v. Riles [14] challenged the use of IQ tests to place blacks in classes for mentally retarded persons in the San Francisco Unified School District. In that case, brought in 1974, a court enjoined any use of standardized tests to place black California students in classes for retarded children. In 1979 a federal appeals court affirmed the district court holding that standardized IQ measures create a disproportionate misclassification of black California children who are then placed in special education classes, and their use was permanently discarded. However, in 1980 a federal court in Illinois held that the existing data do not support a finding that currently used IQ tests are biased against minorities.[15] This question will remain in dispute for the foreseeable future.

A similar California case, *Diana v. State Board of Education*,[16] was brought on behalf of Chicano and Chinese students whose inappropriate placements resulted from the same standardized IQ tests. In a consent agreement entered into before the 504 regulations and 94–142, the school defendants agreed to rework the tests to eliminate cultural bias and to monitor school districts to determine if there is a significant difference between the minority makeup of regular classes and that of special education classes. Similar cases were brought on behalf of Hispanic and black students in Detroit and in New York.

The federal statute prohibiting any discrimination against minorities is Title VI of the Civil Rights Act of 1964, which provides that

> [n]o person in the United States shall, on the ground of race, color, or national origin, be excluded from participation in, be denied the benefits of, or be subjected to discrimination under any program or activity receiving federal financial assistance.[17]

According to HEW guidelines issued in 1970, Title VI is specifically enforceable for minority children with language difficulties. HEW stated that

> where inability to speak and understand the English language excludes national origin minority group children from effective participation in an educational program offered by a school district, a district must take affirmative steps to rectify the language deficiency, in order to open its instructional program to these students. Any ability grouping or tracking system employed by the school system to deal with these special language skill needs of national origin minority group children must be designed to meet such language skill needs as soon as possible and must not operate as an educational dead-end or permanent track.[18]

Furthermore, HEW has issued regulations implementing Title VI for federally funded programs under its jurisdiction. Recipients also may not

> (iii) provide any service, financial aid, or other benefit to an individual which is different or is provided in a different manner, from that provided to others under the program; and (iv) restrict an individual in any way in the enjoyment of any advantage or privilege enjoyed by others receiving any service, financial aid or other benefit under the program.[19]

Reading the HEW guidelines, Title VI, and its implementing regulations together, the Court held in *Lau v. Nichols*[20] that bilingual programs for Chinese-speaking students are required under the law.

Lau became the basis for a number of bilingual programs for language minority students across the country and also served as the partial basis for the Equal Educational Opportunities Act of 1974. This law requires every educational agency, both state and local, "to take appropriate action to overcome language barriers that impede equal participation by its students in its instructional program."[21]

Also based in large part on Title VI is Section 504, the law prohibiting discrimination against qualified handicapped persons in programs receiving federal financial assistance. School districts must provide handicapped school-age children with benefits and services that will help them participate in educational programs. The law also requires that these programs be provided on an equal basis with those offered other students. When a handicapped person is offered a free appropriate program of special education and related services, the school district is required to give great weight to the social and cultural background, including race and language barriers, of the student.[22] This mandate is reflected in the Education for All Handicapped Children Act, and its implementing regulations require that all notices, hearings, and meetings be communicated in the parents' primary language.[23] Unless not feasible, interpreters must be provided for language minority parents, and most important, testing cannot be racially or culturally discriminatory.

To come into compliance with this body of law, school districts may try a wide variety of techniques. For individual students, it is possible that bilingual special education may be required while the student is phased into an English-language program. In other instances, unique needs of a student may require instruction in both English and the native language. In still others, it may be appropriate that the student's instruction is primarily in English. Educators disagree at present regarding which techniques are generally appropriate. Evaluations should reflect a student's language and cultural needs, which may entail testing by a psychologist speaking solely the child's native language. Translating English-language IQ tests into another language is generally not acceptable because of cultural bias. Appropriate opportunities to be mainstreamed with other students who are not handicapped or are of a different cultural background must also be provided as quickly as possible. In addition, it is usually necessary to recruit bilingual personnel, including psychologists, certified special education teachers, paraprofessionals, and other staff necessary to comport with the equal opportunity requirements of both the special education and other antidiscrimination laws. The *Lora*[24] case, recently decided by a federal district judge in New York City, describes in great detail the concerns of minority students in large urban districts in the area of special education. This decision and order mandates appropriate testing and individualized placement for minorities before placement in special classes. *Lora* represents the modern trend of judicial thinking concerning the legal rights of minority children with special needs.

5.3.1. The Courts and Minorities and Special Education: Lora v. Board of Education of the City of New York (456 F.Supp. 1211)

WEINSTEIN, District Judge.

I. INTRODUCTION

Plaintiffs complain that their constitutional and statutory rights are being denied by the procedures and facilities afforded by New York City for the education of children whose emotional problems result in severe acting-out and aggression in school, behavior which may produce danger to others as well as themselves. These children often have severe academic problems. They have been placed in special day schools for the education of the emotionally handicapped. The schools utilize smaller class size, specially trained teachers and support staff, and special facilities, designed to provide a "generally therapeutic" atmosphere.

Racial composition of the pupil population in these special day schools is 68% Black; 27% Hispanic; and 5% other, primarily White (figures as of October 31, 1977). The high percentage of "minorities" in these schools is not a recent phenomenon; rather, a disparate racial composition has remained constant for nearly 15 years. The other major services for children with emotional disturbance, "classes for emotionally handicapped" (CEH classes) have a higher proportion, 20%, of non-minority students. Still higher is the proportion of Whites in the New York City public school equivalent grades: 36% Black, 23% Hispanic and 41% "other."

Starting from this striking racial disparity plaintiffs have added extensive evidence supporting their thesis. They contend that the special day schools are intentionally segregated "dumping grounds" for minorities forced into inadequate facilities without due process. White students with the same problems, it is maintained, are treated more favorably in other settings. Defendants and their witnesses deny any racial bias. They point with considerable pride to the advantages afforded, at substantial taxpayers' expense, in an effort to bring these problem students into the mainstream of education and society.

Laid bare by the dispute is one of the most excruciating issues of our democratic society. Almost every American agrees that the ringing words of the Declaration of Independence, "all men are created equal," mean at least that each person shall have an equal opportunity to develop and exercise his God-given talents. But many children born into deprived social, economic and psychological backgrounds lack the equality of real opportunity they would have had were their familial circumstances more fortunate. Unfavorable environment in such cases overwhelms favorable genes. To afford equality of opportunity so far as we can, we depend primarily on education. The free public system of education is the great equalizer, conceived to allow those born into the lowliest status the opportunity of rising as far as their potential talents, drive and luck will take them. But the system is—and perhaps by its nature must be—inadequate to lift fully the burden of poverty, of discrimination and of ignorance that so many of our children carry.

Depressingly revealed by the record are some of the almost insoluble problems of educating certain of the products of this background—the socially and emotionally maladjusted children who present a physical danger to themselves and others, who cannot learn and who prevent others from learning in a regular school setting. Yet the evidence before us also illustrates how talented and devoted school personnel, sympathetic to this group of children and operating under federal, state and local laws and regulations, can help even those who appeared beyond redemption.

Hope for substantial improvements lies not in the courts but in the hands of those who control society's resources and of those who are trained and dedicated to use pedagogic and therapeutic arts. Nevertheless, since the matter has been properly placed before us for adjudication, we have, under our legal system, no alternative but to address the issues in their limited legal context. The dismal facts, the ennobling aspirations, and the encouraging portents for the future have been revealed by devoted and skillful counsel for both sides.

At the time this suit was commenced in 1975, the plaintiffs could have demonstrated a violation of their rights by clear and convincing evidence. Since then, however, partly as a result of the litigation process itself, substantial improvements have been instituted by defendants. During the course of this law suit many of those charged with supervising the evaluation, placement and education of plaintiffs testified and were forced to face up to and justify shortcomings, and to modify the system as it was. For example, one day school for girls that the Court visited did not measure up to the standards enunciated by those in charge of the program. Partly as a result of colloquy between the Court and witnesses, the school was reexamined and closed. Developments on the administrative front, to be examined in more detail *infra*, have also had an ameliorating effect.

The preponderance of evidence still indicates a degree of deprivation of certain rights of some members of the plaintiff class. Yet the momentum for changes favoring plaintiffs' rights is now so strong that it cannot be said that a claim for powerful equitable relief has been substantiated. The energies of educators and therapists are best devoted to improving the education of the youngsters who need their help, rather than in litigating details of their educational practices. The record suggests that the extensive legislative and administrative regulations recently injected into the system will in due course provide adequate protections for plaintiffs. Time is needed for the educational system to absorb and adjust to the new legal standards. The case will not be dismissed but the remedies granted will be designed to have a minimal disruptive impact on personnel striving to meet plaintiffs' needs under difficult conditions.

II. PROCEDURAL HISTORY

A. *This Case*

The original complaint in this suit was filed in June 1975. The plaintiffs alleged violations of their rights under the Fourth, Eighth, Thirteenth and Fourteenth Amendments, as well as rights guaranteed by the Civil Rights Statutes, 42 U.S.C. §§ 1981, 1983, and 2000d (1974). Subsequently, the pleadings were amended to include claims under the Education of All Handicapped Children Act (20 U.S.C. §§ 1401 *et seq.* 1978, EHA) and the Rehabilitation Act of 1973 (29 U.S.C. §§ 701 *et seq.*, 1975). . . .

Plaintiffs claim, first, that the referral and assignment of students to special day schools is based upon vague and subjective criteria and that the combination of processes, practices and policies has a racially discriminatory effect on Black and Hispanic children. This, it is alleged, constitutes a violation of 42 U.S.C. § 1983 as well as section 2000d of Title VI of the Civil Rights Act of 1964, prohibiting racial discrimination under any program or activity receiving federal financial assistance. Second, plaintiffs allege that they have been denied their rights to due process, equal protection and equal educational opportunity because they have been placed in special day schools with the natural and foreseeable consequences that they will be isolated within a racially segregated system which does not provide them with suitable facilities and instruction. Third, plaintiffs charge that defendants have violated their due process rights by (1) placing students in the special day schools without giving them the opportunity for prior hearings mandated by federal and state law and regulations and (2) failure to reevaluate students already in such schools as required by state regulations, with the result that those who may be ready to return to regular schools are not able to do so. Fourth, plaintiffs invoke jurisdiction under 20 U.S.C. § 1415(e)(4) of the EHA, claiming specific violations of due process rights provided by that statute. Finally, plaintiffs claim that the special day school program affords students only inadequate educational opportunity in violation of § 791 of the Rehabilitation Act of 1973 (29 U.S.C. § 701 *et seq.*) and its accompanying regulations prohibiting discrimination against the handicapped.

This is essentially a constitutional and not a statutory case, involving racial discrimination and denial of educational rights. . . .

Title VI has been held to require satisfactory levels of education for children of all races and ethnic backgrounds. In *Lau v. Nichols*, 414 U.S. 563, 94 S.Ct. 786, 39 L.Ed.2d 1 (1974), the Supreme Court found that the failure to provide language courses for students of Chinese ancestry constituted lack of adequate educational opportunity within the meaning of Title VI. Plaintiffs had shown that no student could receive a high school diploma without meeting standards of proficiency in English. The failure to provide educational facilities tailored to these students' needs thus amounted to foreclosure of any meaningful education. In articulating a standard to be used in Title VI cases, the Court, relying on regulations promulgated in compliance with the Act (45 CRF § 80.3(b)(1) and (2)), noted that:

> Discrimination is barred which has that *effect* even though no purposeful design is present; a recipient may not . . . utilize criteria or methods of administration which have the effect of subjecting individuals to discrimination or have the effect of defeating or substantially impairing accomplishment of the objectives of the program as respect individuals of a particular race, color, or national orgin.

414 U.S. at 568, 94 S.Ct. at 789 (citations omitted, emphasis in original).

More recently, the Tenth Circuit, relying on *Lau v. Nichols*, found that in a primarily Spanish-speaking school a curriculum oriented towards white middle-class pupils violated Title VI. The court noted that the performance of the students in that school was well below what it should have been for students of their age. This was found to be due, at least in part, to the lack of materials reflecting the needs of the minority children. *Serna v. Portales School District*, 449 F.2d 1147 (10th Cir. 1974). See *Soria v. Oxnard Board of Trustees*, 386 F.Supp. 539, 544–45 (D.C.Cal.1974) (Title VI effects standard reiterated; the court noted the defendant's affirmative duty to desegregate its schools, irrespective of any finding of intent to discriminate).

B. Right to Due Process in Procedures

Plaintiff's claim a violation of their due process rights in that pupils have been, and continue to be, transferred to special day schools without adequate prior notice and an opportunity to be heard. This, it is argued, constitutes a violation not only of the due process clause of the 14th Amendment, but also of due process guarantees included in federal and state statutes and regulations. Defendants have two answers to these charges. First, they claim there is no right to notice and hearing prior to a change in educational placement; second, assuming the existence of such a right, they deny that their practices have violated it in any way.

The argument that there is no right to notice and hearing prior to a change in educational setting is without merit; it flies in the face of judicial pronouncements as well as the congressional and state policies outlined in the statutes and regulations. . . .

Placement of children out of the mainstream requires procedural due process protection. The law supports plaintiffs' contention that the following abuses—if established by the evidence—would constitute a violation of due process: (a) use of surreptitious means to obtain parental consent for special day school placement by mailing uninformed parents forms which are signed without full realization of what is involved; (b) denial of plaintiffs' right to a hearing by not appointing a surrogate parent to represent the interests of the child should the parent disagree with the child's objection to placement in a special school or be disinterested in the matter; (c) failure to reevaluate students already placed in these schools without the benefit of the due process protections built into the current regulations; (d) failure to carry out an annual and triennial review of all students currently in the special day schools as provided in the regulations; and (e) failure to provide parents with clinical records upon which recommendations for special day school placement are made so that they are unable to prepare for a hearing to contest the placement.

In *Mills v. Board of Education*, 348 F.Supp. 866, 875 (D.D.C.1972) the court noted that "[d]ue process of law requires a hearing prior to exclusion, termination or classification into a special program" (citations omitted). The court also ordered periodic review of each child's status and of the soundness of present placement. *Id.* at 878. *See Hairston v. Drosick*, 423 F.Supp. 180, 184–85 (S.D.West Virginia 1976) (exclusion of a handicapped child from the regular classroom without procedural safeguards is a violation of constitutional rights as well as of the Rehabilitation Act of 1973).

Pennsylvania Association for Retarded Children v. Pennsylvania, 343 F.Supp. 279 (E.D.Pa.1972) was resolved by a consent decree providing for public education for all retarded children and guaranteeing both prior notice of suggested non-mainstream placement and the opportunity for a hearing to contest the recommendation. In its opinion, the court acknowledged the danger of stigma in labelling a child mentally retarded; it emphasized the need for due process hearings in any instance where the state's action may result in stigmatization. Id. 295. *See New York Association for Retarded Children, Inc. v. Rockefeller*, 357 F.Supp. 752, 762 (E.D.N.Y.1973).

Legal commentators have recognized the dangers of misclassification in special education placement, whether due to misuse of proper criteria, invalidity of such criteria, or the vulnerability of minority group and behavioral problem pupils to misclassification because of impatient or innately biased teachers, and the possibility of stigma attached to special education placement. These possibilities mandate a hearing, involving parent, student, educator and administrator, prior to placement. *See, e.g.,* S. L. Ross, H. G. DeYoung, J. S. Cohen, "Confrontation: Special Education and the Law," in R. E. Schmid, J. Moneypenny, R. Johnston, *Contemporary Issues in Special Education*, 20 (1977); D. Kirp, Wm. Buss and P. Kuriloff, "Legal Reform of Special Education: Empirical Studies and Procedural Proposals," 62 *Cal. L. Rev.* 40, 117–55 (1974); Kirp, "Student Classification, Public Policy and the Courts," 44 *Harv. Educational Review* 7 (1974); Jones, "Coercive Behavior Control in the Schools: Reconciling 'Individually Appropriate' Education with Damaging Changes in Educational Status," 29 *Stan. L. Rev.* 93, 111 (1976). Parents must have adequate access to all records and the opportunity to obtain an independent evaluation of the child should it be desired. D. Kirp, Wm. Buss, P. Kuriloff, *supra* at 128.

Finally, adequate notice is an essential part of due process. As the

Supreme Court noted in *Goss v. Lopez*, a case involving due process requirements prior to school suspension:

> The fundamental requisite of due process of law is the opportunity to be heard . . . a right that has little reality or worth unless one is informed that the matter is pending and can choose for himself whether to . . . contest. . . . Parties whose rights are to be affected are entitled to be heard; and in order that they may enjoy that right they must first be notified.

419 U.S. 565, 579, 95 S.Ct. 729, 738, 42 L.Ed.2d 725 (1974) (citations omitted).

There is no general rule on the details of required notice. Rather, "the timing and content of notice . . . will depend on appropriate accommodation of the competing interests involved." *Goss v. Lopez, supra*, 419 U.S. at 579, 95 S.Ct. at 738–39. *See also Morrissey v. Brewer*, 408 U.S. 471, 481, 92 S.Ct. 2593, 2600, 33 L.Ed.2d 484 (1972). "The very nature of due process negates any concept of inflexible procedures universally applicable to every imaginable situation." *Cafeteria & Restaurant Workers Union v. McElroy*, 367 U.S. 886, 895, 81 S.Ct. 1743, 1748, 6 L.Ed.2d 1230 (1961), *cited in Goss v. Lopez, supra*, 419 U.S. at 578, 95 S.Ct. at 738.

Reinforcing this case law are, of course, the statutory and regulatory requirements already referred to outlining the contours of due process rights to notice and hearing as well as to periodic reevaluations of the appropriateness of special education placement. . . .

2. *Title VI*

To the extent that it has been shown that students have been referred to largely racially segregated schools, many of which have inadequate therapeutic and curricular offerings, we find a denial of equal educational opportunity in violation of Title VI (42 U.S.C. § 2000d (1974)). Coupled with this is a failure to conduct sufficient periodic reevaluations of students in the schools. The lack of objective criteria, which may result in racially discriminatory placement of students in special education programs, along with inadequate notice, lack of reevaluation and deficient programs, have been cited by the United States Department of Health, Education and Welfare as constituting a possible basis for liability under Title VI when accompanied by disproportionate numbers of minority students in a given program. *See* M. Gerry, Memorandum on "Identification of Discrimination in the Assignment of Children to Special Education Programs," Office of Civil Rights, U.S. Department of Health, Education & Welfare (1975); M. Gerry, "Statement of Findings," Office of Civil Rights, United States Department of Health, Education & Welfare (1977); section II B(2), *supra* (fuller explanations of specific charges contained in H.E.W. findings). As noted elsewhere, the evidence reveals that the initial referral as well as the reevaluation and decertification processes have been incomplete, thus failing to provide adequate safeguards against possible racially biased placement and retention. Even though the system is now much improved, many of the students in the special day schools were admitted prior to current reforms. . . .

5.4. SPECIAL EDUCATION MALPRACTICE

Because of numerous state and federal legal requirements, local school district policies, and an increasingly litigious society, teachers faced with the front-line responsibilities for special education students are concerned over the possibility of being sued. Their fears are based on a realization that not every special education goal written in an Individualized Education Program will be met in the case of every exceptional schoolchild, and that an unhappy parent or student will feel the necessity to bring an action for some sort of compensatory damages. Teachers and administrators are somewhat protected by the language of 94–142, which provides that

> each public agency must provide special education and related services to a handi-
> capped child in accordance with an Individualized Education Program. However, [this
> law] does not require that any agency, teacher, or other person be held accountable if
> a child does not achieve the goal projected in the annual goals and objectives.[25]

HEW attempts to explain in its comments that this section merely requires teachers to make good-faith efforts to meet each goal set down in the IEP, but it is not a legally binding contract for every goal to be met by the end of the school year.

That does not meant teachers and administrators will never be sued in a special education situation. So-called educational malpractice cases have been brought over the past several years, but no case in this area appears to have been successful. The original malpractice action, *Peter Doe v. San Francisco Unified School District*,[26] was filed in 1972 on behalf of an eighteen-year-old graduate of that city's schools who sought damages because, he claimed, the school board's negligence deprived him of the ability to attain literacy. At the time of his graduation from high school he was a functional illiterate. After years of litigation, successive courts refused to accept educational malpractice as a legal theory, and his case was dismissed from the courts. His failure to learn was not based on unmet special education goals, but it set the stage for future lawsuits. A New Jersey case sought damages against a school board in a similar situation on behalf of a high school graduate who left school with an inability to read beyond the second-grade level.[27] This case was also dismissed. A Long Island, New York[28] case was brought by a high school graduate who claimed he was "socially promoted" and presented with a diploma despite the fact that he, too, was functionally illiterate. In this case, some claims were made that potential learning disabilities may not have been noticed, but this matter was dismissed by the New York courts.

A case that had some brief success in the educational malpractice field did involve the failure to properly identify and place a student thought initially to be handicapped. In *Hoffman v. Board of Education of the City of New York*,[29] a student was given a Stanford-Binet IQ test upon entering the school system. His score was one point lower than that which would have qualified him for a placement in regular education, and he was placed in a class for mentally retarded students. Because of a substantial speech defect, the administering school psychologist recommended that he be retested within two years, but this recommendation was never carried out. Throughout his entire academic career, Hoffman was placed in special education classes. Although his mother protested the classification, his education was solely tracked in "CRMD," or New York City classes for "Children with Retarded Mental Development." Upon his graduation from high school his mother sought social security benefits because of his handicap, and an IQ test administered by the Social Security Administration indicated that his intelligence was well within the normal range. An action was brought against the Board of Education, and a jury awarded the plaintiff $750,000. On eventual appeal to the New York State Court of Appeals, the highest court in the state, the case was reversed in favor of the Board of Education. Although the case was based solely on New York negligence law, the court majority claimed that education is best left to the discretion of local school boards and that courts may not interfere in their practices. The decision, reached at the end of 1979, would appear to discourage future litigants in the field.

5.4.1. Denying Educational Malpractice Claims: Hoffman v. Board of Education of the City of New York (424 N.Y.S.2d 376)

JASEN, Judge.

The significant issue presented on this appeal is whether considerations of public policy preclude recovery for an alleged failure to properly evaluate the intellectual capacity of a student.

The facts in this case may be briefly stated. Plaintiff Daniel Hoffman entered kindergarten in the New York City school system in September, 1956. Shortly thereafter, plaintiff was examined by Monroe Gottsegen, a certified clinical psychologist in the school system, who determined that plaintiff had an intelligence quotient (IQ) of 74 and recommended that he be placed in a class for Children with Retarded Mental Development (CRMD). Dr. Gottsegen was, however, not certain of his findings. The apparent reason for this uncertainty was that plaintiff suffered from a severe speech defect which had manifested itself long before plaintiff entered the school system. Plaintiff's inability to communicate verbally made it difficult to assess his mental ability by means of the primarily verbal Stanford-Binet Intelligence Test administered by Dr. Gottsegen. As a result, Dr. Gottsegen recommended that plaintiff's intelligence "be re-evaluated within a two-year period so that a more accurate estimation of his abilities can be made."

Pursuant to Dr. Gottsegen's recommendations, plaintiff was placed in a CRMD program. While enrolled in the program, plaintiff's academic progress was constantly monitored through the observation of his teachers and by the use of academic "achievement tests" given twice a year. Although in 1959 and 1960 plaintiff received a "90 percentile" rating as to "reading readiness," indicating that his potential for learning to read was higher than average, the results of his achievement tests consistently indicated that he possessed extremely limited reading and mathematical skills. As a result of plaintiff's poor performance on the standardized achievement tests and, presumably, because his teacher's daily observations confirmed his lack of programs, plaintiff's intelligence was not retested on an examination designed specifically for that purpose.

In 1968, plaintiff was transferred to the Queens Occupational Training Center (OTC), a manual and shop training center for retarded youths. The following year plaintiff's mother requested, for the first time, that plaintiff's intelligence be retested. Plaintiff was administered the Wechsler Intelligence Scale for Adults (WAIS). The result of the test indicated that plaintiff had a "verbal" IQ of 85 and a "performance" IQ of 107 for a "full scale" IQ of 94. In other words, plaintiff's combined score on the WAIS test indicated that he was not retarded. Inasmuch as his course of study at the OTC was designed specifically for retarded youths, plaintiff was no longer qualified to be enrolled. As a result, plaintiff was allowed to complete the spring semester of 1969, but was not allowed to return in the fall.

Thereafter, plaintiff commenced this action against the Board of Education of the City of New York, alleging that the board was negligent in its original assessment of his intellectual ability and that the board negligently failed to retest him pursuant to Dr. Gottsegen's earlier recommendation. Plaintiff claimed that these negligent acts and omissions caused him to be misclassified and improperly enrolled in the CRMD program which allegedly resulted in severe injury to plaintiff's intellectual and emotional well-being and reduced his ability to obtain employment. At trial, the jury awarded plaintiff damages in the amount of $750,000. The Appellate Division affirmed this judgment, two Justices dissenting, as to liability, but would have reversed this judgment and required plaintiff to retry the issue of damages had he not consented to a reduction in the amount of the verdict from $750,000 to $500,000. The Appellate Division predicated its affirmance upon defendants' failure to administer a second intelligence test to plaintiff pursuant to Dr. Gottsegen's recommendation to "re-evaluate" plaintiff's intelligence within two years. The court characterized defendants' failure to retest plaintiff as an affirmative act of negligence, actionable under New York law. There should be a reversal.

At the outset, it should be stated that although plaintiff's complaint does not expressly so state, his cause of action sounds in "educational malpractice." Plaintiff's recitation of specific acts of negligence is, in essence, an attack upon the professional judgment of the board of education grounded upon the board's alleged failure to properly interpret and act upon Dr. Gottsegen's recommendations and its alleged failure to properly assess plaintiff's intellectual status thereafter. As we have recently stated in *Donohue v. Copiague Union Free School Dist.*, 47 N.Y.2d 440, 418 N.Y.S.2d 375, 391

N.E.2d 1352, such a cause of action, although quite possibly cognizable under traditional notions of tort law, should not, as a matter of public policy, be entertained by the courts of this State. . . .

Our decision in *Donohue* was grounded upon the principle that courts ought not interfere with the professional judgment of those charged by the Constitution and by statute with the responsibility for the administration of the schools of this State. . In the present case, the decision of the school officials and educators who classified plaintiff as retarded and continued his enrollment in CRMD classes was based upon the results of a recognized intelligence test administered by a qualified psychologist and the daily observation of plaintiff's teachers. In order to affirm a finding of liability in these circumstances, this court would be required to allow the finder of fact to substitute its judgment for the professional judgment of the board of education as to the type of psychometric devices to be used and the frequency with which such tests are to be given. Such a decision would also allow a court or a jury to second-guess the determinations of each of plaintiff's teachers. To do so would open the door to an examination of the propriety of each of the procedures used in the education of every student in our school system. Clearly, each and every time a student fails to progress academically, it can be argued that he or she would have done better and received a greater benefit if another educational approach or diagnostic tool had been utilized. Similarly, whenever there was a failure to implement a recommendation made by any person in the school system with respect to the evaluation of a pupil or his or her educational program, it could be said, as here, that liability could be predicated on misfeasance. However, the court system is not the proper forum to test the validity of the educational decision to place a particular student in one of the many educational programs offered by the schools of this State. . . .

5.5. GIFTED AND TALENTED CHILDREN

Children who are gifted and/or talented have been increasingly acknowledged by parents and educators to require special instruction in order to obtain equal educational opportunity and reach their fullest potential. These students have long been ignored and underserved, but they are now classified as "exceptional" in half of the states. The realization that individualized and appropriate education must be provided is rapidly increasing involvement among local and state boards of education in gifted education. The traditional view that gifted or talented students should merely be provided with some additional work in regular classes has been and is being discarded; however, as in the case of their handicapped peers, there is no national civil rights protection for this identifiable population. Different states have differing legal approaches to gifted/talented education; some require nothing, others supportive services, and still others accept these students as "exceptional" and provide for their participation in due process and evaluation procedures. In addition, there has been some limited federal recognition and funding for those states that allow for gifted/talented education.

Gifted and talented children are defined in a variety of ways, but Congress defines them as

> children who are identified at the preschool, elementary, or secondary level as possessing demonstrated or potential abilities that give evidence of high performance capability in areas such as intellectual, creative, specific academic, or leadership ability, or in the performing and visual arts, and who by reason thereof, require service, or activities not ordinarily provided by the school. [30]

Depending on the school district in question, gifted children can range as high as 10 percent of the total population. Some districts, citing the high income and intellectual background of their students and parents, have been known to claim substantially higher percentages of gifted children within their jurisdiction. Indeed, one district administrator in a wealthy Philadelphia suburb has remarked that even his learning-impaired students have such substantial educational backgrounds that they perform into the gifted range.

5.5.1. The Federal Laws

After Sputnik was launched by the Soviet Union in 1958, a great furor arose about the need to train the best scientific minds of our youth, and federal involvement in gifted education commenced. The aptly named National Defense and Education Act was passed in 1958, and its provisions included higher-education loans for gifted students. The National/State Leadership Training Institute was then established following the commissioner of education's report to Congress on the state of gifted education in the nation. Eventually, the U.S. Office of Education set up a bureaucracy to cover gifted and talented children.

The 1972 Emergency School Aid Act,[31] a funding law to support desegregation efforts, briefly mentioned the needs of gifted and talented children in its provisions. Finally, a U.S. Office for Gifted and Talented Students was established by the Education Amendments of 1974, from which the definition describing this group was developed. Congress then passed the Gifted and Talented Children's Education Act of 1978 (Title IX of the 1978 Education Amendments), which established a grant-in-aid program to assist state education officials who want to develop and increase programs in school districts, colleges, and other agencies. In passing the law, Congress found that

> (1) the Nation's greatest resource for solving critical national problems in areas of national concern is its gifted and talented children, (2) unless the special abilities of gifted and talented children are developed during their elementary and secondary school years, their special potentials for assisting the nation may be lost, and (3) gifted

and talented children from economically disadvantaged families and areas are not afforded the opportunity to fulfill their special education and valuable potentials, due to inadequate or inappropriate educational services.[32]

Funds are provided for in-service training of personnel, and for aid to assist with local planning, developing, and implementing preschool, elementary, and secondary programs. Fifty percent of funds allocated to states under the law must be for programs that include a component for the location and identification of low-income gifted and talented children. For the first fiscal year in the law's existence, $25 million was appropriated. Figures for later years include increases of $5 million for each year until $50 million is appropriated in fiscal year 1983. It must be emphasized that this is a grant program and not a civil rights law. Grants are not, as in 94–142, contingent on the development of due process procedures; nor, as with 504, does funding hinge on nondiscrimination against the law's beneficiaries. It seems almost inevitable that gifted and talented children will eventually be covered nationally by due process rights and prohibition against discrimination based on their exceptionality. As knowledge concerning their unique needs is developed and disseminated, their needs will, it appears certain, be more universally provided for and protected.

5.5.2. State Laws: A Comparative Approach of Two States

In the absence of a uniform, national law, the efforts of advocates have produced a number of laws and regulations in this area. The approaches of various states can be studied to determine the efforts they have made to serve gifted and talented persons with appropriate educational programs. Two representative states that have made at least some headway are Pennsylvania and New Jersey.

5.5.2a. The Pennsylvania Approach.[33] When special education due process procedures were extended from covering mentally retarded children to all exceptional persons of school age in Pennsylvania, the regulations also mandated protections for gifted students. State Board of Education regulations promulgated in 1975 stated that exceptional persons included gifted and talented persons who "in accordance with standards developed by the Secretary of Education, have outstanding intellectual or creative ability, the development of which requires special activities not ordinarily provided to regular children by local educational agencies."[34] They were covered by state legislation and by the procedures, including a due process hearing and appeal rights, available to all exceptional students and their parents to challenge any aspect of their educational program. Curriculum requirements covering admission and participation of this group in special programs were mandated. In 1978 the secretary of education developed the standards (other, less detailed definitions and procedures had previously existed) that are in effect today.

In this state there are separate definitions for gifted as well as for talented students. "Mentally gifted" includes those who have

> outstanding intellectual and creative ability the development of which requires special activities or services not ordinarily provided in the regular program. Persons shall be assigned to a program for the gifted when they have an IQ of 130 or higher. A limited number of persons with IQ scores lower than 130 may be admitted to gifted programs when other educational criteria in the profile of the person strongly indicate gifted ability. [35]

Talented children are those who have "outstanding talent as identified by a team of educators and professionals competent in the areas of art, music, dance, creative writing, photographic arts, or theater, the development of which requires special activities or services not ordinarily provided in the regular program. . . ."[36] Gifted and talented children are not distinguished under the law from other exceptional children in any major provision, and are protected by such requirements as nondiscrimination in testing and the development of an individualized educational program describing a free, appropriate education program for each student. Despite their equal protection, funding available pursuant to 94–142 is unavailable for gifted programs, and state and local districts are responsible for developing programs based on their own resources.

Parents have been quite properly availing themselves of the available due process hearing device. As in all areas where education funding is difficult to obtain, litigation has resulted in the provision of funds. For example, one local district has filed suit to obtain funding for gifted programs from the State Department of Education. The department refused, asserting that districts must first provide appropriate gifted education programs, despite the cost, and then funding will possibly become available from state sources. A court agreed with the department and ordered the hard-pressed district to develop necessary special education programs.

5.5.2b. New Jersey.[37] New Jersey's approach differs somewhat from Pennsylvania's. The relevant state statute, known as the "thorough and efficient" or "T&E" law, was passed in 1975 and includes general provisions requiring the development of instruction "intended to produce the attainment of reasonable levels of proficiency in the basic communication and computational skills." As is typical of legislative statements of purpose, this statute has its share of general and high-minded pronouncements, such as the mandate for "a breadth of offerings designed to develop the needs and abilities of all pupils," including those who are educationally disadvantaged. State Board of Education regulations do require, in a somewhat general manner, that all school districts provide "opportunities" for gifted and talented students on an individualized basis, to allow each person to "achieve the highest level of attainment of which he is capable."

Unlike Pennsylvania, New Jersey has not issued the sort of substantial and comprehensive regulations and policy guidelines necessary both to provide guidance for school districts and to protect the rights of gifted and talented children. New Jersey local school boards are obligated to provide the State Board of Education with descriptions of their particular policies for identifying these children and for providing programming for them. Even in the absence of detailed state guidelines for the identification and admission of gifted and talented students to programs, local districts were required to provide appropriate programs by 1981.

Staff attorneys for the Education Law Center, a public interest law firm that monitors programs and advocates on behalf of exceptional children in New Jersey, have described the status of gifted and talented programs in New Jersey:

> Despite the T&E law and its regulations, many school districts have not addressed the requirement of developing appropriate educational programs for gifted and talented children. Major reasons for the failure of school districts to provide adequate programs for their gifted and talented students include a lack of agreed upon definitions, standards and the absence of state regulations concerning identification of and educational programming for such students. Although the non-binding state guidelines suggest which personnel should identify and what programs should be provided for gifted and talented children, there are no specific requirements, by practice or regulation, regarding these tasks. However, despite the current absence of standards, because of the T&E law and its regulations, the right to educational opportunities of the gifted and talented does exist and school districts are responsible for the identification and educational programming for these children.
>
> At minimum, procedures to identify gifted and talented children must be reasonable and fair. Therefore, unless the gifted and talented child is identified by proper personnel and procedures, the child may be denied the right to an educational program to which the child is entitled under New Jersey law. Identification procedures cannot discriminate on any basis prohibited by New Jersey law including race, national origin, sex and socioeconomic status.[38]
>
> Some indicators of the reasonableness of identification procedures include the extensive studies regarding identification of the gifted and talented (including the USOE's Report to Congress), surveys of current educational practices in this area and a recognition of the aptitudes and abilities encompassed by all six recognized categories of giftedness and talents. For example, studies indicate that teacher nominations of gifted children are 30% accurate, or only half as accurate as parent or peer nominations. Similar studies indicate that standardized intelligence and achievement tests are unreliable for identifying economically disadvantaged children unless the tests are given by trained personnel and the scores are adapted to reflect the deficiencies in the tests. Moreover, if the identification process does not give attention to all three characteristics of giftedness—above average ability, creativity and task commitment— it ignores the best available research on the topic.[39] Thus, procedures which are inaccurate, unreliable and which cannot be adapted for identification of gifted and talented children should not be used for such purpose.
>
> In addition, the state guidelines recommend, and current federal regulations controlling financial assistance to programs for the gifted and talented require, that multiple criteria be used to identify these children in order to avoid unfair and unreasonable results.
>
> Children identified as gifted and talented are entitled to "educational opportunities" under New Jersey law. Educational opportunities may include many alterna-

tives such as: self-contained classrooms, mentorships, independent study, advanced placement, resource rooms and adapted in-classroom activities. However, the chosen alternative must reflect the learning characteristics and abilities of the gifted child which have been identified. A program appropriate for a child of average abilities would not meet the needs of a gifted and talented child. Proper educational programs for gifted and talented children would, like those for handicapped children, have to meet the special needs of the child in order to meet the requirements of the regulation.

5.6. NOTES

1. 476 F. Supp. 583 (E.D. Pa. 1979).
2. *Id.* at 603.
3. *Id.* at 600.
4. 95 S. Ct. 729 (1975); *see also* Wood v. Strickland, 95 S. Ct. 992 (1975); Ingraham v. Wright, 430 U.S. 651 (1977); Carey v. Piphus, 98 S. Ct. 1042 (1978).
5. 95 S. Ct. at 737.
6. *Id.*
7. 22 Pa. Code § 13.62.
8. 443 F. Supp. 1235 (D. Conn. 1978).
9. No. 77-1360 (D.S.C., Order, Aug. 22, 1977).
10. No. D.C. 75-31-S (N.D. Miss., Jan. 26, 1979).
11. Civil No. 77-2257 (E.D. Pa., filed June 28, 1977).
12. 269 F. Supp. 401 (D.D.C. 1967), *aff'd sub nom.*, Smuck v. Hobson, 408 F.2d 175 (D.C. Cir. 1969).
13. *Id.* at 481.
14. 343 F. Supp. 1306 (N.D. Cal. 1971), *aff'd*, 502 F.2d 963 (9th Cir. 1974) (Order, Oct. 16, 1979); *cf.* Martin Luther King, Jr. Elementary School Children v. Ann Arbor School District Board, 473 F. Supp. 1371 (E.D. Mich. 1979) (teachers must take into account the home language system of minority children when teaching).
15. Parents in Action on Special Education v. Hannon, 49 U.S.L.W. 2087 (N.D. Ill., Aug. 5, 1980).
16. No. C-70-37 RFP (N.D. Cal., Feb. 5, 1970); *see also* Newberg on Class Actions, § 8712, for extensive discussion, cases, and materials cited therein.
17. 42 U.S.C. § 2000d.
18. 35 Fed. Reg. 11595.
19. 34 C.F.R. § 104.3(b).
20. 414 U.S. 563 (1974).
21. 20 U.S.C. § 1703.
22. 34 C.F.R. § 104.35(c).
23. *See, e.g.,* 34 C.F.R. § 300.505.
24. 456 F. Supp. 1211 (E.D.N.Y. 1978).
25. 34 C.F.R. § 300.349.
26. No. 653-312 (Sup. Ct. Cal., filed Nov. 20, 1972).
27. McNeil v. Board of Education, No. L-17297-74 (Sup. Ct., filed January 24, 1975).
28. Donohue v. Copiague Union Free School District, 47 N.Y.2d 440.
39. 424 N.Y.S.2d 376 (Ct. App. 1979).
30. 20 U.S.C. § 3312.
31. 20 U.S.C. §§ 3191 *et seq.*
32. 20 U.S.C. § 3311.

33. *See* 24 P.S. §§ 1371 *et seq.*; 22 Pa. Code §§ 13.1, 13.21–23, 341.1 *et seq.*

34. 22 Pa. Code § 13.1.

35. 22 Pa. Code § 341.1(iv).

36. 22 Pa. Code § 341.1(x).

37. See N.J.S.A. 18A:36–30; N.J.A.C. §§ 6:4–1.1 *et seq.*

38. "No pupil in a public school in this State shall be discriminated against in admission to, or in obtaining any advantages, privileges or course of study of the school by reason of race, color, creed, sex or national origin."

39. *See, e.g.,* Renzulli, *What Makes Giftedness? Reexamining a Definition,* 60 PHI DELTA KAPPA 180 (1978).

FEDERAL REQUIREMENTS FOR THE EDUCATION OF ALL HANDICAPPED CHILDREN (20 U.S.C. §§ 1401–1420)

These laws were drafted in large part before the establishment of the United States Department of Education. All functions of the former Department of Health, Education and Welfare were transferred in this area to the U.S. Secretary of Education. The former Bureau of Education for the Handicapped special education programs are now administered by the Office of Special Education and Rehabilitative Services.

SUBCHAPTER I—GENERAL PROVISIONS

§ 1401. Definitions

As used in this chapter—

(1) The term "handicapped children" means mentally retarded, hard of hearing, deaf, speech impaired, visually handicapped, seriously emotionally disturbed, orthopedically impaired, or other health impaired children, or children with specific learning disabilities, who by reason thereof require special education and related services.

(2) The term "Commissioner" means the Commissioner of Education.

(3) The term "Advisory Committee" means the National Advisory Committee on Handicapped Children.

(4) The term "construction", except where otherwise specified, means (A) erection of new or expansion of existing structures, and the acquisition and installation of equipment therefor; or (B) acquisition of existing structures not owned by any agency or institution making application for assistance under this chapter; or (C) remodeling or alteration (including the acquisition, installation, modernization, or replacement of equipment) of existing structures; or (D) acquisition of land in connection with activities in clauses (A), (B), and (C); or (E) a combination of any two or more of the foregoing.

(5) The term "equipment" includes machinery, utilities, and built-in equipment and any necessary enclosures or structures to house them, and includes all other items necessary for the functioning of a particular facility as a facility for the provision of educational services, including items such as instructional equipment and necessary furniture, printed, published, and audio-visual instructional materials, telecommunications, sensory, and other technological aids and devices, and books, periodicals, documents, and other related materials.

(6) The term "State" means each of the several States, the District of Columbia, the Commonwealth of Puerto Rico, Guam, American Samoa, the Virgin Islands and the Trust Territory of the Pacific Islands.

(7) The term "State educational agency" means the State board of education or other agency or officer primarily responsible for the State supervision of public elementary and secondary schools, or, if there is no such officer or agency, an officer or agency designated by the Governor or by State law.

(8) The term "local educational agency" means a public board of education or other public authority legally constituted within a State for either administrative control or direction of, or to perform a service function for, public elementary or secondary schools in a city, county, township, school district, or other political subdivision of a State, or such combination of school districts or counties as are recognized in a State as an administrative agency for its public elementary or secondary schools. Such term also includes any other public institution or agency having administrative control and direction of a public elementary or secondary school.

(9) The term "elementary school" means a day or residential school which provides elementary education, as determined under State law.

(10) The term "secondary school" means a day or residential school which provides secondary education, as determined under State law, except that it does not include any education provided beyond grade 12.

(11) The term "institution of higher education" means an educational institution in any State which—

(A) admits as regular students only individuals having a certificate of graduation from a high school, or the recognized equivalent of such a certificate;

(B) is legally authorized within such State to provide a program of education beyond high school;

(C) provides an educational program for which it awards a bachelor's degree, or provides not less than a two-year program which is acceptable for full credit toward such a degree, or offers a two-year program in engineering, mathematics, or the physical or biological sciences which is designed to prepare the student to work as a technician and at a semiprofessional level in engineering, scientific, or other technological fields which require the understanding and application of basic engineering, scientific, or mathematical principles or knowledge;

(D) is a public or other nonprofit institution; and

(E) is accredited by a nationally recognized accrediting agency or association listed by the Commissioner pursuant to this paragraph or, if not so accredited, is an institution whose credits are accepted, on transfer, by not less than three institutions which are so accredited, for credit on the same basis as if transferred from an institution so accredited: *Provided, however,* That in the case of an institution offering a two-year program in engineering, mathematics, or the physical or biological sciences which is designed to prepare the student to work as a technician and at a semiprofessional level in engineering, scientific, or technological fields which require the understanding and application of basic engineering, scientific, or mathematical principles or knowledge, if the Commissioner determines that there is no nationally recognized accrediting agency or association qualified to accredit such institutions, he shall appoint an advisory committee, composed of persons specially qualified to evaluate training provided by such institutions, which shall prescribe the standards of content, scope, and quality which must be met in order to qualify such institutions to participate under this Act and shall also determine whether particular institutions meet such standards. For the purposes of this paragraph the Commissioner shall publish a list of nationally recognized accrediting agencies or associations which he determines to be reliable authority as to the quality of education or training offered.

(12) The term "nonprofit" as applied to a school, agency, organization, or institution means a school, agency, organization, or institution owned and operated by one or more nonprofit corporations or associations no part of the net earnings of which inures, or may lawfully inure, to the benefit of any private shareholder or individual.

(13) The term "research and related purposes" means research, research training (including the payment of stipends and allowances), surveys, or demonstrations in the field of education of handicapped children, or the dissemination of information derived therefrom, including (but without limitation) experimental schools.

(14) The term "Secretary" means the Secretary of Health, Education, and Welfare.

(15) The term "children with specific learning disabilities" means those children who have a disorder in one or more of the basic psychological processes involved in understanding or in using language, spoken or written, which disorder may manifest itself in imperfect ability to listen, think, speak, read, write, spell, or do mathematical calculations. Such disorders include such conditions as perceptual handicaps, brain injury, minimal brain dysfunction, dyslexia, and developmental aphasia. Such term does not include children who have learning problems which are primarily the result of visual, hearing, or motor handicaps, of mental retardation, of emotional disturbance, or of environmental, cultural, or economic disadvantage.

(16) The term "special education" means specially designed instruction, at no cost to parents or guardians, to meet the unique needs of a handicapped child, including classroom instruction, instruction in physical education, home instruction, and instruction in hospitals and institutions.

(17) The term "related services" means transportation, and such developmental, corrective, and other supportive services (including speech pathology and audiology, psychological services, physical and occupational therapy, recreation, and medical and counseling services, except that such medical services shall be for diagnostic and evaluation purposes only) as may be required to assist a handicapped child to benefit from special education, and includes the early identification and assessment of handicapping conditions in children.

(18) The term "free appropriate public education" means special education and related services which (A) have been provided at public expense, under public supervision and direction, and without charge, (B) meet the standards of the State educational agency, (C) include an appropriate preschool, elementary, or secondary school education in the State involved, and (D) are provided in conformity with the individualized education program required under section 1414(a)(5) of this title.

(19) The term "individualized education program" means a written statement for each handicapped child developed in any meeting by a representative of the local educational agency or an intermediate educational unit who shall be qualified to provide, or supervise the provision of, specially designed instruction to meet the unique needs of handicapped children, the teacher, the parents or guardian of such child, and, whenever appropriate, such child, which statement shall include (A) a statement of the present levels of educational performance of such child, (B) a statement of annual goals, including short-term instructional objectives, (C) a statement of the specific educational services to be provided to such child, and the extent to which such child will be able to participate in regular educational programs, (D) the projected date for initiation and anticipated duration of such services, and (E) appropriate objective criteria and evaluation procedures and schedules for determining, on at least an annual basis, whether instructional objectives are being achieved.

(20) The term "excess costs" means those costs which are in excess of the average annual per student expenditure in a local educational agency during the preceding school year for an elementary or secondary school student, as may be appropriate, and which shall be computed after deducting (A) amounts received under this subchapter or under title I [20 U.S.C. 241a et seq.] or title VII [20 U.S.C. 880b et seq.] of the Elementary and Secondary Education Act of 1965, and (B) any State or local funds expended for programs which would qualify for assistance under this subchapter or under such titles.

(21) The term "native language" has the meaning given that term by section 703(a)(2) of the Bilingual Education Act [20 U.S.C. 880b-1(a)(2)].

(22) The term "intermediate educational unit" means any public authority, other than a local educational agency, which is under the general supervision of a State educational agency, which is established by State law for the purpose of providing free public education on a regional basis, and which provides special education and related services to handicapped children within that State.

§ 1402. Bureau for education and training of the handicapped; Deputy Commissioner: appointment and compensation; Associate Deputy Commissioner and other assistants to Deputy Commissioner

TRANSFER OF FUNCTIONS

For transfer of functions and offices (relating to education) of the Secretary and Department of Health, Education, and Welfare to the Secretary and Department of Education, and termination of certain offices and positions, see sections 3441 and 3503 of this title.

(a) There shall be, within the Office of Education, a bureau for the education and training of the handicapped which shall be the principal agency in the Office of Education for administering and carrying out programs and projects relating to the education and training of the handicapped, including programs and projects for the training of teachers of the handicapped and for research in such education and training.

(b)(1) The Bureau established under subsection (a) of this section shall be headed by a Deputy Commissioner of Education who shall be appointed by the Commissioner, who shall report directly to the Commissioner, be compensated at the rate specified for, and placed in, grade 18 of the General Schedule set forth in section 5332 of title 5.

(2) In addition to such Deputy Commissioner, there shall be placed in such Bureau five positions for persons to assist the Deputy Commissioner in carrying out his duties, including the position of Associate Deputy Commissioner, and such positions shall be placed in grade 16 of the General Schedule set forth in section 5332 of title 5.

§ 1404. Acquisition of equipment and construction of necessary facilities

(a) Authorization for use of funds

In the case of any program authorized by this chapter, if the Commissioner determines that such program will be improved by permitting the funds authorized for such program to be used for the acquisition of equipment and the construction of necessary facilities, he may authorize the use of such funds for such purposes.

(b) Recovery of payments under certain conditions

If within twenty years after the completion of any construction (except minor remodeling or alteration) for which funds have been paid pursuant to a grant or contract under this chapter the facility constructed ceases to be used for the purposes for which it was constructed, the United States, unless the Secretary determines that there is good cause for releasing the recipient of the funds from its obligation, shall be entitled to recover from the applicant or other owner of the facility an amount which bears the same ratio to the then value of the facility as the amount of such Federal funds bore to the cost of the portion of the facility financed with such funds. Such value shall be determined by agreement of the parties or by action brought in the United States district court for the district in which the facility is situated.

§ 1405. Employment of handicapped individuals

The Secretary shall assure that each recipient of assistance under this chapter shall make positive efforts to employ and advance in employment qualified handicapped individuals in programs assisted under this chapter.

§ 1406. Grants for the removal of architectural barriers; authorization of appropriations

(a) Upon application by any State or local educational agency or intermediate educational unit the Commissioner is authorized to make grants to pay part or all of the cost of altering existing buildings and equipment in the same manner and to the same extent as authorized by the Act approved August 12, 1968 (Pub. Law 90–480) [42 U.S.C. 4151 et seq.], relating to architectural barriers.

(b) For the purpose of carrying out the provisions of this section, there are authorized to be appropriated such sums as may be necessary.

SUBCHAPTER II—ASSISTANCE FOR EDUCATION OF ALL HANDICAPPED CHILDREN

§ 1411. Entitlements and allocations

(a) Formula for determining maximum State entitlement

(1) Except as provided in paragraph (3) and in section 1419 of this title, the maximum amount of the grant to which a State is entitled under this subchapter for any fiscal year shall be equal to—

(A) the number of handicapped children aged three to twenty-one, inclusive, in such State who are receiving special education and related services;

multiplied by—

(B)(i) 5 per centum, for the fiscal year ending September 30, 1978, of the average per pupil expenditure in public elementary and secondary schools in the United States;

(ii) 10 per centum, for the fiscal year ending September 30, 1979, of the average per pupil expenditure in public elementary and secondary schools in the United States;

(iii) 20 per centum, for the fiscal year ending September 30, 1980, of the average per pupil expenditure in public elementary and secondary schools in the United States;

(iv) 30 per centum, for the fiscal year ending September 30, 1981, of the average per pupil expenditure in public elementary and secondary schools in the United States; and

(v) 40 per centum, for the fiscal year ending September 30, 1982, and for each fiscal year thereafter, of the average per pupil expenditure in public elementary and secondary schools in the United States;

except that no State shall receive an amount which is less than the amount which such State received under this subchapter for the fiscal year ending September 30, 1977.

(2) For the purpose of this subsection and subsection (b) through subsection (e) of this section, the term "State" does not include Guam, American Samoa, the Virgin Islands, and the Trust Territory of the Pacific Islands.

(3) The number of handicapped children receiving special education and related services in any fiscal year shall be equal to number of such children receiving special education and related services on December 1 of the fiscal year preceding the fiscal year for which the determination is made.

(4) For purposes of paragraph (1)(B), the term "average per pupil expenditure", in the United States, means the aggregate current expenditures, during the second fiscal year preceding the fiscal year for which the computation is made (or, if satisfactory data for such year are not available at the time of computation, then during the most recent preceding fiscal year for which satisfactory data are available) of all local educational agencies in the United States (which, for purposes of this subsection, means the fifty States and the District of Columbia), as the case may be, plus any direct expenditures by the State for operation of such agencies (without regard to the source of funds from which either of such expenditures are made), divided by the aggregate number of children in average daily attendance to whom such agencies provided free public education during such preceding year.

(5)(A) In determining the allotment of each State under paragraph (1), the Commissioner may not count—

(i) handicapped children in such State under paragraph (1)(A) to the extent the number of such children is greater than 12 per centum of the number of all children aged five to seventeen, inclusive, in such State; and

(ii) handicapped children who are counted under section 241c-1 of this title.

(B) For purposes of subparagraph (A), the number of children aged five to seventeen, inclusive, in any State shall be determined by the Commissioner on the basis of the most recent satisfactory data available to him.

(b) **Distribution and use of grant funds by States for fiscal year ending September 30, 1978**

(1) Of the funds received under subsection (a) of this section by any State for the fiscal year ending September 30, 1978—

(A) 50 per centum of such funds may be used by such State in accordance with the provisions of paragraph (2); and

(B) 50 per centum of such funds shall be distributed by such State pursuant to subsection (d) of this section to local educational agencies and intermediate educational units in such State, for use in accordance with the priorities established under section 1412(3) of this title.

(2) Of the funds which any State may use under paragraph (1)(A)—

(A) an amount which is equal to the greater of—

(i) 5 per centum of the total amount of funds received under this subchapter by such State; or

(ii) $200,000;

may be used by such State for administrative costs related to carrying out sections 1412 and 1413 of this title;

(B) the remainder shall be used by such State to provide support services and direct services, in accordance with the priorities established under section 1412(3) of this title.

(c) **Distribution and use of grant funds by States for fiscal years ending September 30, 1979, and thereafter**

(1) Of the funds received under subsection (a) of this section by any State for the fiscal year ending September 30, 1979, and for each fiscal year thereafter—

(A) 25 per centum of such funds may be used by such State in accordance with the provisions of paragraph (2); and

(B) except as provided in paragraph (3), 75 per centum of such funds shall be distributed by such State pursuant to subsection (d) of this section to local educational agencies and intermediate educational units in such State, for use in accordance with priorities established under section 1412(3) of this title.

(2)(A) Subject to the provisions of subparagraph (B), of the funds which any State may use under paragraph (1)(A)—

(i) an amount which is equal to the greater of—

(I) 5 per centum of the total amount of funds received under this subchapter by such State; or

(II) $200,000;

may be used by such State for administrative costs related to carrying out the provisions of sections 1412 and 1413 of this title; and

(ii) the remainder shall be used by such State to provide support services and direct services, in accordance with the priorities established under section 1412(3) of this title.

(B) The amount expended by any State from the funds available to such State under paragraph (1)(A) in any fiscal year for the provisions of support services or for the provision of direct services shall be matched on a program basis by such State, from funds other than Federal funds, for the provision of support services or for the provision of direct services for the fiscal year involved.

(3) The provisions of section 1413(a)(9) of this title shall not apply with respect to amounts available for use by any State under paragraph (2).

(4)(A) No funds shall be distributed by any State under this subsection in any fiscal year to any local educational agency or intermediate educational unit in such State if—

(i) such local educational agency or intermediate educational unit is entitled, under subsection (d) of this section, to less than $7,500 for such fiscal year; or

(ii) such local educational agency or intermediate educational unit has not submitted an application for such funds which meets the requirements of section 1414 of this title.

(B) Whenever the provisions of subparagraph (A) apply, the State involved shall use such funds to assure the provision of a free appropriate education to handicapped children residing in the area served by such local educational agency or such intermediate educational unit. The provisions of paragraph (2)(B) shall not apply to the use of such funds.

(d) **Allocation of funds within States to local educational agencies and intermediate educational units**

From the total amount of funds available to local educational agencies and intermediate educational units in any State under subsection (b)(1)(B) or subsection (c)(1)(B) of this section, as the case may be, each local educational agency or intermediate educational unit shall be entitled to an amount which bears the same ratio to the total amount available under subsection (b)(1)(B) or subsection (c)(1)(B) of this section, as the case may be, as the number of handicapped children aged three to twenty-one, inclusive, receiving special education and related services in such local educational agency or intermediate educational unit bears to the aggregate number of handicapped children aged three to twenty-one, inclusive, receiving special education and related services in all local educational agencies and intermediate educational units which apply to the State educational agency involved for funds under this subchapter.

(e) **Territories and possessions**

(1) The jurisdictions to which this subsection applies are Guam, American Samoa, the Virgin Islands, and the Trust Territory of the Pacific Islands.

(2) Each jurisdiction to which this subsection applies shall be entitled to a grant for the purposes set forth in section 601(c) in an amount equal to an amount determined by the Commissioner in accordance with criteria based on respective needs, except that the aggregate of the amount to which such jurisdictions are so entitled for any fiscal year shall not exceed an amount equal to 1 per centum of the aggregate of the amounts available to all States under this subchapter for that fiscal year. If the aggregate of the amounts, determined by the

Commissioner pursuant to the preceding sentence, to be so needed for any fiscal year exceeds an amount equal to such 1 per centum limitation, the entitlement of each such jurisdiction shall be reduced proportionately until such aggregate does not exceed such 1 per centum limitation.

(3) The amount expended for administration by each jurisdiction under this subsection shall not exceed 5 per centum of the amount allotted to such jurisdiction for any fiscal year, or $35,000, whichever is greater.

(f) **Indian reservations**

(1) The Commissioner is authorized to make payments to the Secretary of the Interior according to the need for such assistance for the education of handicapped children on reservations serviced by elementary and secondary schools operated for Indian children by the Department of the Interior. The amount of such payment for any fiscal year shall not exceed 1 per centum of the aggregate amounts available to all States under this subchapter for that fiscal year.

(2) The Secretary of the Interior may receive an allotment under this subsection only after submitting to the Commissioner an application which meets the applicable requirements of section 1414(a) of this title and which is approved by the Commissioner. The provisions of section 1416 of this title shall apply to any such application.

(g) **Reductions or increases**

(1) If the sums appropriated for any fiscal year for making payments to States under this subchapter are not sufficient to pay in full the total amounts which all States are entitled to receive under this subchapter for such fiscal year, the maximum amounts which all States are entitled to receive under this subchapter for such fiscal year shall be ratably reduced. In case additional funds become available for making such payments for any fiscal year during which the preceding sentence is applicable, such reduced amounts shall be increased on the same basis as they were reduced.

(2) In the case of any fiscal year in which the maximum amounts for which States are eligible have been reduced under the first sentence of paragraph (1), and in which additional funds have not been made available to pay in full the total of such maximum amounts under the last sentence of such paragraph, the State educational agency shall fix dates before which each local educational agency or intermediate educational unit shall report to the State educational agency on the amount of funds available to the local educational agency or intermediate educational unit, under the provisions of subsection (d) of this section, which it estimates that it will expend in accordance with the provisions of this subchapter. The amounts so available to any local educational agency or intermediate educational unit, or any amount which would be available to any other local educational agency or intermediate educational unit if it were to submit a program meeting the requirements of this subchapter, which the State educational agency determines will not be used for the period of its availability, shall be available for allocation to those local educational agencies or intermediate educational units, in the manner provided by this section, which the State educational agency determines will need

and be able to use additional funds to carry out approved programs.

§ 1412. Eligibility requirements

In order to qualify for assistance under this subchapter in any fiscal year, a State shall demonstrate to the Commissioner that the following conditions are met:

(1) The State has in effect a policy that assures all handicapped children the right to a free appropriate public education.

(2) The State has developed a plan pursuant to section 1413(b) of this title in effect prior to November 29, 1975, and submitted not later than August 21, 1975, which will be amended so as to comply with the provisions of this paragraph. Each such amended plan shall set forth in detail the policies and procedures which the State will undertake or has undertaken in order to assure that—

(A) there is established (i) a goal of providing full educational opportunity to all handicapped children, (ii) a detailed timetable for accomplishing such a goal, and (iii) a description of the kind and number of facilities, personnel, and services necessary throughout the State to meet such a goal;

(B) a free appropriate public education will be available for all handicapped children between the ages of three and eighteen within the State not later than September 1, 1978, and for all handicapped children between the ages of three and twenty-one within the State not later than September 1, 1980, except that, with respect to handicapped children aged three to five and aged eighteen to twenty-one, inclusive, the requirements of this clause shall not be applied in any State if the application of such requirements would be inconsistent with State law or practice, or the order of any court, respecting public education within such age groups in the State;

(C) all children residing in the State who are handicapped, regardless of the severity of their handicap, and who are in need of special education and related services are identified, located, and evaluated, and that a practical method is developed and implemented to determine which children are currently receiving needed special education and related services and which children are not currently receiving needed special education and related services;

(D) policies and procedures are established in accordance with detailed criteria prescribed under section 1417(c) of this title; and

(E) the amendment to the plan submitted by the State required by this section shall be available to parents, guardians, and other members of the general public at least thirty days prior to the date of submission of the amendment to the Commissioner.

(3) The State has established priorities for providing a free appropriate public education to all handicapped children, which priorities shall meet the timetables set forth in clause (B) of paragraph (2) of this section, first with respect to handicapped children who are not receiving an education, and second with respect to handicapped children, within each disability, with the most severe handicaps who are receiving an inadequate education, and has made adequate progress in meeting the timetables set forth in clause (B) of paragraph (2) of this section.

(4) Each local educational agency in the State will maintain records of the individualized education program for each handicapped child, and such program shall be established, reviewed, and revised as provided in section 1414(a)(5) of this title.

(5) The State has established (A) procedural safeguards as required by section 1415 of this title, (B) procedures to assure that, to the maximum extent appropriate, handicapped children, including children in public or private institutions or other care facilities, are educated with children who are not handicapped, and that special classes, separate schooling, or other removal of handicapped children from the regular educational environment occurs only when the nature or severity of the handicap is such that education in regular classes with the use of supplementary aids and services cannot be achieved satisfactorily, and (C) procedures to assure that testing and evaluation materials and procedures utilized for the purposes of evaluation and placement of handicapped children will be selected and administered so as not to be racially or culturally discriminatory. Such materials or procedures shall be provided and administered in the child's native language or mode of communication, unless it clearly is not feasible to do so, and no single procedure shall be the sole criterion for determining an appropriate educational program for a child.

(6) The State educational agency shall be responsible for assuring that the requirements of this subchapter are carried out and that all educational programs for handicapped children within the State, including all such programs administered by any other State or local agency, will be under the general supervision of the persons responsible for educational programs for handicapped children in the State educational agency and shall meet education standards of the State educational agency.

(7) The State shall assure that (A) in carrying out the requirements of this section procedures are established for consultation with individuals involved in or concerned with the education of handicapped children, including handicapped individuals and parents or guardians of handicapped children, and (B) there are public hearings, adequate notice of such hearings, and an opportunity for comment available to the general public prior to adoption of the policies, programs, and procedures required pursuant to the provisions of this section and section 1413 of this title.

§ 1413. State plans

(a) Requisite features

Any State meeting the eligibility requirements set forth in section 1412 of this title and desiring to participate in the program under this subchapter shall submit to the Commissioner, through its State educational agency, a State plan at such time, in such manner, and containing or accompanied by such information, as he deems necessary. Each such plan shall—

(1) set forth policies and procedures designed to assure that funds paid to the State under this subchapter will be expended in accordance with the provisions of this subchapter, with particular attention given to the provisions of sections 1411(b), 1411(c), 1411(d), 1412(2), and 1412(3) of this title;

(2) provide that programs and procedures will be established to assure that funds received by the State or any of its political subdivisions under any other Federal program, including section 241c-1 of this title, section 844a(b)(8) of this title or its successor authority, and section 1262(a)(4)(B) of this title, under which there is specific authority for the provision of assistance for the education of handicapped children, will be utilized by the State, or any of its political subdivisions, only in a manner consistent with the goal of providing a free appropriate public education for all handicapped children, except that nothing in this clause shall be construed to limit the specific requirements of the laws governing such Federal programs;

(3) set forth, consistent with the purposes of this chapter, a description of programs and procedures for (A) the development and implementation of a comprehensive system of personnel development which shall include the inservice training of general and special educational instructional and support personnel, detailed procedures to assure that all personnel necessary to carry out the purposes of this chapter are appropriately and adequately prepared and trained, and effective procedures for acquiring and disseminating to teachers and administrators of programs for handicapped children significant information derived from educational research, demonstration, and similar projects, and (B) adopting, where appropriate, promising educational practices and materials development through such projects;

(4) set forth policies and procedures to assure—

(A) that, to the extent consistent with the number and location of handicapped children in the State who are enrolled in private elementary and secondary schools, provision is made for the participation of such children in the program assisted or carried out under this subchapter by providing for such children special education and related services; and

(B) that (i) handicapped children in private schools and facilities will be provided special education and related services (in conformance with an individualized educational program as required by this subchapter) at no cost to their parents or guardian, if such children are placed in or referred to such schools or facilities by the State or appropriate local educational agency as the means of carrying out the requirements of this subchapter or any other applicable law requiring the provision of special education and related services to all handicapped children within such State, and (ii) in all such instances the State educational agency shall determine whether such schools and facilities meet standards that apply to State and local educational agencies and that children so served have all the rights they would have if served by such agencies;

(5) set forth policies and procedures which assure that the State shall seek to recover any funds made available under this subchapter for services to any child who is determined to be erroneously classified as eligible to be counted under section 1411(a) or 1411(d) of this title;

(6) provide satisfactory assurance that the control of funds provided under this subchapter, and title to property derived therefrom, shall be in a public agency for the uses and purposes provided in this subchapter, and that a public agency will administer such funds and property;

(7) provide for (A) making such reports in such form and containing such information as the Commissioner may require to carry out his functions under this subchapter, and (B) keeping such records and affording such access thereto as the Commissioner may find necessary to assure the correctness and verification of such reports and proper disbursement of Federal funds under this subchapter;

(8) provide procedures to assure that final action with respect to any application submitted by a local educational agency or an intermediate educational unit shall not be taken without first affording the local educational agency or intermediate educational unit involved reasonable notice and opportunity for a hearing;

(9) provide satisfactory assurance that Federal funds made available under this subchapter (A) will not be commingled with State funds, and (B) will be so used as to supplement and increase the level of State and local funds expended for the education of handicapped children and in no case to supplant such State and local funds, except that, where the State provides clear and convincing evidence that all handicapped children have available to them a free appropriate public education, the Commissioner may waive in part the requirement of this clause if he concurs with the evidence provided by the State;

(10) provide, consistent with procedures prescribed pursuant to section 1417(a)(2) of this title, satisfactory assurance that such fiscal control and fund accounting procedures will be adopted as may be necessary to assure proper disbursement of, and accounting for, Federal funds paid under this subchapter to the State, including any such funds paid by the State to local educational agencies and intermediate educational units;

(11) provide for procedures for evaluation at least annually of the effectiveness of programs in meeting the educational needs of handicapped children (including evaluation of individualized education programs), in accordance with such criteria that the Commissioner shall prescribe pursuant to section 1417 of this title; and

(12) provide that the State has an advisory panel, appointed by the Governor or any other official authorized under State law to make such appointments, composed of individuals involved in or concerned with the education of handicapped children, including handicapped individuals, teachers, parents or guardians of handicapped children, State and local education officials, and administrators of programs for handicapped children, which (A) advises the State educational agency of unmet needs within the State in the education of handicapped children, (B) comments publicly on any rules or regulations proposed for issuance by the State regarding the education of handicapped children and the procedures for distribution of funds under this subchapter, and (C) assists the State in developing and reporting such data and evaluations as may assist the Commissioner in the perfor-

mance of his responsibilities under section 1418 of this title.

(b) Additional assurances

Whenever a State educational agency provides free appropriate public education for handicapped children, or provides direct services to such children, such State educational agency shall include, as part of the State plan required by subsection (a) of this section, such additional assurances not specified in such subsection (a) of this section as are contained in section 1414(a) of this title, except that funds available for the provision of such education or services may be expended without regard to the provisions relating to excess costs in section 1414(a) of this title.

(c) Notice and hearing prior to disapproval of plan

The Commissioner shall approve any State plan and any modification thereof which—

(1) is submitted by a State eligible in accordance with section 1412 of this title; and

(2) meets the requirements of subsection (a) and subsection (b) of this section.

The Commissioner shall disapprove any State plan which does not meet the requirements of the preceding sentence, but shall not finally disapprove a State plan except after reasonable notice and opportunity for a hearing to the State.

§ 1414. Application

(a) Requisite features

A local educational agency or an intermediate educational unit which desires to receive payments under section 1411(d) of this title for any fiscal year shall submit an application to the appropriate State educational agency. Such application shall—

(1) provide satisfactory assurance that payments under this subchapter will be used for excess costs directly attributable to programs which—

(A) provide that all children residing within the jurisdiction of the local educational agency or the intermediate educational unit who are handicapped, regardless of the severity of their handicap, and are in need of special education and related services will be identified, located, and evaluated, and provide for the inclusion of a practical method of determining which children are currently receiving needed special education and related services and which children are not currently receiving such education and services;

(B) establish policies and procedures in accordance with detailed criteria prescribed under section 1417(c) of this title;

(C) establish a goal of providing full educational opportunities to all handicapped children, including—

(i) procedures for the implementation and use of the comprehensive system of personnel development established by the State educational agency under section 1413(a)(3) of this title;

(ii) the provision of, and the establishment of priorities for providing, a free appropriate public education to all handicapped children, first with respect to handicapped children who are not receiving an education, and second with respect to handicapped children, within each disability, with the most severe handicaps who are receiving an inadequate education;

(iii) the participation and consultation of the parents or guardian of such children; and

(iv) to the maximum extent practicable and consistent with the provisions of section 1412(5)(B) of this title, the provision of special services to enable such children to participate in regular educational programs;

(D) establish a detailed timetable for accomplishing the goal described in subclause (C); and

(E) provide a description of the kind and number of facilities, personnel, and services necessary to meet the goal described in subclause (C);

(2) provide satisfactory assurance that (A) the control of funds provided under this subchapter, and title to property derived from such funds, shall be in a public agency for the uses and purposes provided in this subchapter, and that a public agency will administer such funds and property, (B) Federal funds expended by local educational agencies and intermediate educational units for programs under this subchapter (i) shall be used to pay only the excess costs directly attributable to the education of handicapped children, and (ii) shall be used to supplement and, to the extent practicable, increase the level of State and local funds expended for the education of handicapped children, and in no case to supplant such State and local funds, and (C) State and local funds will be used in the jurisdiction of the local educational agency or intermediate educational unit to provide services in program areas which, taken as a whole, are at least comparable to services being provided in areas of such jurisdiction which are not receiving funds under this subchapter;

(3)(A) provide for furnishing such information (which, in the case of reports relating to performance, is in accordance with specific performance criteria related to program objectives), as may be necessary to enable the State educational agency to perform its duties under this subchapter, including information relating to the educational achievement of handicapped children participating in programs carried out under this subchapter; and

(B) provide for keeping such records, and provide for affording such access to such records, as the State educational agency may find necessary to assure the correctness and verification of such information furnished under subclause (A);

(4) provide for making the application and all pertinent documents related to such application available to parents, guardians, and other members of the general public, and provide that all evaluations and reports required under clause (3) shall be public information;

(5) provide assurances that the local educational agency or intermediate educational unit will establish, or revise, whichever is appropriate, an individualized education program for each handicapped child at the beginning of each school year and will then review and, if appropriate revise, its provi-

sions periodically, but not less than annually;

(6) provide satisfactory assurance that policies and programs established and administered by the local educational agency or intermediate educational unit shall be consistent with the provisions of paragraph (1) through paragraph (7) of section 1412 and section 1413(a) of this title; and

(7) provide satisfactory assurance that the local educational agency or intermediate educational unit will establish and maintain procedural safeguards in accordance with the provisions of sections 1412(5)(B), 1412(5)(C), and 1415 of this title.

(b) **Approval by State educational agencies of applications submitted by local educational agencies or intermediate educational units; notice and hearing**

(1) A State educational agency shall approve any application submitted by a local educational agency or an intermediate educational unit under subsection (a) of this section if the State educational agency determines that such application meets the requirements of subsection (a) of this section, except that no such application may be approved until the State plan submitted by such State educational agency under subsection (a) of this section is approved by the Commissioner under section 1413(c) of this title. A State educational agency shall disapprove any application submitted by a local educational agency or an intermediate educational unit under subsection (a) of this section if the State educational agency determines that such application does not meet the requirements of subsection (a) of this section.

(2)(A) Whenever a State educational agency, after reasonable notice and opportunity for a hearing, finds that a local educational agency or an intermediate educational unit, in the administration of an application approved by the State educational agency under paragraph (1), has failed to comply with any requirement set forth in such application, the State educational agency, after giving appropriate notice to the local educational agency or the intermediate educational unit, shall—

(i) make no further payments to such local educational agency or such intermediate educational unit under section 1420 of this title until the State educational agency is satisfied that there is no longer any failure to comply with the requirement involved; or

(ii) take such finding into account in its review of any application made by such local educational agency or such intermediate educational unit under subsection (a) of this section.

(B) The provisions of the last sentence of section 1416(a) of this title shall apply to any local educational agency or any intermediate educational unit receiving any notification from a State educational agency under this paragraph.

(3) In carrying out its functions under paragraph (1), each State educational agency shall consider any decision made pursuant to a hearing held under section 1415 of this title which is adverse to the local educational agency or intermediate educational unit involved in such decision.

(c) **Consolidated applications**

(1) A State educational agency may, for purposes of the consideration and approval of ap-

plications under this section, require local educational agencies to submit a consolidated application for payments if such State educational agency determines that any individual application submitted by any such local educational agency will be disapproved because such local educational agency is ineligible to receive payments because of the application of section 1411(c)(4)(A)(i) of this title or such local educational agency would be unable to establish and maintain programs of sufficient size and scope to effectively meet the educational needs of handicapped children.

(2)(A) In any case in which a consolidated application of local educational agencies is approved by a State educational agency under paragraph (1), the payments which such local educational agencies may receive shall be equal to the sum of payments to which each such local educational agency would be entitled under section 1411(d) of this title if an individual application of any such local educational agency had been approved.

(B) The State educational agency shall prescribe rules and regulations with respect to consolidated applications submitted under this subsection which are consistent with the provisions of paragraph (1) through paragraph (7) of section 1412 and section 1413(a) of this title and which provide participating local educational agencies with joint responsibilities for implementing programs receiving payments under this subchapter.

(C) In any case in which an intermediate educational unit is required pursuant to State law to carry out the provisions of this subchapter, the joint responsibilities given to local educational agencies under subparagraph (B) shall not apply to the administration and disbursement of any payments received by such intermediate educational unit. Such responsibilities shall be carried out exclusively by such intermediate educational unit.

(d) **Special education and related services provided directly by State educational agencies; regional or State centers**

Whenever a State educational agency determines that a local educational agency—

(1) is unable or unwilling to establish and maintain programs of free appropriate public education which meet the requirements established in subsection (a) of this section;

(2) is unable or unwilling to be consolidated with other local educational agencies in order to establish and maintain such programs; or

(3) has one or more handicapped children who can best be served by a regional or State center designed to meet the needs of such children;

the State educational agency shall use the payments which would have been available to such local educational agency to provide special education and related services directly to handicapped children residing in the area served by such local educational agency. The State educational agency may provide such education and services in such manner, and at such locations (including regional or State centers), as it considers appropriate, except that the manner in which such education and services are provided shall be consistent with the requirements of this subchapter.

(e) **Reallocation of funds**

Whenever a State educational agency determines that a local educational agency is adequately providing a free appropriate public education to all handicapped children residing in the area served by such agency with State and local funds otherwise available to such agency, the State educational agency may reallocate funds (or such portion of those funds as may not be required to provide such education and services) made available to such agency, pursuant to section 1411(d) of this title, to such other local educational agencies within the State as are not adequately providing special education and related services to all handicapped children residing in the areas served by such other local educational agencies.

(f) **Programs using State or local funds**

Notwithstanding the provisions of subsection (a)(2)(B)(ii) of this section, any local educational agency which is required to carry out any program for the education of handicapped children pursuant to a State law shall be entitled to receive payments under section 1411(d) of this title for use in carrying out such program, except that such payments may not be used to reduce the level of expenditures for such program made by such local educational agency from State or local funds below the level of such expenditures for the fiscal year prior to the fiscal year for which such local educational agency seeks such payments.

§ 1415. Procedural safeguards

(a) **Establishment and maintenance**

Any State educational agency, any local educational agency, and any intermediate educational unit which receives assistance under this subchapter shall establish and maintain procedures in accordance with subsection (b) through subsection (e) of this section to assure that handicapped children and their parents or guardians are guaranteed procedural safeguards with respect to the provision of free appropriate public education by such agencies and units.

(b) **Required procedures; hearing**

(1) The procedures required by this section shall include, but shall not be limited to—

(A) an opportunity for the parents or guardian of a handicapped child to examine all relevant records with respect to the identification, evaluation, and educational placement of the child, and the provision of a free appropriate public education to such child, and to obtain an independent educational evaluation of the child;

(B) procedures to protect the rights of the child whenever the parents or guardian of the child are not known, unavailable, or the child is a ward of the State, including the assignment of an individual (who shall not be an employee of the State educational agency, local educational agency, or intermediate educational unit involved in the education or care of the child) to act as a surrogate for the parents or guardian;

(C) written prior notice to the parents or guardian of the child whenever such agency or unit—

(i) proposes to initiate or change, or

(ii) refuses to initiate or change,

the identification, evaluation, or educational placement of the child or the provision of a free appropriate public education to the child;

(D) procedures designed to assure that the notice required by clause (C) fully inform the parents or guardian, in the parents' or guardian's native language, unless it clearly is not feasible to do so, of all procedures available pursuant to this section; and

(E) an opportunity to present complaints with respect to any matter relating to the identification, evaluation, or educational placement of the child, or the provision of a free appropriate public education to such child.

(2) Whenever a complaint has been received under paragraph (1) of this subsection, the parents or guardian shall have an opportunity for an impartial due process hearing which shall be conducted by the State educational agency or by the local educational agency or intermediate educational unit, as determined by State law or by the State educational agency. No hearing conducted pursuant to the requirements of this paragraph shall be conducted by an employee of such agency or unit involved in the education or care of the child.

(c) Review of local decision by State educational agency

If the hearing required in paragraph (2) of subsection (b) of this section is conducted by a local educational agency or an intermediate educational unit, any party aggrieved by the findings and decision rendered in such a hearing may appeal to the State educational agency which shall conduct an impartial review of such hearing. The officer conducting such review shall make an independent decision upon completion of such review.

(d) Enumeration of rights accorded parties to hearings

Any party to any hearing conducted pursuant to subsections (b) and (c) of this section shall be accorded (1) the right to be accompanied and advised by counsel and by individuals with special knowledge or training with respect to the problems of handicapped children, (2) the right to present evidence and confront, cross-examine, and compel the attendance of witnesses, (3) the right to a written or electronic verbatim record of such hearing, and (4) the right to written findings of fact and decisions (which findings and decisions shall also be transmitted to the advisory panel established pursuant to section 1413(a)(12) of this title).

(e) Civil action; jurisdiction

(1) A decision made in a hearing conducted pursuant to paragraph (2) of subsection (b) of this section shall be final, except that any party involved in such hearing may appeal such decision under the provisions of subsection (c) and paragraph (2) of this subsection. A decision made under subsection (c) of this section shall be final, except that any party may bring an action under paragraph (2) of this subsection.

(2) Any party aggrieved by the findings and decision made under subsection (b) of this section who does not have the right to an appeal under subsection (c) of this section, and any party aggrieved by the findings and decision under subsection (c) of this section, shall have the right to bring a civil action with respect to the complaint presented pursuant to this section, which action may be brought in any State court of competent jurisdiction or in a district court of the United States without regard to the amount in controversy. In any action brought under this paragraph the court shall receive the records of the administrative proceedings, shall hear additional evidence at the request of a party, and, basing its decision on the preponderance of the evidence, shall grant such relief as the court determines is appropriate.

(3) During the pendency of any proceedings conducted pursuant to this section, unless the State or local educational agency and the parents or guardian otherwise agree, the child shall remain in the then current educational placement of such child, or, if applying for initial admission to a public school, shall, with the consent of the parents or guardian, be placed in the public school program until all such proceedings have been completed.

(4) The district courts of the United States shall have jurisdiction of actions brought under this subsection without regard to the amount in controversy.

§ 1416. Withholding of payments; judicial review

(a) Whenever the Commissioner, after reasonable notice and opportunity for hearing to the State educational agency involved (and to any local educational agency or intermediate educational unit affected by any failure described in clause (2)), finds—

(1) that there has been a failure to comply substantially with any provision of section 1412 or section 1413 of this title, or

(2) that in the administration of the State plan there is a failure to comply with any provision of this subchapter or with any requirements set forth in the application of a local educational agency or intermediate educational unit approved by the State educational agency pursuant to the State plan, the Commissioner (A) shall, after notifying the State educational agency, withhold any further payments to the State under this subchapter, and (B) may, after notifying the State educational agency, withhold further payments to the State under the Federal programs specified in section 1413(a)(2) of this title within his jurisdiction, to the extent that funds under such programs are available for the provision of assistance for the education of handicapped children. If the Commissioner withholds further payments under clause (A) or clause (B) he may determine that such withholding will be limited to programs or projects under the State plan, or portions thereof, affected by the failure, or that the State educational agency shall not make further payments under this subchapter to specified local educational agencies or intermediate educational units affected by the failure. Until the Commissioner is satisfied that there is no longer any failure to comply with the provisions of this subchapter, as specified in clause (1) or clause (2), no further payments shall be made to the State under this subchapter or under the Federal programs specified in section 1413(a)(2) of this title within his jurisdiction to the extent that funds under such programs are available for the provision of assistance for the education of handicapped children, or payments by the State educational agency under this subchapter shall be limited to local educational agencies and intermediate educational units whose actions did not cause or were not involved in the failure, as the case may be. Any State educational agency, local educational agency, or intermediate educational unit in receipt of a notice pursuant to the first sentence of this subsection shall, by means of a public notice, take such measures as may be necessary to bring the pendency of an action pursuant to this subsection to the attention of

the public within the jurisdiction of such agency or unit.

(b)(1) If any State is dissatisfied with the Commissioner's final action with respect to its State plan submitted under section 1413 of this title, such State may, within sixty days after notice of such action, file with the United States court of appeals for the circuit in which such State is located a petition for review of that action. A copy of the petition shall be forthwith transmitted by the clerk of the court to the Commissioner. The Commissioner thereupon shall file in the court the record of the proceedings on which he based his action, as provided in section 2112 of title 28.

(2) The findings of fact by the Commissioner, if supported by substantial evidence, shall be conclusive; but the court, for good cause shown, may remand the case to the Commissioner to take further evidence, and the Commissioner may thereupon make new or modified findings of fact and may modify his previous action, and shall file in the court the record of the further proceedings. Such new or modified findings of fact shall likewise be conclusive if supported by substantial evidence.

(3) Upon the filing of such petition, the court shall have jurisdiction to affirm the action of the Commissioner or to set it aside, in whole or in part. The judgment of the court shall be subject to review by the Supreme Court of the United States upon certiorari or certification as provided in section 1254 of title 28.

§ 1417. Administration

(a) Duties of Commissioner

(1) In carrying out his duties under this subchapter, the Commissioner shall—

(A) cooperate with, and furnish all technical assistance necessary, directly or by grant or contract, to the States in matters relating to the education of handicapped children and the execution of the provisions of this subchapter;

(B) provide such short-term training programs and institutes as are necessary;

(C) disseminate information, and otherwise promote the education of all handicapped children within the States; and

(D) assure that each State shall, within one year after November 29, 1975, provide certification of the actual number of handicapped children receiving special education and related services in such State.

(2) As soon as practicable after November 29, 1975, the Commissioner shall, by regulation, prescribe a uniform financial report to be utilized by State educational agencies in submitting State plans under this subchapter in order to assure equity among the States.

(b) Rules and regulations

In carrying out the provisions of this subchapter, the Commissioner (and the Secretary, in carrying out the provisions of subsection (c) of this section) shall issue, not later than January 1, 1977, amend, and revoke such rules and regulations as may be necessary. No other less formal method of implementing such provisions is authorized.

(c) Protection of rights and privacy of parents and students

The Secretary shall take appropriate action, in accordance with the provisions of section 1232g of this title, to assure the protection of the confidentiality of any personally identifiable data, information, and records collected or maintained by the Commissioner and by State and local educational agencies pursuant to the provisions of this subchapter.

(d) Hiring of qualified personnel

The Commissioner is authorized to hire qualified personnel necessary to conduct data collection and evaluation activities required by subsections (b), (c) and (d) of section 1418 of this title and to carry out his duties under subsection (a)(1) of this section without regard to the provisions of title 5 relating to appointments in the competitive service and without regard to chapter 51 and subchapter III of chapter 53 of such title relating to classification and general schedule pay rates except that no more than twenty such personnel shall be employed at any time.

§ 1418. Evaluation

(a) Duty of Commissioner

The Commissioner shall measure and evaluate the impact of the program authorized under this subchapter and the effectiveness of State efforts to assure the free appropriate public education of all handicapped children.

(b) Studies and investigations

The Commissioner shall conduct, directly or by grant or contract, such studies, investigations, and evaluations as are necessary to assure effective implementation of this subchapter. In carrying out his responsibilities under this section, the Commissioner shall—

(1) through the National Center for Education Statistics, provide to the appropriate committees of each House of the Congress and to the general public at least annually, and shall update at least annually, programmatic information concerning programs and projects assisted under this subchapter and other Federal programs supporting the education of handicapped children, and such information from State and local educational agencies and other appropriate sources necessary for the implementation of this subchapter, including—

(A) the number of handicapped children in each State, within each disability, who require special education and related services;

(B) the number of handicapped children in each State, within each disability, receiving a free appropriate public education and the number of handicapped children who need and are not receiving a free appropriate public education in each such State;

(C) the number of handicapped children in each State, within each disability, who are participating in regular educational programs, consistent with the requirements of section 1412(5)(B) and section 1414(a)(1)(C)(iv) of this title, and the number of handicapped children who have been placed in separate classes or separate school facilities, or who have been otherwise removed from the regular education environment;

(D) the number of handicapped children who are enrolled in public or private institutions in each State and who are receiving a free appropriate public education, and the number of handicapped children who are in such institutions and who are not receiving a free appropriate public education;

(E) the amount of Federal, State, and local expenditures in each State specifically available for special education and related services; and

(F) the number of personnel, by disability category, employed in the education of handicapped children, and the estimated number of additional personnel needed to adequately carry out the policy established by this chapter; and

(2) provide for the evalution of programs and projects assisted under this subchapter through—

(A) the development of effective methods and procedures for evaluation;

(B) the testing and validation of such evaluation methods and procedures; and

(C) conducting actual evaluation studies designed to test the effectiveness of such programs and projects.

(c) Data sample

In developing and furnishing information under subclause (E) of clause (1) of subsection (b) of this section, the Commissioner may base such information upon a sampling of data available from State agencies, including the State educational agencies, and local educational agencies.

(d) Annual reports to Congressional Committees

(1) Not later than one hundred twenty days after the close of each fiscal year, the Commissioner shall transmit to the appropriate committees of each House of the Congress a report on the progress being made toward the provision of free appropriate public education to all handicapped children, including a detailed description of all evaluation activities conducted under subsection (b) of this section.

(2) The Commissioner shall include in each such report—

(A) an analysis and evaluation of the effectiveness of procedures undertaken by each State educational agency, local educational agency, and intermediate educational unit to assure that handicapped children receive special education and related services in the least restrictive environment commensurate with their needs and to improve programs of instruction for handicapped children in day or residential facilities;

(B) any recommendations for change in the provisions of this subchapter, or any other Federal law providing support for the education of handicapped children; and

(C) an evaluation of the effectiveness of the procedures undertaken by each such agency or unit to prevent erroneous classification of children as eligible to be counted under section 1411 of this title, including actions undertaken by the Commissioner to carry out provisions of this chapter relating to such erroneous classification.

In order to carry out such analyses and evaluations, the Commissioner shall conduct a statistically valid survey for assessing the effectiveness of individualized educational programs.

(e) Authorization of appropriations

There are authorized to be appropriated for each fiscal year such sums as may be necessary to carry out the provisions of this section.

§ 1419. Incentive grants

(a) Authority to make grants

The Commissioner shall make a grant to any State which—

(1) has met the eligibility requirements of section 1412 of this title;

(2) has a State plan approved under section 1413 of this title; and

(3) provides special education and related services to handicapped children aged three to five, inclusive, who are counted for the purposes of section 1411(a)(1)(A) of this title.

The maximum amount of the grant for each fiscal year which a State may receive under this section shall be $300 for each such child in that State.

(b) Application

Each State which—

(1) has met the eligibility requirements of section 1412 of this title,

(2) has a State plan approved under section 1413 of this title, and

(3) desires to receive a grant under this section,

shall make an application to the Commissioner at such time, in such manner, and containing or accompanied by such information, as the Commissioner may reasonably require.

(c) Payment

The Commissioner shall pay to each State having an application approved under subsection (b) of this section the amount to which the State is entitled under this section, which amount shall be used for the purpose of providing the services specified in clause (3) of subsection (a) of this section.

(d) Ratable reduction or increase of payments

If the sums appropriated for any fiscal year for making payments to States under this section are not sufficient to pay in full the maximum amounts which all States may receive under this subchapter for such fiscal year, the maximum amounts which all States may receive under this subchapter for such fiscal year shall be ratably reduced. In case additional funds become available for making such payments for any fiscal year during which the preceding sentence is applicable, such reduced amounts shall be increased on the same basis as they were reduced.

(e) Authorization of appropriations

In addition to the sums necessary to pay the entitlements under section 1411 of this title, there are authorized to be appropriated for each fiscal year such sums as may be necessary to carry out the provisions of this section.

§ 1420. Payments

(a) The Commissioner shall make payments to each State in amounts which the State educational agency of such State is eligible to receive under this subchapter. Any State educational agency receiving payments under this subsection shall distribute payments to the local educational agencies and intermediate educational units of such State in amounts which such agencies and units are eligible to receive under this subchapter after the State educational agency has approved applications of such agencies or units for payments in accordance with section 1414(b) of this title.

(b) Payments under this subchapter may be made in advance or by way of reimbursement and in such installments as the Commissioner may determine necessary.

P.L. 94–142 REGULATIONS (34 C.F.R. PART 300)

These regulations were formerly known as 45 C.F.R. part 121a. All previous references to "45 C.F.R." should now be read as "34 C.F.R."; all references to "121a" should be designated as "300" when the regulations are discussed or cited in writing.

PART 121a—ASSISTANCE TO STATES FOR EDUCATION OF HANDICAPPED CHILDREN

Subpart A—General

PURPOSE, APPLICABILITY, AND GENERAL PROVISIONS REGULATIONS

Sec.
121a.1 Purpose.
121a.2 Applicability to State, local, and private agencies.
121a.3 Regulations that apply to assistance to States for education of handicapped children.

DEFINITIONS

121a.4 Free appropriate public education.
121a.5 Handicapped children.
121a.6 Include.
121a.7 Intermediate educational unit.
121a.8 Local educational agency.
121a.9 Native language.
121a.10 Parent.
121a.11 Public agency.
121a.12 Qualified.
121a.13 Related services.
121a.14 Special education.

Subpart B—State Annual Program Plans and Local Applications

ANNUAL PROGRAM PLANS—GENERAL

121a.110 Condition of assistance.
121a.111 Contents of plan.

ANNUAL PROGRAM PLANS—CONTENTS

121a.121 Right to a free appropriate public education.
121a.122 Timeliness and ages for free appropriate public education.
121a.123 Full educational opportunity goal.
121a.124 Full educational opportunity goal—data requirement.
121a.125 Full educational opportunity goal—timetable.
121a.126 Full educational opportunity goal—facilities, personnel, and services.
121a.127 Priorities.
121a.128 Identification, location, and evaluation of handicapped children.
121a.129 Confidentiality of personally identifiable information.
121a.130 Individualized education programs.
121a.131 Procedural safeguards.
121a.132 Least restrictive environment.
121a.133 Protection in evaluation procedures.
121a.134 Responsibility of State educational agency for all educational programs.
121a.135 [Reserved]

AUTHORITY: Part of the Education of the Handicapped Act, Pub. L. 91-230, Title VI, as amended, 89 Stat. 776-794 (20 U.S.C. 1411-1420), unless otherwise noted.

SOURCE: 42 FR 42476, Aug. 23, 1977, unless otherwise noted.

Subpart A—General

PURPOSE, APPLICABILITY, AND GENERAL
PROVISIONS REGULATIONS

§ 121a.1   Purpose.

The purpose of this part is:

(a) To insure that all handicapped children have available to them a free appropriate public education which includes special education and related services to meet their unique needs,

(b) To insure that the rights of handicapped children and their parents are protected,

(c) To assist States and localities to provide for the education of all handicapped children, and

(d) To assess and insure the effectiveness of efforts to educate those children.

(20 U.S.C. 1401 Note)

§ 121a.2   Applicability to State, local, and private agencies.

(a) *States.* This part applies to each State which receives payments under Part B of the Education of the Handicapped Act.

(b) *Public agencies within the State.* The annual program plan is submitted by the State educational agency on behalf of the State as a whole. Therefore, the provisions of this part apply to all political subdivisions of the State that are involved in the education of handicapped children. These would include:

(1) The State educational agency, (2) local educational agencies and intermediate educational units, (3) other State agencies and schools (such as Departments of Mental Health and Welfare and State schools for the deaf or blind), and (4) State correctional facilities.

(c) *Private schools and facilities.* Each public agency in the State is responsible for insuring that the rights and protections under this part are given to children referred to or placed in private schools and facilities by that public agency. (See §§ 121a.400-121a.403)

(20   U.S.C.   1412(1),   (6);   1413(a); 1413(a)(4)(B))

Comment. The requirements of this part are binding on each public agency that has direct or delegated authority to provide special education and related services in a State that receives funds under Part B of the Act, regardless of whether that agency is receiving funds under Part B.

§ 121a.3 **Regulations that apply to assistance to States for education of handicapped children.**

(a) *Regulations.* The following regulations apply to this program of Assistance to States for Education of Handicapped Children.

(1) The Education Division General Administrative Regulations (EDGAR) in 45 CFR Part 100b (State-Administered Programs) and Part 100c (Definitions).

(2) The regulations in this Part 121a.

(b) *How to use regulations; how to apply for funds.* The "Introduction to Regulations of the Education Division" at the beginning of EDGAR includes general information to assist in—

(1) Using regulations that apply to Education Division programs; and

(2) Applying for assistance under an Education Division program.

(20 U.S.C. 1221e-3(a)(1))

DEFINITIONS

Comment. Definitions of terms that are used throughout these regulations are included in this subpart. Other terms are defined in the specific subparts in which they are used. Below is a list of those terms and the specific sections and subparts in which they are defined:

Consent (Section 121a.500 of Subpart E)
Destruction (Section 121a.560 of Subpart E)
Direct services (Section 121a.370(b)(1) of Subpart C)
Evaluation (Section 121a.500 of Subpart E)
First priority children (Section 121a.320(a) of Subpart C)
Independent educational evaluation (Section 121a.503 of Subpart E)
Individualized education program (Section 121a.340 of Subpart C)
Participating agency (Section 121a.560 of Subpart E)
Personally identifiable (Section 121a.500 of Subpart E)
Private school handicapped children (Section 121a.450 of Subpart D)
Public expense (Section 121a.503 of Subpart E)
Second priority children (Section 121a.320(b) of Subpart C)
Special definition of "State" (Section 121a.700 of Subpart G)

Support services (Section 121a.370(b)(2) of Subpart C)

[42 FR 42476, Aug. 23, 1977, as amended at 45 FR 22531, Apr. 3, 1980]

§ 121a.4 **Free appropriate public education.**

As used in this part, the term "free appropriate public education" means special education and related services which:

(a) Are provided at public expense, under public supervision and direction, and without charge.

(b) Meet the standards of the State educational agency, including the requirements of this part,

(c) Include preschool, elementary school, or secondary school education in the State involved, and

(d) Are provided in conformity with an individualized education program which meets the requirements under §§ 121a.340–121a.349 of Subpart C.

(20 U.S.C. 1401(18))

§ 121a.5 **Handicapped children.**

(a) As used in this part, the term "handicapped children" means those children evaluated in accordance with §§ 121a.530–121a.534 as being mentally retarded, hard of hearing, deaf, speech impaired, visually handicapped, seriously emotionally disturbed, orthopedically impaired, other health impaired, deaf-blind, multi-handicapped, or as having specific learning disabilities, who because of those impairments need special education and related services.

(b) The terms used in this definition are defined as follows:

(1) "Deaf" means a hearing impairment which is so severe that the child is impaired in processing linguistic information through hearing, with or without amplification, which adversely affects educational performance.

(2) "Deaf-blind" means concomitant hearing and visual impairments, the combination of which causes such severe communication and other developmental and educational problems that they cannot be accommodated in special education programs solely for deaf or blind children.

(3) "Hard of Hearing" means a hearing impairment, whether permanent or fluctuating, which adversely affects a child's educational performance but

which is not included under the definition of "deaf" in this section.

(4) "Mentally retarded" means significantly subaverage general intellectual functioning existing concurrently with deficits in adaptive behavior and manifested during the developmental period, which adversely affects a child's educational performance.

(5) "Multihandicapped" means concomitant impairments (such as mentally retarded—blind, mentally retarded-orthopedically impaired, etc.), the combination of which causes such severe educational problems that they cannot be accommodated in special education programs solely for one of the impairments. The term does not include deaf-blind children.

(6) "Orthopedically impaired" means a severe orthopedic impairment which adversely affects a child's educational performance. The term includes impairments caused by congenital anomaly (e.g., clubfoot, absence of some member, etc.), impairments caused by disease (e.g. poliomyelitis, bone tuberculosis, etc.), and impairments from other causes (e.g., cerebral palsy, amputations, and fractures or burns which cause contractures).

(7) *
limited strength, vitality or alertness, due to chronic or acute health problems such as a heart condition, tuberculosis, rheumatic fever, nephritis, asthma, sickle cell anemia, hemophilia, epilepsy, lead poisoning, leukemia, or diabetes, which adversely affects a child's educational performance.

(8) "Seriously emotionally disturbed" is defined as follows:

(i) The term means a condition exhibiting one or more of the following characteristics over a long period of time and to a marked degree, which adversely affects educational performance:

(A) An inability to learn which cannot be explained by intellectual, sensory, or health factors;

(B) An inability to build or maintain satisfactory interpersonal relationships with peers and teachers;

(C) Inappropriate types of behavior

or feelings under normal circumstances;

(D) A general pervasive mood of unhappiness or depression; or

(E) A tendency to develop physical symptoms or fears associated with personal or school problems.

(ii) The term includes children who are schizophrenic   . The term does not include children who are socially maladjusted, unless it is determined that they are seriously emotionally disturbed.

(9) "Specific learning disability" means a disorder in one or more of the basic psychological processes involved in understanding or in using language, spoken or written, which may manifest itself in an imperfect ability to listen, think, speak, read, write, spell, or to do mathematical calculations. The term includes such conditions as perceptual handicaps, brain injury, minimal brain dysfunction, dyslexia, and developmental aphasia. The term does not include children who have learning problems which are primarily the result of visual, hearing, or motor handicaps, of mental retardation of emotional disturbance or of environmental, cultural, or economic disadvantage.

(10) "Speech impaired" means a communication disorder such as stuttering, impaired articulation, a language impairment, or a voice impairment, which adversely affects a child's educational performance.

(11) "Visually handicapped" means a visual impairment which, even with correction, adversely affects a child's educational performance. The term includes both partially seeing and blind children.

(20 U.S.C. 1401(1), (15))

[42 FR 42476, Aug. 23, 1977, as amended at 42 FR 65083, Dec. 29, 1977]

§ 121a.6 Include.

As used in this part, the term "include" means that the items named are not all of the possible items that are covered, whether like or unlike the ones named.

(20 U.S.C. 1417(b))

§ 121a.7 Intermediate educational unit.

As used in this part, the term "intermediate educational unit" means any

---

*"Other health impaired" means (i) having an autistic condition which is manifested by severe communication and other developmental and educational problems: or (ii) having

public authority, other than a local educational agency, which:

(a) Is under the general supervision of a State educational agency;

(b) Is established by State law for the purpose of providing free public education on a regional basis; and

(c) Provides special education and related services to handicapped children within that State.

(20 U.S.C. 1401 (22))

§ 121a.8   Local educational agency.

(a) [Reserved]

(b) For the purposes of this part, the term "local educational agency" also includes intermediate educational units.

(20 U.S.C. 1401 (8))

[42 FR 42476, Aug. 23, 1977, as amended at 45 FR 22531, Apr. 3, 1980]

§ 121a.9   Native language.

As used in this part, the term "native language" has the meaning given that term by section 703(a)(2) of the Bilingual Education Act, which provides as follows:

The term "native language", when used with reference to a person of limited English-speaking ability, means the language normally used by that person, or in the case of a child, the language normally used by the parents of the child.

(20 U.S.C. 880b-1(a)(2); 1401(21))

Comment. Section 602(21) of the Education of the Handicapped Act states that the term "native language" has the same meaning as the definition from the Bilingual Education Act. (The term is used in the prior notice and evaluation sections under § 121a.505(b)(2) and § 121a.532(a)(1) of Subpart E.) In using the term, the Act does not prevent the following means of communication:

(1) In all direct contact with a child (including evaluation of the child), communication would be in the language normally used by the child and not that of the parents, if there is a difference between the two.

(2) If a person is deaf or blind, or has no written language, the mode of communication would be that normally used by the person (such as sign language, braille, or oral communication).

§ 121a.10   Parent.

As used in this part, the term "parent" means a parent, a guardian, a

person acting as a parent of a child, or a surrogate parent who has been appointed in accordance with § 121a.514. The term does not include the State if the child is a ward of the State.

(20 U.S.C. 1415)

Comment. The term "parent" is defined to include persons acting in the place of a parent, such as a grandmother or stepparent with whom a child lives, as well as persons who are legally responsible for a child's welfare.

§ 121a.11   Public agency.

As used in this part, the term "public agency" includes the State educational agency, local educational agencies, intermediate educational units, and any other political subdivisions of the State which are responsible for providing education to handicapped children.

(20 U.S.C. 1412(2)(B); 1412(6); 1413(a))

§ 121a.12   Qualified.

As used in this part, the term "qualified" means that a person has met State educational agency approved or recognized certification, licensing, registration, or other comparable requirements which apply to the area in which he or she is providing special education or related services.

(20 U.S.C. 1417(b))

§ 121a.13   Related services.

(a) As used in this part, the term "related services" means transportation and such developmental, corrective, and other supportive services as are required to assist a handicapped child to benefit from special education, and includes speech pathology and audiology, psychological services, physical and occupational therapy, recreation, early identification and assessment of disabilities in children, counseling services, and medical services for diagnostic or evaluation purposes. The term also includes school health services, social work services in schools, and parent counseling and training.

(b) The terms used in this definition are defined as follows:

(1) "Audiology" includes:

(i) Identification of children with hearing loss;

(ii) Determination of the range, nature, and degree of hearing loss, including referral for medical or other professional attention for the habilitation of hearing;

(iii) Provision of habilitative activities, such as language habilitation, auditory training, speech reading (lipreading), hearing evaluation, and speech conservation;

(iv) Creation and administration of programs for prevention of hearing loss;

(v) Counseling and guidance of pupils, parents, and teachers regarding hearing loss; and

(vi) Determination of the child's need for group and individual amplification, selecting and fitting an appropriate aid, and evaluating the effectiveness of amplification.

(2) "Counseling services" means services provided by qualified social workers, psychologists, guidance counselors, or other qualified personnel.

(3) "Early identification" means the implementation of a formal plan for identifying a disability as early as possible in a child's life.

(4) "Medical services" means services provided by a licensed physician to determine a child's medically related handicapping condition which results in the child's need for special education and related services.

(5) "Occupational therapy" includes:

(i) Improving, developing or restoring functions impaired or lost through illness, injury, or deprivation;

(ii) Improving ability to perform tasks for independent functioning when functions are impaired or lost; and

(iii) Preventing, through early intervention, initial or further impairment or loss of function.

(6) "Parent counseling and training" means assisting parents in understanding the special needs of their child and providing parents with information about child development.

(7) "Physical therapy" means services provided by a qualified physical therapist.

(8) "Psychological services" include:

(i) Administering psychological and educational tests, and other assessment procedures;

(ii) Interpreting assessment results;

(iii) Obtaining, integrating, and interpreting information about child behavior and conditions relating to learning.

(iv) Consulting with other staff members in planning school programs to meet the special needs of children as indicated by psychological tests, interviews, and behavioral evaluations; and

(v) Planning and managing a program of psychological services, including psychological counseling for children and parents.

(9) "Recreation" includes:

(i) Assessment of leisure function;

(ii) Therapeutic recreation services;

(iii) Recreation programs in schools and community agencies; and

(iv) Leisure education.

(10) "School health services" means services provided by a qualified school nurse or other qualified person.

(11) "Social work services in schools" include:

(i) Preparing a social or developmental history on a handicapped child;

(ii) Group and individual counseling with the child and family;

(iii) Working with those problems in a child's living situation (home, school, and community) that affect the child's adjustment in school; and

(iv) Mobilizing school and community resources to enable the child to receive maximum benefit from his or her educational program.

(12) "Speech pathology" includes:

(i) Identification of children with speech or language disorders;

(ii) Diagnosis and appraisal of specific speech or languge disorders;

(iii) Referral for medical or other professional attention necessary for the habilitation of speech or language disorders;

(iv) Provisions of speech and language services for the habilitation or prevention of communicative disorders; and

(v) Counseling and guidance of parents, children, and teachers regarding speech and language disorders.

(13) "Transportation" includes:

(i) Travel to and from school and between schools,

(ii) Travel in and around school buildings, and

(iii) Specialized equipment (such as special or adapted buses, lifts, and ramps), if required to provide special transportation for a handicapped child.

(20 U.S.C. 1401 (17))

Comment. With respect to related services, the Senate Report states:

The Committee bill provides a definition of "related services," making clear that all such related services may not be required for each individual child and that such term includes early identification and assessment of handicapping conditions and the provision of services to minimize the effects of such conditions.

(Senate Report No. 94-168, p. 12 (1975))

The list of related services is not exhaustive and may include other developmental, corrective, or supportive services (such as artistic and cultural programs, and art, music, and dance therapy), if they are required to assist a handicapped child to benefit from special education.

There are certain kinds of services which might be provided by persons from varying professional backgrounds and with a variety of operational titles, depending upon requirements in individual States. For example, counseling services might be provided by social workers, psychologists, or guidance counselors; and psychological testing might be done by qualified psychological examiners, psychometrists, or psychologists, depending upon State standards.

Each related service defined under this part may include appropriate administrative and supervisory activities that are necessary for program planning, management, and evaluation.

§ 121a.14   Special education.

(a) (1) As used in this part, the term "special education" means specially designed instruction, at no cost to the parent, to meet the unique needs of a handicapped child, including classroom instruction, instruction in physical education, home instruction, and instruction in hospitals and institutions.

(2) The term includes speech pathology, or any other related service, if the service consists of specially designed instruction, at no cost to the parents, to meet the unique needs of a handicapped child, and is considered "special education" rather than a "related service" under State standards.

(3) The term also includes vocational education if it consists of specially de-

signed instruction, at no cost to the parents, to meet the unique needs of a handicapped child.

(b) The terms in this definition are defined as follows:

(1) "At no cost" means that all specially designed instruction is provided without charge, but does not preclude incidental fees which are normally charged to non-handicapped students or their parents as a part of the regular education program.

(2) "Physical education" is defined as follows:

(i) The term means the development of:

(A) Physical and motor fitness;

(B) Fundamental motor skills and patterns; and

(C) Skills in aquatics, dance, and individual and group games and sports (including intramural and lifetime sports).

(ii) The term includes special physical education, adapted physical education, movement education, and motor development.

(20 U.S.C. 1401 (16))

(3) "Vocational education" means organized educational programs which are directly related to the preparation of individuals for paid or unpaid employment, or for additional preparation for a career requiring other than a baccalaureate or advanced degree.

(20 U.S.C. 1401 (16))

Comment. (1) The definition of "special education" is a particularly important one under these regulations, since a child is not handicapped unless he or she needs special education. (See the definition of "handicapped children" in § 121a.5.) The definition of "related services" (section 121a.13) also depends on this definition, since a related service must be necessary for a child to benefit from special education. Therefore, if a child does not need special education, there can be no "related services," and the child (because not "handicapped") is not covered under the Act.

(2) The above definition of vocational education is taken from the Vocational Education Act of 1963, as amended by Pub. L. 94-482. Under that Act, "vocational education" includes industrial arts and consumer and homemaking education programs.

Subpart B—State Annual Program Plans and Local Applications

ANNUAL PROGRAM PLANS—GENERAL

§ 121a.110   Condition of assistance.

In order to receive funds under Part B of the Act for any fiscal year, a State must submit an annual program plan to the Commissioner through its State educational agency.

(20 U.S.C. 1232c(b), 1412, 1413)

§ 121a.111   Contents of plan.

Each annual program plan must contain the provisions required in this subpart.

(20 U.S.C. 1412, 1413, 1232c(b))

ANNUAL PROGRAM PLANS—CONTENTS

§ 121a.121   Right to a free appropriate public education.

(a) Each annual program plan must include information which shows that the State has in effect a policy which insures that all handicapped children have the right to a free appropriate public education within the age ranges and timelines under § 121a.122.

(b) The information must include a copy of each State statute, court order, State Attorney General opinion, and other State document that shows the source of the policy.

(c) The information must show that the policy:

(1) Applies to all public agencies in the State;

(2) Applies to all handicapped children;

(3) Implements the priorities established under § 121a.127(a)(1) of this subpart; and

(4) Establishes timeliness for implementing the policy, in accordance with § 121a.122.

(20 U.S.C. 1412(1)(2)(B), (6); 1413(a)(3))

§ 121a.122   Timeliness and ages for free appropriate public education.

(a) General. Each annual program plan must include in detail the policies and procedures which the State will undertake or has undertaken in order to insure that a free appropriate public education is available for all handicapped children aged three through eighteen within the State not later than September 1, 1978, and for all handicapped children aged three through twenty-one within the State not later than September 1, 1980.

(b) Documents relating to timeliness. Each annual program plan must include a copy of each statute, court order, attorney general decision, another State document which demonstrates that the State has established timelines in accordance with paragraph (a) of this section

(c) Exception. The requirement in paragraph (a) of this section does not apply to a State with respect to handicapped children aged three, four, five, eighteen, nineteen, twenty, or twenty-one to the extent that the requirement would be inconsistent with State law or practice, or the order of any court, respecting public education for one or more of those age groups in the State.

(d) Documents relating to exceptions. Each annual program plan must:

(1) Describe in detail the extent to which the exception in paragraph (c) of this section applies to the State, and

(2) Include a copy of each State law, court order, and other document which provides a basis for the exception.

(20 U.S.C. 1412(2)(B))

§ 121a.123   Full educational opportunity goal.

Each annual program plan must include in detail the policies and procedures which the State will undertake, or has undertaken, in order to insure that the State has a goal of providing full educational opportunity to all handicapped children aged birth through twenty-one.

(20 U.S.C. 1412(2)(A))

§ 121a.124   Full educational opportunity goal—data requirement.

Beginning with school year 1978–1979, each annual program plan must contain the following information:

(a) The estimated number of handicapped children who need special education and related services.

(b) For the current school year:

(1) The number of handicapped children aged birth through two, who are receiving special education and related services; and

(2) The number of handicapped children:

(i) Who are receiving a free appropriate public education,

(ii) Who need, but are not receiving a free appropriate public education,

(iii) Who are enrolled in public private institutions who are receiving a free appropriate public education, and

(iv) Who are enrolled in public and private institutions and are not receiving a free appropriate public education.

(c) The estimated numbers of handicapped children who are expected to receive special education and related services during the next school year.

(d) A description of the basis used to determine the data required under this section.

(e) The data required by paragraphs (a), (b), and (c) of this section must be provided:

(1) For each disability category (except for children aged birth through two), and

(2) For each of the following age ranges: birth through two, three through five, six through seventeen, and eighteen through twenty-one.

(20 U.S.C. 1412(2)(A))

Comment. In Part B of the Act, the term "disability" is used interchangeably with "handicapping condition". For consistency in this regulation, a child with a "disability" means a child with one of the impairments listed in the definition of "handicapped children" in § 121a.5, if the child needs special education because of the impairment. In essence, there is a continuum of impairments. When an impairment is of such a nature that the child needs special education, it is referred to as a disability, in these regulations, and the child is a "handicapped" child.

States should note that data required under this section are not to be transmitted to the Commissioner in personally identifiable form. Generally, except for such purposes as monitoring and auditing, neither the States nor the Federal Government should have to collect data under this part in personally identifiable form.

§ 121a.125 Full educational opportunity goal—timetable.

(a) *General requirement.* Each annual program plan must contain a detailed timetable for accomplishing the goal of providing full educational opportunity for all handicapped children.

(b) *Content of timetable.* (1) The timetable must indicate what percent of the total estimated number of handicapped children the State expects to have full educational opportunity in each succeeding school year.

(2) The data required under this paragraph must be provided:

(i) For each disability category (except for children aged birth through two), and

(ii) For each of the following age ranges: birth through two, three through five, six through seventeen, and eighteen through twenty-one.

(20 U.S.C. 1412(2)(A))

§ 121a.126 Full educational opportunity goal—facilities, personnel, and services.

(a) *General requirement.* Each annual program plan must include a description of the kind and number of facilities, personnel, and services necessary throughout the State to meet the goal of providing full educational opportunity for all handicapped children. The State educational agency shall include the data required under paragraph (b) of this section and whatever additional data are necessary to meet the requirement.

(b) *Statistical description.* Each annual program plan must include the following data:

(1) The number of additional special class teachers, resource room teachers, and itinerant or consultant teachers needed for each disability category and the number of each of these who are currently employed in the State.

(2) The number of other additional personnel needed, and the number currently employed in the State, including school psychologists, school social workers, occupational therapists, physical therapists, home-hospital teachers, speech-language pathologists, audiologists, teacher aides, vocational education teachers, work study

coordinators, physical education teachers, therapeutic recreation specialists, diagnostic personnel, supervisors, and other instructional and noninstructional staff.

(3) The total number of personnel reported under paragraphs (b) (1) and (2) of this section, and the salary costs of those personnel.

(4) The number and kind of facilities needed for handicapped children and the number and kind currently in use in the State, including regular classes serving handicapped children, self-contained classes on a regular school campus, resource rooms, private special education day schools, public special education day schools, private special education residential schools, public special education residential schools, hospital programs, occupational therapy facilities, physical therapy facilities, public sheltered workshops, private sheltered workshops, and other types of facilities.

(5) The total number of transportation units needed for handicapped children, the number of transportation units designed for handicapped children which are in use in the State, and the number of handicapped children who use these units to benefit from special education.

(c) *Data categories.* The data required under paragraph (b) of this section must be provided as follows:

(1) Estimates for serving all handicapped children who require special education and related services,

(2) Current year data, based on the actual numbers of handicapped children receiving special education and related services (as reported under Subpart G), and

(3) Estimates for the next school year.

(d) *Rationale.* Each annual program plan must include a description of the means used to determine the number and salary costs of personnel.

(20 U.S.C. 1412(2)(A))

§ 121a.127 **Priorities.**

(a) *General requirement.* Each annual program plan must include information which shows that:

(1) The State has established priorities which meet the requirements

under §§ 121a.320–121a.324 of Subpart C.

(2) The State priorities meet the timelines under § 121a.122 of this subpart, and

(3) The State has made progress in meeting those timelines.

(b) *Child data.* (1) Each annual program plan must show the number of handicapped children known by the State to be in each of the first two priority groups named in §§ 121a.321 of Subpart C:

(i) By disability category, and

(ii) By the age ranges in § 121a.124(e) (2) of this subpart.

(c) *Activities and resources.* Each annual program plan must show for each of the first two priority groups:

(1) The programs, services, and activities that are being carried out in the State,

(2) The Federal, State, and local resources that have been committed during the current school year, and

(3) The programs, services, activities, and resources that are to be provided during the next school year.

(20 U.S.C. 1412(3))

§ 121a.128 **Identification, location, and evaluation of handicapped children.**

(a) *General requirement.* Each annual program plan must include in detail the policies and procedures which the State will undertake or has undertaken to insure that:

(1) All children who are handicapped, regardless of the severity of their handicap, and who are in need of special education and related services are identified, located, and evaluated; and

(2) A practical method is developed and implemented to determine which children are currently receiving needed special education and related services and which children are not currently receiving needed special education and related services.

(b) *Information.* Each annual program plan must:

(1) Designate the State agency (if other than the State educational agency) responsible for coordinating the planning and implementation of the policies and procedures under paragraph (a) of this section;

(2) Name each agency that participates in the planning and implementation and describe the nature and extent of its participation;

(3) Describe the extent to which:

(i) The activities described in paragraph (a) of this section have been achieved under the current annual program plan, and

(ii) The resources named for these activities in that plan have been used;

(4) Describe each type of activity to be carried out during the next school year, including the role of the agency named under paragraph (b)(1) of this section, timelines for completing those activities, resources that will be used, and expected outcomes;

(5) Describe how the policies and procedures under paragraph (a) of this section will be monitored to insure that the State educational agency obtains:

(i) The number of handicapped children within each disability category that have been identified, located, and evaluated, and

(ii) Information adequate to evaluate the effectiveness of those policies and procedures; and

(6) Describe the method the State uses to determine which children are currently receiving special education and related services and which children are not receiving special education and related services.

(20 U.S.C. 1412(2)(C))

Comment. The State is responsible for insuring that all handicapped children are identified, located, and evaluated, including children in all public and private agencies and institutions in the State. Collection and use of data are subject to the confidentiality requirements in §§ 121a.560–121a.576.

§ 121a.129 Confidentiality of personally identifiable information.

(a) Each annual program plan must include in detail the policies and procedures which the State will undertake or has undertaken in order to insure the protection of the confidentiality of any personally identifiable information collected, used, or maintained under this part.

(b) The Commissioner shall use the criteria in §§ 121a.560–121a.576 of Subpart E to evaluate the policies and procedures of the State under paragraph (a) of this section.

(20 U.S.C. 1412(2)(D); 1417(c))

Comment. The confidentiality regulations were published in the FEDERAL REGISTER in final form on February 27, 1976 (41 FR 8603–8610), and met the requirements of Part B of the Act, as amended by Pub. L. 94–142. Those regulations are incorporated in § 121a.560–121a.576 of Subpart E.

§ 121a.130 Individualized education programs.

(a) Each annual program plan must include information which shows that each public agency in the State maintains records of the individualized education program for each handicapped child, and each public agency establishes, reviews, and revises each program as provided in Subpart C.

(b) Each annual program plan must include:

(1) A copy of each State statute, policy, and standard that regulates the manner in which individualized education programs are developed, implemented, reviewed, and revised, and

(2) The procedures which the State educational agency follows in monitoring and evaluating those programs.

(20 U.S.C. 1412(4))

§ 121a.131 Procedural safeguards.

Each annual program plan must include procedural safeguards which insure that the requirements in §§ 121a.500–121a.514 of Subpart E are met.

(20 U.S.C. 1412(5)(A))

§ 121a.132 Least restrictive environment.

(a) Each annual program plan must include procedures which insure that the requirements in §§ 121a.550–121a.556 of Subpart E are met.

(b) Each annual program plan must include the following information:

(1) The number of handicapped children in the State, within each disability category, who are participating in regular education programs, consistent with §§ 121a.550–121a.556 of Subpart E.

(2) The number of handicapped children who are in separate classes or separate school facilities, or who are

otherwise removed from the regular education environment.

(20 U.S.C. 1412(5)(B))

§ 121a.133   Protection in evaluation procedures.

Each annual program plan must include procedures which insure that the requirements in §§ 121a.530-121a.534 of Subpart E are met.

(10 U.S.C. 1412(5)(C))

§ 121a.134   Responsibility of State educational agency for all educational programs.

(a) Each annual program plan must include information which shows that the requirements in § 121a.600 of Subpart F are met.

(b) The information under paragraph (a) of this section must include a copy of each State statute, State regulation, signed agreement between respective agency officials, and any other document that shows compliance with that paragraph.

(20 U.S.C. 1412(6))

§ 121a.135   [Reserved]

§ 121a.136   Implementation procedures—State educational agency.

Each annual program plan must describe the procedures the State educational agency follows to inform each public agency of its responsibility for insuring effective implementation of procedural safeguards for the handicapped children served by that public agency.

(20 U.S.C. 1412(6))

§ 121a.137   Procedures for consultation.

Each annual program plan must include an assurance that in carrying out the requirements of section 612 of the Act, procedures are established for consultation with individuals involved in or concerned with the education of handicapped children, including handicapped individuals and parents of handicapped children.

(20 U.S.C. 1412(7)(A))

§ 121a.138   Other Federal programs.

Each annual program plan must provide that programs and procedures are established to insure that funds received by the State or any public agency in the State under any other Federal program, including section 121 of the Elementary and Secondary Education Act of 1965 (20 U.S.C. 241e-2), section 305(b)(8) of that Act (20 U.S.C. 844a(b)(8)) or Title IV-C of that Act (20 U.S.C. 1831), and section 110(a) of the Vocational Education Act of 1963, under which there is specific authority for assistance for the education of handicapped children, are used by the State, or any public agency in the State, only in a manner consistent with the goal of providing free appropriate public education for all handicapped children, except that nothing in this section limits the specific requirements of the laws governing those Federal programs.

(20 U.S.C. 1413(a)(2))

§ 121a.139   Comprehensive system of personnel development.

Each annual program plan must include the material required under §§ 121a.380-121a.387 of Subpart C.

(20 U.S.C. 1413(a)(3))

§ 121a.140   Private schools.

Each annual program plan must include policies and procedures which insure that the requirements of Subpart D are met.

(20 U.S.C. 1413(a)(4))

§ 121a.141   Recovery of funds for misclassified children.

Each annual program plan must include policies and procedures which insure that the State seeks to recover any funds provided under Part B of the Act for services to a child who is determined to be erroneously classified as eligible to be counted under section 611 (a) or (d) of the Act.

(20 U.S.C. 1413(a)(5))

§ 121a.142   [Reserved]

§ 121a.143   [Reserved]

§ 121a.144   Hearing on application.

Each annual program plan must include procedures to insure that the State educational agency does not take any final action with respect to an application submitted by a local educational agency before giving the local educational agency reasonable notice and an opportunity for a hearing.

(20 U.S.C. 1413(a)(8))

§ 121a.145 Prohibition of commingling.

Each annual program plan must provide assurance satisfactory to the Commissioner that funds provided under Part B of the Act are not commingled with State funds.

(20 U.S.C. 1413(a)(9))

Comment. This assurance is satisfied by the use of a separate accounting system that includes an "audit trail" of the expenditure of the Part B funds. Separate bank accounts are not required. (See 45 CFR 100b, Subpart F (Cash Depositories))

§ 121a.146 Annual evaluation.

Each annual program plan must include procedures for evaluation at least annually of the effectiveness of programs in meeting the educational needs of handicapped children, including evaluation of individualized education programs.

(20 U.S.C. 1413(a)(11))

§ 121a.147 State advisory panel.

Each annual program plan must provide that the requirements of §§ 121a.650–121a.653 of Subpart F are met.

(20 U.S.C. 1413(a)(12))

§ 121a.148 Policies and procedures for use of Part B funds.

Each annual program plan must set forth policies and procedures designed to insure that funds paid to the State under Part B of the Act are spent in accordance with the provisions of Part B, with particular attention given to sections 611(b), 611(c), 611(d), 612(2), and 612(3) of the Act.

(20 U.S.C. 1413(a)(1))

§ 121a.149 Description of use of Part B funds.

(a) *State allocation.* Each annual program plan must include the following information about the State's use of funds under § 121a.370 of Subpart C and § 121a.620 of Subpart F:

(1) A list of administrative positions, and a description of duties for each person whose salary is paid in whole or in part with those funds.

(2) For each position, the percentage of salary paid with those funds.

(3) A description of each administrative activity the State educational agency will carry out during the next school year with those funds.

(4) A description of each direct service and each support service which the State educational agency will provide during the next school year with those funds, and the activities the State advisory panel will undertake during that period with those funds.

(b) *Local educational agency allocation.* Each annual program plan must include:

(1) An estimate of the number and percent of local educational agencies in the State which will receive an allocation under this part (other than local educational agencies which submit a consolidated application),

(2) An estimate of the number of local educational agencies which will receive an allocation under a consolidated application,

(3) An estimate of the number of consolidated applications and the average number of local educational agencies per application, and

(4) A description of direct services the State educational agency will provide under § 121a.360 of Subpart C.

(20 U.S.C. 1232c(b)(1)(B)(ii))

§ 121a.150 [Reserved]

§ 121a.151 Additional information if the State educational agency provides direct services.

If a State educational agency provides free appropriate public education for handicapped children or provides them with direct services, its annual program plan must include the information required under §§ 121a.226–121a.228, 121a.231, and 121a.235.

(20 U.S.C. 1413(b))

LOCAL EDUCATIONAL AGENCY APPLICATIONS—GENERAL

§ 121a.180 Submission of application.

In order to receive payments under Part B of the Act for any fiscal year a local educational agency must submit an application to the State educational agency.

(20 U.S.C. 1414(a))

§ 121a.181 [Reserved]

§ 121a.182 The excess cost requirement.

A local educational agency may only use funds under Part B of the Act for the excess costs of providing special education and related services for handicapped children.

(20 U.S.C. 1414 (a)(1), (a)(2)(B)(i))

§ 121a.183 Meeting the excess cost requirement.

(a) A local educational agency meets the excess cost requirement if it has on the average spent at least the amount determined under § 121a.184 for the education of each of its handicapped children. This amount may not include capital outlay or debt service.

(20 U.S.C. 1402(20); 1414(a)(1))

Comment. The excess cost requirement means that the local educational agency must spend a certain minimum amount for the education of its handicapped children before Part B funds are used. This insures that children served with Part B funds have at least the same average amount spent on them, from sources other than Part B, as do the children in the school district taken as a whole.

The minimum amount that must be spent for the education of handicapped children is computed under a statutory formula. Section 121a.184 implements this formula and gives a step-by-step method to determine the minimum amount. Excess costs are those costs of special education and related services which exceed the minimum amount. Therefore, if a local educational agency can show that it has (on the average) spent the minimum amount for the education of each of its handicapped children, it has met the excess cost requirement, and all additional costs are excess costs. Part B funds can then be used to pay for these additional costs, subject to the other requirements of Part B (priorities, etc.). In the "Comment" under § 121a.184, there is an example of how the minimum amount is computed.

[42 FR 42476, Aug. 23, 1977, as amended at 45 FR 22531, Apr. 3, 1980]

§ 121a.184 Excess costs—computation of minimum amount.

The minimum average amount a local educational agency must spend under § 121a.183 for the education of each of its handicapped children is computed as follows:

(a) Add all expenditures of the local educational agency in the preceding school year, except capital outlay and debt service:

(1) For elementary school students, if the handicapped child is an elementary school student, or

(2) For secondary school students, if the handicapped child is a secondary school student.

(b) From this amount, subtract the total of the following amounts spent for elementary school students or for secondary school students, as the case may be:

(1) Amounts the agency spent in the preceding school year from funds awarded under Part B of the Act and Titles I and VII of the Elementary and Secondary Education Act of 1965, and

(2) Amounts from State and local funds which the agency spent in the preceding school year for:

(i) Programs for handicapped children,

(ii) Programs to meet the special educational needs of educationally deprived children, and

(iii) Programs of bilingual education for children with limited English-speaking ability.

(c) Divide the result under paragraph (b) of this section by the average number of students enrolled in the agency in the preceding school year:

(1) In its elementary schools, if the handicapped child is an elementary school student, or

(2) In its secondary schools, if the handicapped child is a secondary school student.

(20 U.S.C. 1414(a)(1))

Comment. The following is an example of how a local educational agency might compute the average minimum amount it must spend for the education of each of its handicapped children, under § 121a.183. This example follows the formula in § 121a.184. Under the statute and regulations, the local educational agency must make one computation for handicapped children in its elementary schools and a separate computation for handicapped children in its secondary schools. The computation for handicapped elementary school students would be done as follows:

a. First, the local educational agency must determine its total amount of expenditures for elementary school students from all sources—local, State, and Federal (including Part B)—in the preceding school year. Only capital outlay and debt service are excluded.

Example: A local educational agency spent the following amounts last year for elementary school students (including its handicapped elementary school students):

(1) From local tax funds	$2,750,000
(2) From State funds	7,000,000
(3) From Federal funds	750,000
	10,500,000

Of this total, $500,000 was for capital outlay and debt service relating to the education of elementary school students. This must be subtracted from total expenditures:

	$10,500,000
	−500,000
Total expenditures for elementary school students (less capital outlay and debt service)	= 10,000,000

b. Next, the local educational agency must subtract amounts spent for:

(1) Programs for handicapped children;

(2) Programs to meet the special education needs of educationally deprived children; and

(3) Programs of bilingual education for children with limited English-speaking ability.

These are funds which the local educational agency actually spent, not funds received last year but carried over for the current school year.

Example: The local educational agency spent the following amounts for elementary school students last year:

(1) From funds under Title I of the Elementary and Secondary Education Act of 1965	$300,000
(2) From a special State program for educationally deprived children	200,000
(3) From a grant under Part B	200,000
(4) From State funds for the education of handicapped children	500,000
(5) From a locally-funded program for handicapped children	250,000
(6) From a grant for a bilingual education program under Title VII of the Elementary and Secondary Education Act of 1965	150,000
Total	1,600,000

(A local educational agency would also include any other funds it spent from Federal, State, or local sources for the three basic purposes: handicapped children, educationally deprived children, and bilingual educa-

tion for children with limited English-speaking ability.)

This amount is subtracted from the local educational agency's total expenditure for elementary school students computed above:

$10,000,000
−1,600,000
8,400,000

c. The local educational agency next must divide by the average number of students enrolled in the elementary schools of the agency last year (including its handicapped students).

Example: Last year, an average of 7,000 students were enrolled in the agency's elementary schools. This must be divided into the amount computed under the above paragraph:

$8,400,000/7,000$ students = $1,200/student

This figure is in the minimum amount the local educational agency must spend (on the average) for the education of each of its handicapped students. Funds under Part B may be used only for costs over and above this minimum. In this example, if the local educational agency has 100 handicapped elementary school students, it must keep records adequate to show that it has spent at least $120,000 for the education of those students (100 students times $1,200/student), not including capital outlay and debt service.

This $120,000 may come from any funds except funds under Part B, subject to any legal requirements that govern the use of those other funds.

If the local educational agency has handicapped secondary school students, it must do the same computation for them. However the amounts used in the computation would be those the local educational agency spent last year for the education of secondary school students, rather than for elementary school students.

§ 121a.185 **Computation of excess costs— consolidated application.**

The minimum average amount under § 121a.183 where two or more local educational agencies submit a consolidated application, is the average of the combined minimum average amounts determined under § 121a.184 in those agencies for elementary or secondary school students, as the case may be.

(20 U.S.C. 1414(a)(1))

§ 121a.186   Excess costs—limitation on use of Part B funds.

(a) The excess cost requirement prevents a local educational agency from using funds provided under Part B of the Act to pay for all of the costs directly attributable to the education of a handicapped child, subject to paragraph (b) of this section.

(b) The excess cost requirement does not prevent a local educational agency from using Part B funds to pay for all of the costs directly attributable to the education of a handicapped child in any of the age ranges three, four, five, eighteen, nineteen, twenty, or twenty-one, if no local or State funds are available for non-handicapped children in that age range. However, the local educational agency must comply with the non-supplanting and other requirements of this part in providing the education and services.

(20 U.S.C. 1402(20); 1414(a)(1))

§ 121a.190   Consolidated applications.

(a) [Reserved]

(b) *Required applications.* A State educational agency may require local educational agencies to submit a consolidated application for payments under Part B of the Act if the State educational agency determines that an individual application submitted by a local educational agency will be disapproved because:

(1) The agency's entitlement is less than the $7,500 minimum required by section 611(c)(4)(A)(i) of the Act (§ 121a.360(a)(1) of Subpart C); or

(2) The agency is unable to establish and maintain programs of sufficient size and scope to effectively meet the educational needs of handicapped children.

(c) *Size and scope of program.* The State educational agency shall establish standards and procedures for determinations under paragraph (b)(2) of this section.

(20 U.S.C. 1414(c)(1))

[42 FR 42476, Aug. 23, 1977, as amended at 45 FR 22531, Apr. 3, 1980]

§ 121a.191   [Reserved]

§ 121a.192   State regulation of consolidated applications.

(a) The State educational agency shall issue regulations with respect to consolidated applications submitted under this part.

(b) The State educational agency's regulations must:

(1) Be consistent with section 612 (1)-(7) and section 613(a) of the Act, and

(2) Provide participating local educational agencies with joint responsibilities for implementing programs receiving payments under this part.

(20 U.S.C. 1414(c)(2)(B))

(c) If an intermediate educational unit is required under State law to carry out this part, the joint responsibilities given to local educational agencies under paragraph (b)(2) of this section do not apply to the administration and disbursement of any payments received by the intermediate educational unit. Those administrative responsibilities must be carried out exclusively by the intermediate educational unit.

(20 U.S.C. 1414(c)(2)(C))

§ 121a.193   State educational agency approval; disapproval.

(a)-(b) [Reserved]

(c) In carrying out its functions under this section, each State educational agency shall consider any decision resulting from a hearing under §§ 121a.506–121a.513 of Subpart E which is adverse to the local educational agency involved in the decision.

(20 U.S.C. 1414(b)(3))

[42 FR 42476, Aug. 23, 1977, as amended at 45 FR 22531, Apr. 3, 1980]

§ 121a.194   Withholding.

(a) If a State educational agency, after giving reasonable notice and an opportunity for a hearing to a local educational agency, decides that the local educational agency in the administration of an application approved by the State educational agency has failed to comply with any requirement in the application, the State educational agency, after giving notice to the local educational agency, shall:

(1) Make no further payments to the local educational agency until the State educational agency is satisfied that there is no longer any failure to comply with the requirement; or

(2) Consider its decision in its review of any application made by the local educational agency under § 121a.180;

(3) Or both.

(b) Any local educational agency receiving a notice from a State educational agency under paragraph (a) of this section is subject to the public notice provision in § 121a.592.

(20 U.S.C. 1414(b)(2))

LOCAL EDUCATIONAL AGENCY
APPLICATIONS—CONTENTS

§ 121a.220   Child identification.

Each application must include procedures which insure that all children residing within the jurisdiction of the local educational agency who are handicapped, regardless of the severity of their handicap, and who are in need of special education and related services are identified, located, and evaluated, including a practical method of determining which children are currently receiving needed special education and related services and which children are not currently receiving needed special education and related services.

(20 U.S.C. 1414(a)(1)(A))

Comment. The local educational agency is responsible for insuring that all handicapped children within its jurisdiction are identified, located, and evaluated, including children in all public and private agencies and institutions within that jurisdiction. Collection and use of data are subject to the confidentiality requirements in §§ 121a.560-121a.576 of Subpart E.

§ 121a.221   Confidentiality of personally identifiable information.

Each application must include policies and procedures which insure that the criteria in §§ 121a.560-121a.574 of Subpart E are met.

(20 U.S.C. 1414(a)(1)(B))

§ 121a.222   Full educational opportunity goal; timetable.

Each application must: (a) Include a goal of providing full educational opportunity to all handicapped children, aged birth through 21, and

(b) Include a detailed timetable for accomplishing the goal.

(20 U.S.C. 1414(a)(1) (C), (D))

§ 121a.223   Facilities, personnel, and services.

Each application must provide a description of the kind and number of facilities, personnel, and services necessary to meet the goal in § 121a.222.

(20 U.S.C. 1414(a)(1)(E))

§ 121a.224   Personnel development.

Each application must include procedures for the implementation and use of the comprehensive system of personnel development established by the State educational agency under § 121a.140.

(20 U.S.C. 1414(a)(1)(C)(i))

§ 121a.225   Priorities.

Each application must include priorities which meet the requirements of §§ 121a.320-121a.324.

(20 U.S.C. 1414(a)(1)(C)(ii))

§ 121a.226   Parent involvement.

Each application must include procedures to insure that, in meeting the goal under § 121a.222, the local educational agency makes provision for participation of and consultation with parents or guardians of handicapped children.

(20 U.S.C. 1414(a)(1)(C)(iii))

§ 121a.227   Participation in regular education programs.

(a) Each application must include procedures to insure that to the maximum extent practicable, and consistent with §§ 1212a.550-121a.553 of Subpart E, the local educational agency provides special services to enable handicapped children to participate in regular educational programs.

(b) Each application must describe:

(1) The types of alternative placements that are available for handicapped children, and

(2) The number of handicapped children within each disability category who are served in each type of placement.

(20 U.S.C. 1414(a)(1)(C)(iv))

§ 121a.228 [Reserved]

§ 121a.229 Excess cost.

Each application must provide assurance satisfactory to the State educational agency that the local educational agency uses funds provided under Part B of the Act only for costs which exceed the amount computed under § 121a.184 and which are directly attributable to the education of handicapped children.

(20 U.S.C. 1414(a)(2)(B))

§ 121a.230 Nonsupplanting.

(a) Each application must provide assurance satisfactory to the State educational agency that the local educational agency uses funds provided under Part B of the Act to supplement and, to the extent practicable, increase the level of State and local funds expended for the education of handicapped children, and in no case to supplant those State and local funds.

(b) To meet the requirement in paragraph (a) of this section:

(1) The total amount or average per capita amount of State and local school funds budgeted by the local educational agency for expenditures in the current fiscal year for the education of handicapped children must be at least equal to the total amount or average per capita amount of State and local school funds actually expended for the education of handicapped children in the most recent preceding fiscal year for which the information is available. Allowance may be made for:

(i) Decreases in enrollment of handicapped children; and

(ii) Unusually large amounts of funds expended for such long-term purposes as the acquisition of equipment and the construction of school facilities; and

(2) The local educational agency must not use Part B funds to displace State or local funds for any particular cost.

(20 U.S.C. 1414(a)(2)(B))

Comment. Under statutes such as Title I of the Elementary and Secondary Education Act of 1965, as amended, the requirement is to not supplant funds that "would" have been expended if the Federal funds were not available. The requirement under Part B, however, is to not supplant funds which have been "expended." This use of the past tense suggests that the funds referred to are those which the State or local agency actually spent at some time before the use of the Part B funds. Therefore, in judging compliance with this requirement, the Commissioner looks to see if Part B funds are used for any costs which were previously paid for with State or local funds.

The nonsupplanting requirement prohibits a local educational agency from supplanting State and local funds with Part B funds on either an aggregate basis or for a given expenditure. This means that if an LEA spent $100,000 for special education in FY 1977, it must budget at least $100,000 in FY 1978, unless one of the conditions in § 121a.230(b)(1) applies.

Whether a local educational agency supplants with respect to a particular cost would depend on the circumstances of the expenditure. For example, if a teacher's salary has been switched from local funding to Part B funding, this would appear to be supplanting. However, if that teacher was taking over a different position (such as a resource room teacher, for example), it would not be supplanting. Moreover, it might be important to consider whether the particular action of a local educational agency led to an increase in services for handicapped children over that which previously existed. The intent of the requirement is to insure that Part B funds are used to increase State and local efforts and are not used to take their place. Compliance would be judged with this aim in mind. The supplanting requirement is not intended to inhibit better services to handicapped children.

§ 121a.231 Comparable services.

(a) Each application must provide assurance satisfactory to the State educational agency that the local educational agency meets the requirements of this section.

(b) A local educational agency may not use funds under Part B of the Act to provide services to handicapped children unless the agency uses State and local funds to provide services to those children which, taken as a whole, are at least comparable to services provided to other handicapped children in that local educational agency.

(c) Each local educational agency shall maintain records which show that the agency meets the requirement in paragraph (b) of this section.

(20 U.S.C. 1414(a)(2)(C))

Comment. Under the "comparability" requirement, if State and local funds are used to provide certain services, those services must be provided with State and local funds to all handicapped children in the local educational agency who need them. Part B funds may then be used to supplement existing services, or to provide additional services to meet special needs. This, of course, is subject to the other requirements of the Act, including the priorities under §§ 121a.320–121a.324.

§§ 121a.232–121a.234 [Reserved]

§ 121a.235 Individualized education program.

Each application must include procedures to assure that the local educational agency complies with §§ 121a.340–121a.349 of Subpart C.

(20 U.S.C. 1414(a)(5))

§ 121a.236 [Reserved]

§ 121a.237 Procedural safeguards.

Each application must provide assurance satisfactory to the State educational agency that the local educational agency has procedural safeguards which meet the requirements of §§ 121a.500–121a.514 of Subpart E.

(20 U.S.C. 1414(a)(7))

§ 121a.238 Use of Part B funds.

Each application must describe how the local educational agency will use the funds under Part B of the Act during the next school year.

(20 U.S.C. 1414(a))

§ 121a.239 [Reserved]

§ 121a.240 Other requirements.

Each local application must include additional procedures and information which the State educational agency may require in order to meet the State annual program plan requirements under §§ 121a.120–121a.151.

(20 U.S.C. 1414(a)(6))

APPLICATION FROM SECRETARY OF INTERIOR

§ 121a.260 Submission of annual application; approval.

In order to receive payments under this part, the Secretary of Interior shall submit an annual application which:

(a) Meets applicable requirements of section 614(a) of the Act;

(b) Includes monitoring procedures which are consistent with § 121a.601; and

(c) Includes other material as agreed to by the Commissioner and the Secretary of Interior.

(20 U.S.C. 1411(f))

§ 121a.261 Public participation.

In the development of the application for the Department of Interior, the Secretary of Interior shall provide for public participation consistent with §§ 121a.280–121a.284.

(20 U.S.C. 1411(f))

§ 121a.262 Use of Part B funds.

(a) The Department of Interior may use five percent of its payments in any fiscal year, or $200,000, whichever is greater, for administrative costs in carrying out the provisions of this part.

(b) The remainder of the payments to the Secretary of the Interior in any fiscal year must be used in accordance with the priorities under §§ 121a.320–121a.324 of Subpart C.

(20 U.S.C. 1411(f))

§ 121a.263 Applicable regulations.

The Secretary of the Interior shall comply with the requirements under Subparts C, E, and F.

(20 U.S.C. 1411(f)(2))

PUBLIC PARTICIPATION

§ 121a.280 Public hearings before adopting an annual program plan.

(a) Prior to its adoption of an annual program plan, the State educational agency shall:

(1) Make the plan available to the general public,

(2) Hold public hearings, and

(3) Provide an opportunity for comment by the general public on the plan.

(20 U.S.C. 1412(7))

§ 121a.281 Notice.

(a) The State educational agency shall provide notice to the general public of the public hearings.

(b) The notice must be in sufficient detail to inform the public about:

(1) The purpose and scope of the annual program plan and its relation to Part B of the Education of the Handicapped Act,

(2) The availability of the annual program plan,

(3) The date, time, and location of each public hearing,

(4) The procedures for submitting written comments about the plan, and

(5) The timetable for developing the final plan and submitting it to the Commissioner for approval.

(c) The notice must be published or announced:

(1) In newspapers or other media, or both, with circulation adequate to notify the general public about the hearings, and (2) Enough in advance of the date of the hearings to afford interested parties throughout the State a reasonable opportunity to participate.

(20 U.S.C. 1412(7))

§ 121a.282 Opportunity to participate; comment period.

(a) The State educational agency shall conduct the public hearings at times and places that afford interested parties throughout the State a reasonable opportunity to participate.

(b) The plan must be available for comment for a period of at least 30 days following the date of the notice under § 121a.281.

(20 U.S.C. 1412(7))

§ 121a.283 Review of public comments before adopting plan.

Before adopting its annual program plan, the State educational agency shall:

(a) Review and consider all public comments, and

(b) Make any necessary modifications in the plan.

(20 U.S.C. 1412(7))

§ 121a.284 Publication and availability of approved plan.

After the Commissioner approves an annual program plan, the State educational agency shall give notice in newspapers or other media, or both, that the plan is approved. The notice must name places throughout the State where the plan is available for access by any interested person.

(20 U.S.C. 1412(7))

Subpart C—Services

FREE APPROPRIATE PUBLIC EDUCATION

§ 121a.300 Timeliness for free appropriate public education.

(a) *General.* Each State shall insure that free appropriate public education is available to all handicapped children aged three through eighteen within the State not later than September 1, 1978, and to all handicapped children aged three through twenty-one within the State not later than September 1, 1980.

(b) *Age ranges 3-5 and 18-21.* This paragraph provides rules for applying the requirement in paragraph (a) of this section to handicapped children aged three, four, five, eighteen, nineteen, twenty, and twenty-one:

(1) If State law or a court order requires the State to provide education for handicapped children in any disability category in any of these age groups, the State must make a free appropriate public education available to all handicapped children of the same age who have that disability.

(2) If a public agency provides education to non-handicapped children in any of these age groups, it must make a free appropriate public education available to at least a proportionate number of handicapped children of the same age.

(3) If a public agency provides education to 50 percent or more of its handicapped children in any disability category in any of these age groups, it

must make a free appropriate public education available to all of its handicapped children of the same age who have that disability.

(4) If a public agency provides education to a handicapped child in any of these age groups, it must make a free appropriate public education available to that child and provide that child and his or her parents all of the rights under Part B of the Act and this part.

(5) A State is not required to make a free appropriate public education available to a handicapped child in one of these age groups if:

(i) State law expressly prohibits, or does not authorize, the expenditure of public funds to provide education to nonhandicapped children in that age group; or

(ii) The requirement is inconsistent with a court order which governs the provision of free public education to handicapped children in that State.

(20 U.S.C. 1412(2)(B); Sen. Rept. No. 94-168 p. 19 (1975))

Comment. 1. The requirement to make free appropriate public education available applies to all handicapped children within the State who are in the age ranges required under § 121a.300 and who need special education and related services. This includes handicapped children already in school and children with less severe handicaps, who are not covered under the priorities under § 121a.321.

2. In order to be in compliance with § 121a.300, each State must insure that the requirement to identify, locate, and evaluate all handicapped children is fully implemented by public agencies throughout the State. This means that before September 1, 1978, every child who has been referred or is on a waiting list for evaluation (including children in school as well as those not receiving an education) must be evaluated in accordance with §§ 121a.530-121a.533 of Subpart E. If, as a result of the evaluation, it is determined that a child needs special education and related services, an individualized education program must be developed for the child by September 1 1978, and all other applicable requirements of this part must be met.

3. The requirement to identify, locate, and evaluate handicapped children (commonly referred to as the "child find system") was enacted on August 21, 1974, under Pub. L. 93-380. While each State needed time to establish and implement its child find system, the four year period between August 21, 1974, and September 1, 1978, is considered

to be sufficient to insure that the system is fully operational and effective on a State-wide basis.

Under the statute, the age range for the child find requirement (0-21) is greater than the mandated age range for providing free appropriate public education (FAPE). One reason for the broader age requirement under "child find" is to enable States to be aware of and plan for younger children who will require special education and related services. It also ties in with the full educational opportunity goal requirement, which has the same age range as child find. Moreover, while a State is not required to provide "FAPE" to handicapped children below the age ranges mandated under § 121a.300, the State may, at its discretion, extend services to those children, subject to the requirements on priorities under §§ 121a.320-121a.324.

§ 121a.301   Free appropriate public education—methods and payments.

(a) Each State may use whatever State, local, Federal, and private sources of support are available in the State to meet the requirements of this part. For example, when it is necessary to place a handicapped child in a residential facility, a State could use joint agreements between the agencies involved for sharing the cost of that placement.

(b) Nothing in this part relieves an insurer or similar third party from an otherwise valid obligation to provide or to pay for services provided to a handicapped child.

(20 U.S.C. 1401 (18); 1412(2)(B))

§ 121a.302   Residential placement.

If placement in a public or private residential program is necessary to provide special education and related services to a handicapped child, the program, including non-medical care and room and board, must be at no cost to the parents of the child.

(20 U.S.C. 1412(2)(B); 1413(a)(4)(B))

Comment. This requirement applies to placements which are made by public agencies for educational purposes, and includes placements in State-operated schools for the handicapped, such as a State school for the deaf or blind.

§ 121a.303   Proper functioning of hearing aids.

Each public agency shall insure that the hearing aids worn by deaf and hard of hearing children in school are functioning properly.

(20 U.S.C. 1412(2)(B))

Comment. The report of the House of Representatives on the 1978 appropriation bill includes the following statement regarding hearing aids:

In its report on the 1976 appropriation bill the Committee expressed concern about the condition of hearing aids worn by children in public schools. A study done at the Committee's direction by the Bureau of Education for the Handicapped reveals that up to one-third of the hearing aids are malfunctioning. Obviously, the Committee expects the Office of Education will ensure that hearing impaired school children are receiving adequate professional assessment, follow-up and services.

(House Report No. 95-381, p. 67 (1977))

§ 121a.304 **Full educational opportunity goal.**

(a) Each State educational agency shall insure that each public agency establishes and implements a goal of providing full educational opportunity to all handicapped children in the area served by the public agency.

(b) Subject to the priority requirements under §§ 121a.320-121a.324, a State or local educational agency may use Part B funds to provide facilities, personnel, and services necessary to meet the full educational opportunity goal.

(20 U.S.C. 1412(2)(A); 1414(a)(1)(C))

Comment. In meeting the full educational opportunity goal, the Congress also encouraged local educational agencies to include artistic and cultural activities in programs supported under this part, subject to the priority requirements under §§ 121a.320-121a.324. This point is addressed in the following statements from the Senate Report on Pub. L. 94-142:

The use of the arts as a teaching tool for he handicapped has long been recognized ιs a viable, effective way not only of teaching special skills, but also of reaching youngsters who had otherwise been unteachable. The Committee envisions that programs under this bill could well include an arts component and, indeed, urges that local educational agencies include the arts in programs for the handicapped funded under this Act. Such a program could cover both appreciation of the arts by the handicapped youngsters, and the utilization of the arts as a teaching tool per se.

Museum settings have often been another effective tool in the teaching of handicapped children. For example, the Brooklyn Museum has been a leader in developing exhibits utilizing the heightened tactile sensory skill of the blind. Therefore, in light of the national policy concerning the use of museums in Federally supported education programs enunciated in the Education Amendments of 1974, the Committee also urges local educational agencies to include museums in programs for the handicapped funded under this Act.

(Senate Report No. 94-168, p. 13 (1975))

§ 121a.305 **Program options.**

Each public agency shall take steps to insure that its handicapped children have available to them the variety of educational programs and services available to non-handicapped children in the area served by the agency, including art, music, industrial arts, consumer and homemaking education, and vocational education.

(20 U.S.C. 1412(2)(A); 1414(a)(1)(C))

Comment. The above list of program options is not exhaustive, and could include any program or activity in which nonhandicapped students participate. Moreover, vocational education programs must be specially designed if necessary to enable a handicapped student to benefit fully from those programs; and the set-aside funds under the Vocational Education Act of 1963, as amended by Pub. L. 94-482, may be used for this purpose. Part B funds may also be used, subject to the priority requirements under §§ 121a.320-121a.324.

§ 121a.306 **Nonacademic services.**

(a) Each public agency shall take steps to provide nonacademic and extracurricular services and activities in such manner as is necessary to afford handicapped children an equal opportunity for participation in those services and activities.

(b) Nonacademic and extracurricular services and activities may include counseling services, athletics, transportation, health services, recreational activities, special interest groups or clubs sponsored by the public agency, referrals to agencies which provide assistance to handicapped persons, and employment of students, including both employment by the public agency and assistance in making outside employment available.

(20 U.S.C. 1412(2)(A); 1414(a)(1)(C))

§ 121a.307   Physical education.

(a) *General.* Physical education services, specially designed if necessary, must be made available to every handicapped child receiving a free appropriate public education.

(b) *Regular physical education.* Each handicapped child must be afforded the opportunity to participate in the regular physical education program available to non-handicapped children unless:

(1) The child is enrolled full time in a separate facility; or

(2) The child needs specially designed physical education, as prescribed in the child's individualized education program.

(c) *Special physical education.* If specially designed physical education is prescribed in a child's individualized education program, the public agency responsible for the education of that child shall provide the services directly, or make arrangements for it to be provided through other public or private programs.

(d) *Education in separate facilities.* The public agency responsible for the education of a handicapped child who is enrolled in a separate facility shall insure that the child receives appropriate physical education services in compliance with paragraphs (a) and (c) of this section.

(20 U.S.C. 1401(16); 1412(5)(B); 1414(a)(6))

Comment. The Report of the House of Representatives on Pub. L. 94-142 includes the following statement regarding physical education:

Special education as set forth in the Committee bill includes instruction in physical education, which is provided as a matter of course to all non-handicapped children enrolled in public elementary and secondary schools. The Committee is concerned that although these services are available to and required of all children in our school systems, they are often viewed as a luxury for handicapped children.

* * * * *

The Committee expects the Commissioner of Education to take whatever action is necessary to assure that physical education services are available to all handicapped children, and has specifically included physical education within the definition of special education to make clear that the Committee expects such services, specially de-

signed where necessary, to be provided as an integral part of the educational program of every handicapped child.

(House Report No. 94-332, p. 9 (1975))

PRIORITIES IN THE USE OF PART B FUNDS

§ 121a.320   Definitions of "first priority children" and "second priority children."

For the purposes of §§ 121a.321-121a.324, the term:

(a) "First priority children" means handicapped children who:

(1) Are in an age group for which the State must make available free appropriate public education under § 121a.300; and

(2) Are not receiving any education.

(b) "Second priority children" means handicapped children, within each disability, with the most severe handicaps who are receiving an inadequate education.

(20 U.S.C. 1412(3))

Comment. After September 1, 1978, there should be no second priority children, since States must insure, as a condition of receiving Part B funds of fiscal year 1979, that all handicapped children will have available a free appropriate public education by that date.

NOTE: The term "free appropriate public education," as defined in § 121a.4 of Subpart A, means "special education and related services which * * * are provided in conformity with an individualized education program * * *."

New "First priority children" will continue to be found by the State after September 1, 1978 through on-going efforts to identify, locate, and evaluate all handicapped children.

§ 121a.321   Priorities.

(a) Each State and local educational agency shall use funds provided under Part B of the Act in the following order of priorities:

(1) To provide free appropriate public education to first priority children, including the identification, location, and evaluation of first priority children.

(2) To provide free appropriate public education to second priority children, including the identification, location, and evaluation of second priority children.

(3) To meet the other requirements in this part.

(b) The requirements of paragraph (a) of this section do not apply to funds which the State uses for administration under § 121a.620.

(20 U.S.C. 1411 (b)(1)(B), (b)(2)(B), (c)(1)(B), (c)(2)(A)(ii))

(c) State and local educational agencies may not use funds under Part B of the Act for preservice training.

(20 U.S.C. 1413(a)(3); Senate Report No. 94-168, p. 34 (1975))

Comment. Note that a State educational agency as well as local educational agencies must use Part B funds (except the portion used for State administration) for the priorities. A State may have to set aside a portion of its Part B allotment to be able to serve newly identified first priority children. After September 1, 1978, Part B funds may be used:

(1) To continue supporting child identification, location, and evaluation activities;

(2) To provide free appropriate public education to newly identified first priority children;

(3) To meet the full educational opportunities goal required under § 121a.304, including employing additional personnel and providing inservice training, in order to increase the level, intensity and quality of services provided to individual handicapped children; and

(4) To meet the other requirements of Part B.

§ 121a.322 First priority children—school year 1977-1978.

(a) In school year 1977-1978, if a major component of a first priority child's proposed educational program is not available (for example, there is no qualified teacher), the public agency responsible for the child's education shall:

(1) Provide an interim program of services for the child; and

(2) Develop an individualized education program for full implementation no later than September 1, 1978.

(b) A local educational agency may use Part B funds for training or other support services in school year 1977-1978 only if all of its first priority children have available to them at least an interim program of services.

(c) A State educational agency may use Part B funds for training or other support services in school year 1977-1978 only if all first priority children in the State have available to them at least an interim program of services.

(20 U.S.C. 1411 (b), (c))

Comment. This provision is intended to make it clear that a State or local educational agency may not delay placing a previously unserved (first priority) child until it has, for example, implemented an inservice training program. The child must be placed. After the child is in at least an interim program, the State or local educational agency may use Part B funds for training or other support services needed to provide that child with a free appropriate public education.

§ 121a.323 Services to other children.

If a State or a local educational agency is providing free appropriate public education to all of its first priority children, that State or agency may use funds provided under Part B of the Act:

(a) To provide free appropriate public education to handicapped children who are not receiving any education and who are in the age groups not covered under § 121a.300 in that State; or

(b) To provide free appropriate public education to second priority children; or

(c) Both.

(20 U.S.C. 1411 (b)(1)(B), (b)(2)(B), (c)(2)(A)(ii))

§ 121a.324 Application of local educational agency to use funds for the second priority.

A local educational agency may use funds provided under Part B of the Act for second priority children, if it provides assurance satisfactory to the State educational agency in its application (or an amendment to its application):

(a) That all first priority children have a free appropriate public education available to them;

(b) That the local educational agency has a system for the identification, location, and evaluation of handicapped children, as described in its application; and

(c) That whenever a first priority child is identified, located, and evaluated, the local educational agency makes available a free appropriate public education to the child.

(20 U.S.C. 1411 (b)(1)(B), (c)(1)(B); 1414(a)(1)(C)(ii))

INDIVIDUALIZED EDUCATION PROGRAMS

§ 121a.340 Definition.

As used in this part, the term "individualized education program" means a written statement for a handicapped child that is developed and implemented in accordance with §§ 121a.341–121a.349.

(20 U.S.C. 1401(19))

§ 121a.341 State educational agency responsibility.

(a) *Public agencies.* The State educational agency shall insure that each public agency develops and implements an individualized education program for each of its handicapped children.

(b) *Private schools and facilities.* The State educational agency shall insure that an individualized education program is developed and implemented for each handicapped child who:

(1) Is placed in or referred to a private school or facility by a public agency; or

(2) Is enrolled in a parochial or other private school and receives special education or related services from a public agency.

(20 U.S.C. 1412 (4), (6); 1413(a)(4))

Comment. This section applies to all public agencies, including other State agencies (e.g., departments of mental health and welfare), which provide special education to a handicapped child either directly, by contract or through other arrangements. Thus, if a State welfare agency contracts with a private school or facility to provide special education to a handicapped child, that agency would be responsible for insuring that an individualized education program is developed for the child.

§ 121a.342 When individualized education programs must be in effect.

(a) On October 1, 1977, and at the beginning of each school year thereafter, each public agency shall have in effect an individualized education program for every handicapped child who

is receiving special education from that agency.

(b) An individualized education program must:

(1) Be in effect before special education and related services are provided to a child; and

(2) Be implemented as soon as possible following the meetings under § 121a.343.

(20 U.S.C. 1412 (2)(B), (4), (6); 1414(a)(5); Pub. L. 94-142, Sec. 8(c) (1975))

Comment. Under paragraph (b)(2), it is expected that a handicapped child's individualized education program (IEP) will be implemented immediately following the meetings under § 121a.343. An exception to this would be (1) when the meetings occur during the summer or a vacation period, or (2) where there are circumstances which require a short delay (e.g., working out transportation arrangements). However, there can be no undue delay in providing special education and related services to the child.

§ 121a.343 Meetings.

(a) *General.* Each public agency is responsible for initiating and conducting meetings for the purpose of developing, reviewing, and revising a handicapped child's individualized education program.

(b) *Handicapped children currently served.* If the public agency has determined that a handicapped child will receive special education during school year 1977-1978, a meeting must be held early enough to insure that an individualized education program is developed by October 1, 1977.

(c) *Other handicapped children.* For a handicapped child who is not included under paragraph (b) of this action, a meeting must be held within thirty calendar days of a determination that the child needs special education and related services.

(d) *Review.* Each public agency shall initiate and conduct meetings to periodically review each child's individualized education program and if appropriate revise its provisions. A meeting must be held for this purpose at least once a year.

(20 U.S.C. 1412(2)(B), (4), (6); 1414(a)(5))

Comment. The dates on which agencies must have individualized education programs (IEPs) in effect are specified in § 121a.342 (October 1, 1977, and the beginning of each school year thereafter). However-er, except for new handicapped children (i.e., those evaluated and determined to need special education after October 1, 1977), the timing of meetings to develop, review, and revise IEPs is left to the discretion of each agency.

In order to have IEPs in effect by the dates in § 121a.342, agencies could hold meetings at the end of the school year or during the summer preceding those dates. In meeting the October 1, 1977 timeline, meetings could be conducted up through the October 1 date. Thereafter, meetings may be held any time throughout the year, as long as IEPs are in effect at the beginning of each school year.

The statute requires agencies to hold a meeting at least once each year in order to review, and if appropriate revise, each child's IEP. The timing of those meetings could be on the anniversary date of the last IEP meeting on the child, but this is left to the discretion of the agency.

§ 121a.344 Participants in meetings.

(a) *General.* The public agency shall insure that each meeting includes the following participants:

(1) A representative of the public agency, other than the child's teacher, who is qualified to provide, or supervise the provision of, special education.

(2) The child's teacher.

(3) One or both of the child's parents, subject to § 121a.345.

(4) The child, where appropriate.

(5) Other individuals at the discretion of the parent or agency.

(b) *Evaluation personnel.* For a handicapped child who has been evaluated for the first time, the public agency shall insure:

(1) That a member of the evaluation team participates in the meeting; or

(2) That the representative of the public agency, the child's teacher, or some other person is present at the meeting, who is knowledgeable about the evaluation procedures used with the child and is familiar with the results of the evaluation.

(20 U.S.C. 1401(19); 1412 (2)(B), (4), (6); 1414(a)(5))

Comment. 1. In deciding which teacher will participate in meetings on a child's individualized education program, the agency may wish to consider the following possibilities:

(a) For a handicapped child who is receiving special education, the "teacher" could be the child's special education teacher. If the child's handicap is a speech impairment, the "teacher" could be the speech-language pathologist.

(b) For a handicapped child who is being considered for placement in special education, the "teacher" could be the child's regular teacher, or a teacher qualified to provide education in the type of program in which the child may be placed, or both.

(c) If the child is not in school or has more than one teacher, the agency may designate which teacher will participate in the meeting.

2. Either the teacher or the agency representative should be qualified in the area of the child's suspected disability.

3. For a child whose primary handicap is a speech impairment, the evaluation personnel participating under paragraph (b)(1) of this section would normally be the speech-language pathologist.

§ 121a.345 Parent participation.

(a) Each public agency shall take steps to insure that one or both of the parents of the handicapped child are present at each meeting or are afforded the opportunity to participate, including:

(1) Notifying parents of the meeting early enough to insure that they will have an opportunity to attend; and

(2) Scheduling the meeting at a mutually agreed on time and place.

(b) The notice under paragraph (a)(1) of this section must indicate the purpose, time, and location of the meeting, and who will be in attendance.

(c) If neither parent can attend, the public agency shall use other methods to insure parent participation, including individual or conference telephone calls.

(d) A meeting may be conducted without a parent in attendance if the public agency is unable to convince the parents that they should attend. In this case the public agency must have a record of its attempts to arrange a mutually agreed on time and place such as:

(1) Detailed records of telephone calls made or attempted and the results of those calls.

(2) Copies of correspondence sent to the parents and any responses received, and

(3) Detailed records of visits made to the parent's home or place of employment and the results of those visits.

(e) The public agency shall take whatever action is necessary to insure that the parent understands the proceedings at a meeting, including arranging for an interpreter for parents who are deaf or whose native language is other than English.

(f) The public agency shall give the parent, on request, a copy of the individualized education program.

(20 U.S.C. 1401(19); 1412 (2)(B), (4), (6); 1414(a)(5))

Comment. The notice in paragraph (a) could also inform parents that they may bring other people to the meeting. As indicated in paragraph (c), the procedure used to notify parents (whether oral or written or both) is left to the discretion of the agency, but the agency must keep a record of its efforts to contact parents.

§ 121a.346 Content of individualized education program.

The individualized education program for each child must include:

(a) A statement of the child's present levels of educational performance;

(b) A statement of annual goals, including short term instructional objectives;

(c) A statement of the specific special education and related services to be provided to the child, and the extent to which the child will be able to participate in regular educational programs;

(d) The projected dates for initiation of services and the anticipated duration of the services; and

(e) Appropriate objective criteria and evaluation procedures and schedules for determining, on at least an annual basis, whether the short term instructional objectives are being achieved.

(20 U.S.C. 1401(19); 1412 (2)(B), (4), (6); 1414(a)(5); Senate Report No. 94-168, p. 11 (1975))

§ 121a.347 Private school placements.

(a) *Developing individualized education programs.* (1) Before a public agency places a handicapped child in, or refers a child to, a private school or facility, the agency shall initiate and conduct a meeting to develop an individualized education program for the child in accordance with § 121a.343.

(2) The agency shall insure that a representative of the private school facility attends the meeting. If the representative cannot attend, the agency shall use other methods to insure participation by the private school or facility, including individual or conference telephone calls.

(3) The public agency shall also develop an individualized educational program for each handicapped child who was placed in a private school or facility by the agency before the effective date of these regulations.

(b) *Reviewing and revising individualized education programs.* (1) After a handicapped child enters a private school or facility, any meetings to review and revise the child's individualized education program may be initiated and conducted by the private school or facility at the discretion of the public agency.

(2) If the private school or facility initiates and conducts these meetings, the public agency shall insure that the parents and an agency representative:

(i) Are involved in any decision about the child's individualized education program; and

(ii) Agree to any proposed changes in the program before those changes are implemented.

(c) *Responsibility.* Even if a private school or facility implements a child's individualized education program, responsibility for compliance with this part remains with the public agency and the State educational agency.

(20 U.S.C. 1413(a)(4)(B))

§ 121a.348 Handicapped children in parochial or other private schools.

If a handicapped child is enrolled in a parochial or other private school and receives special education or related services from a public agency, the public agency shall:

(a) Initiate and conduct meetings to develop, review, and revise an individualized education program for the child, in accordance with § 121a.343; and

(b) Insure that a representative of the parochial or other private school attends each meeting. If the representative cannot attend, the agency shall use other methods to insure participation by the private school, including individual or conference telephone calls.

(20 U.S.C. 1413(a)(4)(A))

§ 121a.349 Individualized education program—accountability.

Each public agency must provide special education and related services to a handicapped child in accordance with an individualized education program. However, Part B of the Act does not require that any agency, teacher, or other person be held accountable if a child does not achieve the growth projected in the annual goals and objectives.

(20 U.S.C. 1412(2)(B); 1414(a) (5), (6); Cong. Rec. at H7152 (daily ed., July 21, 1975))

Comment. This section is intended to relieve concerns that the individualized education program constitutes a guarantee by the public agency and the teacher that a child will progress at a specified rate. However, this section does not relieve agencies and teachers from making good faith efforts to assist the child in achieving the objectives and goals listed in the individualized education program. Further, the section does not limit a parent's right to complain and ask for revisions of the child's program, or to invoke due process procedures, if the parent feels that these efforts are not being made.

DIRECT SERVICE BY THE STATE EDUCATIONAL AGENCY

§ 121a.360 Use of local educational agency allocation for direct services.

(a) A State educational agency may not distribute funds to a local educational agency, and shall use those funds to insure the provision of a free appropriate public education to handicapped children residing in the area served by the local educational agency, if the local educational agency, in any fiscal year:

(1) Is entitled to less than $7,500 for that fiscal year (beginning with fiscal year 1979);

(2) Does not submit an application that meets the requirements of §§ 121a.220–121a.240;

(3) Is unable or unwilling to establish and maintain programs of free appropriate public education;

(4) Is unable or unwilling to be consolidated with other local educational agencies in order to establish and maintain those programs; or

(5) Has one or more handicapped children who can best be served by a regional or State center designed to meet the needs of those children.

(b) In meeting the requirements of paragraph (a) of this section, the State educational agency may provide special education and related services directly, by contract, or through other arrangements.

(c) The excess cost requirements under §§ 121a.182–121a.186 do not apply to the State educational agency.

(20 U.S.C. 1411(c)(4); 1413(b); 1414(d))

Comment. Section 121a.360 is a combination of three provisions in the statute (Sections 611(c)(4), 613(b), and 614(d)). This section focuses mainly on the State's administration and use of local entitlements under Part B.

The State educational agency, as a recipient of Part B funds is responsible for insuring that all public agencies in the State comply with the provisions of the Act, regardless of whether they receive Part B funds. If a local educational agency elects not to apply for its Part B entitlement, the State would be required to use those funds to insure that a free appropriate public education (FAPE) is made available to children residing in the area served by that local agency. However, if the local entitlement is not sufficient for this purpose, additional State or local funds would have to be expended in order to insure that "FAPE" and the other requirements of the Act are met. Moreover, if the local educational agency is the recipient of any other Federal funds, it would have to be in compliance with Subpart D of the regulations for section 504 of the Rehabilitation Act of 1973 (45 CFR Part 84). It should be noted that the term "FAPE" has different meanings under Part B and section 504. For example, under Part B, "FAPE" is a statutory term which requires special education and related services to be provided in accordance with an individualized education program (IEP). However, under section 504, each recipient must provide an education which includes services that are "designed to meet individual educational needs of handicapped persons as adequately as the needs of nonhandicapped persons are met * * *" Those regulations state that implementation of an IEP, in accordance with Part B, is one means of meeting the "FAPE" requirement.

§ 121a.361 Nature and location of services.

The State educational agency may provide special education and related services under § 121a.360(a) in the manner and at the location it considers appropriate. However, the manner in which the education and services are provided must be consistent with the requirements of this part (including the least restrictive environment provisions in §§ 121a.550–121a.556 of Subpart E).

(20 U.S.C. 1414(d))

§ 121a.370 Use of State educational agency allocation for direct and support services.

(a) The State shall use the portion of its allocation it does not use for administration to provide support services and direct services in accordance with the priority requirements under §§ 121a.320–121a.324.

(b) For the purposes of paragraph (a) of this section:

(1) "Direct services" means services provided to a handicapped child by the State directly, by contract, or through other arrangements.

(2) "Support services" includes implementing the comprehensive system of personnel development under §§ 121a.380–121a.388, recruitment and training of hearing officers and surrogate parents, and public information and parent training activities relating to a free appropriate public education for handicapped children.

(20 U.S.C. 1411(b)(2), (c)(2))

§ 121a.371 State matching.

Beginning with the period July 1, 1978–June 30, 1979, and for each following year, the funds that a State uses for direct and support services under § 121a.370 must be matched on a program basis by the State from funds other than Federal funds. This requirement does not apply to funds that the State uses under § 121a.360.

(20 U.S.C. 1411(c)(2)(B), (c)(4)(B))

Comment. The requirement in § 121a.371 would be satisfied if the State can document that the amount of State funds expended for each major program area (e.g., the comprehensive system of personnel development) is at least equal to the expenditure of Federal funds in that program area.

§ 121a.372 Applicability of nonsupplanting requirement.

Beginning with funds appropriated for Fiscal Year 1979 and for each fol-

lowing Fiscal Year, the requirement in section 613(a)(9) of the Act, which prohibits supplanting with Federal funds, does not apply to funds that the State uses from its allocation under § 121a.706(a) of Subpart G for administration, direct services, or support services.

(20 U.S.C. 1411(c)(3))

COMPREHENSIVE SYSTEM OF PERSONNEL DEVELOPMENT

§ 121a.380 Scope of system.

Each annual program plan must include a description of programs and procedures for the development and implementation of a comprehensive system of personnel development which includes:

(a) The inservice training of general and special educational instructional, related services, and support personnel;

(b) Procedures to insure that all personnel necessary to carry out the purposes of the Act are qualified (as defined in § 121a.12 of Subpart A) and that activities sufficient to carry out this personnel development plan are scheduled; and

(c) Effective procedures for acquiring and disseminating to teachers and administrators of programs for handicapped children significant information derived from educational research, demonstration, and similar projects, and for adopting, where appropriate, promising educational practices and materials developed through those projects.

(20 U.S.C. 1413(a)(3))

§ 121a.381 Participation of other agencies and institutions.

(a) The State educational agency must insure that all public and private institutions of higher education, and other agencies and organizations (including representatives of handicapped, parent, and other advocacy organizations) in the state which have an interest in the preparation of personnel for the education of handicapped children, have an opportunity to participate fully in the development, review, and annual updating of the comprehensive system of personnel development.

(b) The annual program plan must describe the nature and extent of participation under paragraph (a) of this section and must describe responsibilities of the State educational agency, local educational agencies, public and private institutions of higher education, and other agencies:

(1) With respect to the comprehensive system as a whole, and

(2) With respect to the personnel development plan under § 121a.383.

(20 U.S.C. 1412(7)(A); 1413(a)(3))

§ 121a.382   Inservice training.

(a) As used in this section, "inservice training" means any training other than that received by an individual in a full-time program which leads to a degree.

(b) Each annual program plan must provide that the State educational agency:

(1) Conducts an annual needs assessment to determine if a sufficient number of qualified personnel are available in the State; and

(2) Initiates inservice personnel development programs based on the assessed needs of State-wide significance related to the implementation of the Act.

(c) Each annual program plan must include the results of the needs assessment under paragraph (b)(1) of this section, broken out by need for new personnel and need for retrained personnel.

(d) The State educational agency may enter into contracts with institutions of higher education, local educational agencies or other agencies, institutions, or organizations (which may include parent, handicapped, or other advocacy organizations), to carry out:

(1) Experimental or innovative personnel development programs;

(2) Development or modification of instructional materials; and

(3) Dissemination of significant information derived from educational research and demonstration projects.

(e) Each annual program plan must provide that the State educational agency insures that ongoing inservice training programs are available to all personnel who are engaged in the edu-

cation of handicapped children, and that these programs include:

(1) The use of incentives which insure participation by teachers (such as released time, payment for participation, options for academic credit, salary step credit, certification renewal, or updating professional skills);

(2) The involvement of local staff; and

(3) The use of innovative practices which have been found to be effective.

(f) Each annual program plan must:

(1) Describe the process used in determining the inservice training needs of personnel engaged in the education of handicapped children;

(2) Identify the areas in which training is needed (such as individualized education programs, non-discriminatory testing, least restrictive environment, procedural safeguards, and surrogate parents);

(3) Specify the groups requiring training (such as special teachers, regular teachers, administrators, psychologists, speech-language pathologists, audiologists, physical education teachers, therapeutic recreation specialists, physical therapists, occupational therapists, medical personnel, parents, volunteers, hearing officers, and surrogate parents);

(4) Describe the content and nature of training for each area under paragraph (f)(2) of this section;

(5) Describe how the training will be provided in terms of (i) geographical scope (such as Statewide, regional, or local), and (ii) staff training source (such as college and university staffs, State and local educational agency personnel, and non-agency personnel);

(6) *Specify:* (i) The funding sources to be used, and

(ii) The time frame for providing it; and

(7) Specify procedures for effective evaluation of the extent to which program objectives are met.

(20 U.S.C. 1413(a)(3))

§ 121a.383   Personnel development plan.

Each annual program plan must: (a) Include a personnel development plan which provides a structure for personnel planning and focuses on preservice and inservice education needs;

(b) Describe the results of the needs assessment under § 121a.382(b)(1) with respect to identifying needed areas of training, and assigning priorities to those areas; and

(c) Identify the target populations for personnel development, including general education and special education instructional and administrative personnel, support personnel, and other personnel (such as paraprofessionals, parents, surrogate parents, and volunteers).

(20 U.S.C. 1413(a)(3))

§ 121a.384 Dissemination.

(a) Each annual program plan must include a description of the State's procedures for acquiring, reviewing, and disseminating to general and special educational instructional and support personnel, administrators of programs for handicapped children, and other interested agencies and organizations (including parent, handicapped, and other advocacy organizations) significant information and promising practices derived from educational research, demonstration, and other projects.

(b) Dissemination includes:

(1) Making those personnel, administrators, agencies, and organizations aware of the information and practices;

(2) Training designed to enable the establishment of innovative programs and practices targeted on identified local needs; and

(3) Use of instructional materials and other media for personnel development and instructional programming.

(20 U.S.C. 1413(a)(3))

§ 121a.385 Adoption of educational practices.

(a) Each annual program plan must provide for a statewide system designed to adopt, where appropriate, promising educational practices and materials proven effective through research and demonstration.

(b) Each annual program plan must provide for thorough reassessment of educational practices used in the State.

(c) Each annual program plan must provide for the identification of State, local, and regional resources (human and material) which will assist in meeting the State's personnel preparation needs.

(20 U.S.C. 1413(a)(3))

§ 121a.386 [Reserved]

§ 121a.387 Technical assistance to local educational agencies.

Each annual program plan must include a description of technical assistance that the State educational agency gives to local educational agencies in their implementation of the State's comprehensive system of personnel development.

(20 U.S.C. 1413(a)(3))

Subpart D—Private Schools

HANDICAPPED CHILDREN IN PRIVATE SCHOOLS PLACED OR REFERRED BY PUBLIC AGENCIES

§ 121a.400 Applicability of §§ 121a.401–121a.403.

Sections 121a.401–121a.403 apply only to handicapped children who are or have been placed in or referred to a private school or facility by a public agency as a means of providing special education and related services.

(20 U.S.C. 1413(a)(4)(B))

§ 121a.401 Responsibility of State educational agency.

Each State educational agency shall insure that a handicapped child who is placed in or referred to a private school or facility by a public agency:

(a) Is provided special education and related services:

(1) In conformance with an individualized education program which meets the requirements under §§ 121a.340–121a.349 of Subpart C;

(2) At no cost to the parents; and

(3) At a school or facility which meets the standards that apply to State and local educational agencies (including the requirements in this part); and

(b) Has all of the rights of a handicapped child who is served by a public agency.

(20 U.S.C. 1413(a)(4)(B))

§ 121a.402 Implementation by State educational agency.

In implementing § 121a.401, the State educational agency shall:

(a) Monitor compliance through procedures such as written reports, on-site visits, and parent questionnaires;

(b) Disseminate copies of applicable standards to each private school and facility to which a public agency has referred or placed a handicapped child; and

(c) Provide an opportunity for those private schools and facilities to participate in the development and revision of State standards which apply to them.

(20 U.S.C. 1413(a)(4)(B))

§ 121a.403 Placement of children by parents.

(a) If a handicapped child has available a free appropriate public education and the parents choose to place the child in a private school or facility, the public agency is not required by this part to pay for the child's education at the private school or facility. However, the public agency shall make services available to the child as provided under §§ 121a.450–121a.460.

(b) Disagreements between a parent and a public agency regarding the availability of a program appropriate for the child, and the question of financial responsibility, are subject to the due process procedures under §§ 121a.500–121a.514 of Subpart E.

(20 U.S.C. 1412(2)(B); 1415)

HANDICAPPED CHILDREN IN PRIVATE SCHOOLS NOT PLACED OR REFERRED BY PUBLIC AGENCIES

§ 121a.450 Definition of "private school handicapped children."

As used in §§ 121a.451–121a.452, "private school handicapped children" means handicapped children enrolled in private schools or facilities other than handicapped children covered under §§ 121a.400–121a.403.

(20 U.S.C. 1413(a)(4)(A))

[45 FR 22531, Apr. 3, 1980]

§ 121a.451 State educational agency responsibility.

The State educational agency shall insure that—

(a) To the extent consistent with their number and location in the State, provision is made for the participation of private school handicapped children in the program assisted or carried out under this part by providing them with special education and related services; and

(b) The requirements in 45 CFR 100b.651–100b.663 of EDGAR are met.

(20 U.S.C. 1413(a)(4)(A))

[45 FR 22531, Apr. 3, 1980]

§ 121a.452 Local educational agency responsibility.

(a) Each local educational agency shall provide special education and related services designed to meet the needs of private school handicapped children residing in the jurisdiction of the agency.

(20 U.S.C. 1413(a)(4)(A); 1414(a)(6))

[42 FR 42476, Aug. 23, 1977, as amended at 45 FR 22531, Apr. 3, 1980]

Subpart E—Procedural Safeguards

DUE PROCESS PROCEDURES FOR PARENTS AND CHILDREN

§ 121a.500 Definitions of "consent", "evaluation", and "personally identifiable".

As used in this part: "Consent" means that: (a) The parent has been fully informed of all information relevant to the activity for which consent is sought, in his or her native language, or other mode of communication;

(b) The parent understands and agrees in writing to the carrying out of the activity for which his or her consent is sought, and the consent describes that activity and lists the records (if any) which will be released and to whom; and

(c) The parent understands that the granting of consent is voluntary on the part of the parent and may be revoked at any time.

"Evaluation" means procedures used in accordance with §§ 121a.530–121a.534 to determine whether a child is handicapped and the nature and extent of the special education and related services that the child needs. The term means procedures used selectively with an individual child and does not include basic tests administered to or procedures used with all children in a school, grade, or class.

"Personally identifiable" means that information includes:

(a) The name of the child, the child's parent, or other family member;

(b) The address of the child;

(c) A personal identifier, such as the child's social security number or student number; or

(d) A list of personal characteristics or other information which would make it possible to identify the child with reasonable certainty.

(20 U.S.C. 1415, 1417(c))

§ 121a.501 General responsibility of public agencies.

Each State educational agency shall insure that each public agency establishes and implements procedural safeguards which meet the requirements of §§ 121a.500–121a.514.

(20 U.S.C. 1415(a))

§ 121a.502 Opportunity to examine records.

The parents of a handicapped child shall be afforded, in accordance with the procedures in §§ 121a.562–121a.569 an opportunity to inspect and review all education records with respect to:

(a) The identification, evaluation, and educational placement of the child, and

(b) The provision of a free appropriate public education to the child.

(20 U.S.C. 1415(b)(1)(A))

§ 121a.503 Independent educational evaluation.

(a) *General.* (1) The parents of a handicapped child have the right under this part to obtain an independent educational evaluation of the child, subject to paragraphs (b) through (e) of this section.

(2) Each public agency shall provide to parents, on request, information about where an independent educational evaluation may be obtained.

(3) For the purposes of this part:

(i) "Independent educational evaluation" means an evaluation conducted by a qualified examiner who is not employed by the public agency responsible for the education of the child in question.

(ii) "Public expense" means that the public agency either pays for the full cost of the evaluation or insures that the evaluation is otherwise provided at no cost to the parent, consistent with § 121a.301 of Subpart C.

(b) *Parent right to evaluation at public expense.* A parent has the right to an independent educational evaluation at public expense if the parent disagrees with an evaluation obtained by the public agency. However, the public agency may initiate a hearing under § 121a.506 of this subpart to show that its evaluation is appropriate. If the final decision is that the evaluation is appropriate, the parent still has the right to an independent educational evaluation, but not at public expense.

(c) *Parent initiated evaluations.* If the parent obtains an independent educational evaluation at private expense, the results of the evaluation:

(1) Must be considered by the public agency in any decision made with respect to the provision of a free appropriate public education to the child, and

(2) May be presented as evidence at a hearing under this subpart regarding that child.

(d) *Requests for evaluations by hearing officers.* If a hearing officer requests an independent educational evaluation as part of a hearing, the cost of the evaluation must be at public expense.

(e) *Agency criteria.* Whenever an independent evaluation is at public expense, the criteria under which the evaluation is obtained, including the location of the evaluation and the qualifications of the examiner, must be the same as the criteria which the public agency uses when it initiates an evaluation.

(20 U.S.C. 1415(b)(1)(A))

§ 121a.504   Prior notice; parent consent.

(a) *Notice.* Written notice which meets the requirements under § 121a.505 must be given to the parents of a handicapped child a reasonable time before the public agency:

(1) Proposes to initiate or change the identification, evaluation, or educational placement of the child or the provision of a free appropriate public education to the child, or

(2) Refuses to initiate or change the identification, evaluation, or educational placement of the child or the provision of a free appropriate public education to the child.

(b) *Consent.* (1) Parental consent must be obtained before:

(i) Conducting a preplacement evaluation; and

(ii) Initial placement of a handicapped child in a program providing special education and related services.

(2) Except for preplacement evaluation and initial placement, consent may not be required as a condition of any benefit to the parent or child.

(c) *Procedures where parent refuses consent.* (1) Where State law requires parental consent before a handicapped child is evaluated or initially provided special education and related services, State procedures govern the public agency in overriding a parent's refusal to consent.

(2) (i) Where there is no State law requiring consent before a handicapped child is evaluated or initially provided special education and related services, the public agency may use the hearing procedures in §§ 121a.506–121a.508 to determine if the child may be evaluated or initially provided special education and related services without parental consent.

(ii) If the hearing officer upholds the agency, the agency may evaluate or initially provide special education and related services to the child without the parent's consent, subject to the parent's rights under §§ 121a.510–121a.513.

(20 U.S.C. 1415(b)(1)(C), (D))

Comment. 1. Any changes in a child's special education program, after the initial placement, are not subject to parental consent under Part B, but are subject to the prior notice requirement in paragraph (a)

and the individualized education program requirements in Subpart C.

2. Paragraph (c) means that where State law requires parental consent before evaluation or before special education and related services are initially provided, and the parent refuses (or otherwise withholds) consent, State procedures, such as obtaining a court order authorizing the public agency to conduct the evaluation or provide the education and related services, must be followed.

If, however, there is no legal requirement for consent outside of these regulations, the public agency may use the due process procedures under this subpart to obtain a decision to allow the evaluation or services without parental consent. The agency must notify the parent of its actions, and the parent has appeal rights as well as rights at the hearing itself.

§ 121a.505   Content of notice.

(a) The notice under § 121a.504 must include:

(1) A full explanation of all of the procedural safeguards available to the parents under Subpart E;

(2) A description of the action proposed or refused by the agency, an explanation of why the agency proposes or refuses to take the action, and a description of any options the agency considered and the reasons why those options were rejected;

(3) A description of each evaluation procedure, test, record, or report the agency uses as a basis for the proposal or refusal; and

(4) A description of any other factors which are relevant to the agency's proposal or refusal.

(b) The notice must be:

(1) Written in language understandable to the general public, and

(2) Provided in the native language of the parent or other mode of communication used by the parent, unless it is clearly not feasible to do so.

(c) If the native language or other mode of communication of the parent is not a written language, the State or local educational agency shall take steps to insure:

(1) That the notice is translated orally or by other means to the parent in his or her native language or other mode of communication;

(2) That the parent understands the content of the notice, and

(3) That there is written evidence that the requirements in paragraphs

(c) (1) and (2) of this section have been met.

(20 U.S.C. 1415(b)(1)(D))

§ 121a.506   Impartial due process hearing.

(a) A parent or a public educational agency may initiate a hearing on any of the matters described in § 121a.504(a) (1) and (2).

(b) The hearing must be conducted by the State educational agency or the public agency directly responsible for the education of the child, as determined under State statute, State regulation, or a written policy of the State educational agency.

(c) The public agency shall inform the parent of any free or low-cost legal and other relevant services available in the area if:

(1) The parent requests the information; or

(2) The parent or the agency initiates a hearing under this section.

(20 U.S.C. 1416(b)(2))

Comment: Many States have pointed to the success of using mediation as an intervening step prior to conducting a formal due process hearing. Although the process of mediation is not required by the statute or these regulations, an agency may wish to suggest mediation in disputes concerning the identification, evaluation, and educational placement of handicapped children, and the provision of a free appropriate public education to those children. Mediations have been conducted by members of State educational agencies or local educational agency personnel who were not previously involved in the particular case. In many cases, mediation leads to resolution of differences between parents and agencies without the development of an adversarial relationship and with minimal emotional stress. However, mediation may not be used to deny or delay a parent's rights under this subpart.

§ 121a.507   Impartial hearing officer.

(a) A hearing may not be conducted:

(1) By a person who is an employee of a public agency which is involved in the education or care of the child, or

(2) By any person having a personal or professional interest which would conflict with his or her objectivity in the hearing.

(b) A person who otherwise qualifies to conduct a hearing under paragraph (a) of this section is not an employee of the agency solely because he or she is paid by the agency to serve as a hearing officer.

(c) Each public agency shall keep a list of the persons who serve as hearing officers. The list must include a statement of the qualifications of each of those persons.

(20 U.S.C. 1414(b)(2))

§ 121a.508   Hearing rights.

(a) Any party to a hearing has the right to:

(1) Be accompanied and advised by counsel and by individuals with special knowledge or training with respect to the problems of handicapped children;

(2) Present evidence and confront, cross-examine, and compel the attendance of witnesses;

(3) Prohibit the introduction of any evidence at the hearing that has not been disclosed to that party at least five days before the hearing;

(4) Obtain a written or electronic verbatim record of the hearing;

(5) Obtain written findings of fact and decisions. (The public agency shall transmit those findings and decisions, after deleting any personally identifiable information, to the State advisory panel established under Subpart F).

(b) Parents involved in hearings must be given the right to:

(1) Have the child who is the subject of the hearing present; and

(2) Open the hearing to the public.

(20 U.S.C. 1415(d))

§ 121a.509   Hearing decision; appeal.

A decision made in a hearing conducted under this subpart is final, unless a party to the hearing appeals the decision under § 121a.510 or § 121a.511.

(20 U.S.C. 1415(c))

§ 121a.510   Administrative appeal; impartial review.

(a) If the hearing is conducted by a public agency other than the State educational agency, any party aggrieved by the findings and decision in the hearing may appeal to the State educational agency.

(b) If there is an appeal, the State educational agency shall conduct an impartial review of the hearing. The official conducting the review shall:

(1) Examine the entire hearing record;

(2) Insure that the procedures at the hearing were consistent with the requirements of due process;

(3) Seek additional evidence if necessary. If a hearing is held to receive additional evidence, the rights in § 121a.508 apply;

(4) Afford the parties an opportunity for oral or written argument, or both, at the discretion of the reviewing official;

(5) Make an independent decision on completion of the review; and

(6) Give a copy of written findings and the decision to the parties.

(c) The decision made by the reviewing official is final, unless a party brings a civil action under § 121a.512.

(20 U.S.C. 1415 (c), (d); H. Rep. No. 94-664, at p. 49 (1975))

Comment. 1. The State educational agency may conduct its review either directly or through another State agency acting on its behalf. However, the State educational agency remains responsible for the final decision on review.

2. All parties have the right to continue to be represented by counsel at the State administrative review level, whether or not the reviewing official determines that a further hearing is necessary. If the reviewing official decides to hold a hearing to receive additional evidence, the other rights in § 121a.508, relating to hearings, also apply.

§ 121a.511   Civil action.

Any party aggrieved by the findings and decision made in a hearing who does not have the right to appeal under § 121a.510 of this subpart, and any party aggrieved by the decision of a reviewing officer under § 121a.510 has the right to bring a civil action under section 615(e)(2) of the Act.

(20 U.S.C. 1415)

§ 121a.512   Timeliness and convenience of hearings and reviews.

(a) The public agency shall insure that not later than 45 days after the receipt of a request for a hearing:

(1) A final decision is reached in the hearing; and

(2) A copy of the decision is mailed to each of the parties.

(b) The State educational agency shall insure that not later than 30 days after the receipt of a request for a review:

(1) A final decision is reached in the review; and

(2) A copy of the decision is mailed to each of the parties.

(c) A hearing or reviewing officer may grant specific extensions of time beyond the periods set out in paragraphs (a) and (b) of this section at the request of either party.

(d) Each hearing and each review involving oral arguments must be conducted at a time and place which is reasonably convenient to the parents and child involved.

(20 U.S.C. 1415)

§ 121a.513   Child's status during proceedings.

(a) During the pendency of any administrative or judicial proceeding regarding a complaint, unless the public agency and the parents of the child agree otherwise, the child involved in the complaint must remain in his or her present educational placement.

(b) If the complaint involves an application for initial admission to public school, the child, with the consent of the parents, must be placed in the public school program until the completion of all the proceedings.

(20 U.S.C. 1415(e)(3))

Comment. Section 121a.513 does not permit a child's placement to be changed during a complaint proceeding, unless the parents and agency agree otherwise. While the placement may not be changed, this does not preclude the agency from using its normal procedures for dealing with children who are endangering themselves or others.

§ 121a.514   Surrogate parents.

(a) *General.* Each public agency shall insure that the rights of a child are protected when:

(1) No parent (as defined in § 121a.10) can be identified;

(2) The public agency, after reasonable efforts, cannot discover the whereabouts of a parent; or

(3) The child is a ward of the State under the laws of that State.

(b) *Duty of public agency.* The duty of a public agency under paragraph (a) of this section includes the assignment of an individual to act as a surrogate for the parents. This must include a method (1) for determining whether a child needs a surrogate parent, and (2) for assigning a surrogate parent to the child.

(c) *Criteria for selection of surrogates.* (1) The public agency may select a surrogate parent in any way permitted under State law.

(2) Public agencies shall insure that a person selected as a surrogate:

(i) Has no interest that conflicts with the interest of the child he or she represents; and

(ii) Has knowledge and skills, that insure adequate representation of the child.

(d) *Non-employee requirement; compensation.* (1) A person assigned as a surrogate may not be an employee of a public agency which is involved in the education or care of the child.

(2) A person who otherwise qualifies to be a surrogate parent under paragraphs (c) and (d)(1) of this section, is not an employee of the agency solely because he or she is paid by the agency to serve as a surrogate parent.

(e) *Responsibilities.* The surrogate parent may represent the child in all matters relating to:

(1) The identification, evaluation, and educational placement of the child, and

(2) The provision of a free appropriate public education to the child.

(20 U.S.C. 1415(b)(1)(B))

PROTECTION IN EVALUATION
PROCEDURES

§ 121a.530   General.

(a) Each State educational agency shall insure that each public agency establishes and implements procedures which meet the requirements of §§ 121a.530–121a.534.

(b) Testing and evaluation materials and procedures used for the purposes of evaluation and placement of handicapped children must be selected and administered so as not to be racially or culturally discriminatory.

(20 U.S.C. 1412(5)(C))

§ 121a.531   Preplacement evaluation.

Before any action is taken with respect to the initial placement of a handicapped child in a special education program, a full and individual evaluation of the child's educational needs must be conducted in accordance with the requirements of § 121a.532.

(20 U.S.C. 1412(5)(C))

§ 121a.532   Evaluation procedures.

State and local educational agencies shall insure, at a minimum, that:

(a) Tests and other evaluation materials:

(1) Are provided and administered in the child's native language or other mode of communication, unless it is clearly not feasible to do so;

(2) Have been validated for the specific purpose for which they are used; and

(3) Are administered by trained personnel in conformance with the instructions provided by their producer;

(b) Tests and other evaluation materials include those tailored to assess specific areas of educational need and not merely those which are designed to provide a single general intelligence quotient;

(c) Tests are selected and administered so as best to ensure that when a test is administered to a child with impaired sensory, manual, or speaking skills, the test results accurately reflect the child's aptitude or achievement level or whatever other factors the test purports to measure, rather than reflecting the child's impaired sensory, manual, or speaking skills (except where those skills are the factors which the test purports to measure);

(d) No single procedure is used as the sole criterion for determining an appropriate educational program for a child; and

(e) The evaluation is made by a multidisciplinary team or group of persons, including at least one teacher or other specialist with knowledge in the area of suspected disability.

(f) The child is assessed in all areas related to the suspected disability, including, where appropriate, health, vision, hearing, social and emotional status, general intelligence, academic performance, communicative status, and motor abilities.

(20 U.S.C. 1412(5)(C))

Comment. Children who have a speech impairment as their primary handicap may not need a complete battery of assessments (e.g., psychological, physical, or adaptive behavior). However, a qualified speech-language pathologist would (1) evaluate each speech impaired child using procedures that are appropriate for the diagnosis and appraisal of speech and language disorders, and (2) where necessary, make referrals for additional assessments needed to make an appropriate placement decision.

§ 121a.533 Placement procedures.

(a) In interpreting evaluation data and in making placement decisions, each public agency shall:

(1) Draw upon information from a variety of sources, including aptitude and achievement tests, teacher recommendations, physical condition, social or cultural background, and adaptive behavior;

(2) Insure that information obtained from all of these sources is documented and carefully considered;

(3) Insure that the placement decision is made by a group of persons, including persons knowledgeable about the child, the meaning of the evaluation data, and the placement options; and

(4) Insure that the placement decision is made in conformity with the least restrictive environment rules in §§ 121a.550–121a.554.

(b) If a determination is made that a child is handicapped and needs special education and related services, an individualized education program must be developed for the child in accordance with §§ 121a.340–121a.349 of Subpart C.

(20 U.S.C. 1412(5)(C); 1414(a)(5))

Comment. Paragraph (a)(1) includes a list of examples of sources that may be used by a public agency in making placement decisions. The agency would not have to use all the sources in every instance. The point of the requirement is to insure that more than one source is used in interpreting evaluation data and in making placement decisions. For example, while all of the named sources would have to be used for a child whose suspected disability is mental retardation, they

would not be necessary for certain other handicapped children, such as a child who has a severe articulation disorder as his primary handicap. For such a child, the speech-language pathologist, in complying with the multisource requirement, might use (1) a standardized test of articulation, and (2) observation of the child's articulation behavior in conversational speech.

§ 121a.534 Reevaluation.

Each State and local educational agency shall insure:

(a) That each handicapped child's individualized education program is reviewed in accordance with §§ 121a.340–121a.349 of Subpart C, and

(b) That an evaluation of the child, based on procedures which meet the requirements under § 121a.532, is conducted every three years or more frequently if conditions warrant or if the child's parent or teacher requests an evaluation.

(20 U.S.C. 1412(5)(c))

ADDITIONAL PROCEDURES FOR EVALUATING SPECIFIC LEARNING DISABILITIES

§ 121a.540 Additional team members.

In evaluating a child suspected of having a specific learning disability, in addition to the requirements of § 121a.532, each public agency shall include on the multidisciplinary evaluation team:

(a) (1) The child's regular teacher; or

(2) If the child does not have a regular teacher, a regular classroom teacher qualified to teach a child of his or her age; or

(3) For a child of less than school age, an individual qualified by the State educational agency to teach a child of his or her age; and

(b) At least one person qualified to conduct individual diagnostic examinations of children, such as a school psychologist, speech-language pathologist, or remedial reading teacher.

(20 U.S.C. 1411 note)

[42 FR 65083, Dec. 29, 1977]

§ 121a.541 Criteria for determining the existence of a specific learning disability.

(a) A team may determine that a child has a specific learning disability if:

(1) The child does not achieve commensurate with his or her age and ability levels in one or more of the areas listed in paragraph (a)(2) of this section, when provided with learning experiences appropriate for the child's age and ability levels; and

(2) The team finds that a child has a severe discrepancy between achievement and intellectual ability in one or more of the following areas:

(i) Oral expression;
(ii) Listening comprehension;
(iii) Written expression;
(iv) Basic reading skill;
(v) Reading comprehension;
(vi) Mathematics calculation; or
(vii) Mathematics reasoning.

(b) The team may not identify a child as having a specific learning disability if the severe discrepancy between ability and achievement is primarily the result of:

(1) A visual, hearing, or motor handicap;
(2) Mental retardation;
(3) Emotional disturbance; or
(4) Environmental, cultural or economic disadvantage.

(20 U.S.C. 1411 note)

[42 FR 65083, Dec. 29, 1977]

§ 121a.542 Observation.

(a) At least one team member other than the child's regular teacher shall observe the child's academic performance in the regular classroom setting.

(b) In the case of a child of less than school age or out of school, a team member shall observe the child in an environment appropriate for a child of that age.

(20 U.S.C. 1411 note)

[42 FR 65083, Dec. 29, 1977]

§ 121a.543 Written report.

(a) The team shall prepare a written report of the results of the evaluation.

(b) The report must include a statement of:

(1) Whether the child has a specific learning disability;
(2) The basis for making the determination;
(3) The relevant behavior noted during the observation of the child;
(4) The relationship of that behavior to the child's academic functioning;

(5) The educationally relevant medical findings, if any;

(6) Whether there is a severe discrepancy between achievement and ability which is not correctable without special education and related services; and

(7) The determination of the team concerning the effects of environmental, cultural, or economic disadvantage.

(c) Each team member shall certify in writing whether the report reflects his or her conclusion. If it does not reflect his or her conclusion, the team member must submit a separage statement presenting his or her conclusions.

(20 U.S.C. 1411 note)

[42 FR 65083, Dec. 29, 1977]

LEAST RESTRICTIVE ENVIRONMENT

§ 121a.550 General.

(a) Each State educational agency shall insure that each public agency establishes and implements procedures which meet the requirements of §§ 121a.550–121a.556.

(b) Each public agency shall insure:

(1) That to the maximum extent appropriate, handicapped children, including children in public or private institutions or other care facilities, are educated with children who are not handicapped, and

(2) That special classes, separate schooling or other removal of handicapped children from the regular educational environment occurs only when the nature or severity of the handicap is such that education in regular classes with the use of supplementary aids and services cannot be achieved satisfactorily.

(20 U.S.C. 1412(5)(B); 1414(a)(1)(C)(iv))

§ 121a.551 Continuum of alternative placements.

(a) Each public agency shall insure that a continuum of alternative placements is available to meet the needs of handicapped children for special education and related services.

(b) The continuum required under paragraph (a) of this section must:

(1) Include the alternative placements listed in the definition of spe-

cial education under § 121a.13 of Subpart A (instruction in regular classes, special classes, special schools, home instruction, and instruction in hospitals and institutions), and

(2) Make provision for supplementary services (such as resource room or itinerant instruction) to be provided in conjunction with regular class placement.

(20 U.S.C. 1412(5)(B))

§ 121a.552   Placements.

Each public agency shall insure that:

(a) Each handicapped child's educational placement: (1) Is determined at least annually,

(2) Is based on his or her individualized education program, and

(3) Is as close as possible to the child's home;

(b) The various alternative placements included under § 121a.551 are available to the extent necessary to implement the individualized education program for each handicapped child;

(c) Unless a handicapped child's individualized education program requires some other arrangement, the child is educated in the school which he or she would attend if not handicapped; and

(d) In selecting the least restrictive environment, consideration is given to any potential harmful effect on the child or on the quality of services which he or she needs.

(20 U.S.C. 1412(5)(B))

Comment. Section 121a.552 includes some of the main factors which must be considered in determining the extent to which a handicapped child can be educated with children who are not handicapped. The overriding rule in this section is that placement decisions must be made on an individual basis. The section also requires each agency to have various alternative placements available in order to insure that each handicapped child receives an education which is appropriate to his or her individual needs.

The analysis of the regulations for Section 504 of the Rehabilitation Act of 1973 (45 CFR Part 84—Appendix, Paragraph 24) includes several points regarding educational placements of handicapped children which are pertinent to this section:

1. With respect to determining proper placements, the analysis states: "* * * it should be stressed that, where a handi-

capped child is so disruptive in a regular classroom that the education of other students is significantly impaired, the needs of the handicapped child cannot be met in that environment. Therefore regular placement would not be appropriate to his or her needs * * *."

2. With respect to placing a handicapped child in an alternate setting, the analysis states that among the factors to be considered in placing. a child is the need to place the child as close to home as possible. Recipients are required to take this factor into account in making placement decisions. The parent's right to challenge the placement of their child extends not only to placement in special classes or separate schools, but also to placement in a distant school, particularly in a residential program. An equally appropriate education program may exist closer to home; and this issue may be raised by the parent under the due process provisions of this subpart.

§ 121a.553   Nonacademic settings.

In providing or arranging for the provision of nonacademic and extracurricular services and activities, including meals, recess periods, and the services and activities set forth in § 121a.306 of Subpart C, each public agency shall insure that each handicapped child participates with nonhandicapped children in those services and activities to the maximum extent appropriate to the needs of that child.

(20 U.S.C. 1412(5)(B))

Comment. Section 121a.553 is taken from a new requirement in the final regulations for Section 504 of the Rehabilitation Act of 1973. With respect to this requirement, the analysis of the Section 504 Regulations includes the following statement: "[A new paragraph] specifies that handicapped children must also be provided nonacademic services in as integrated a setting as possible. This requirement is especially important for children whose educational needs necessitate their being solely with other handicapped children during most of each day. To the maximum extent appropriate, children in residential settings are also to be provided opportunities for participation with other children." (45 CFR Part 84—Appendix, Paragraph 24.)

§ 121a.554   Children in public or private institutions.

Each State educational agency shall make arrangements with public and private institutions (such as a memorandum of agreement or special implementation procedures) as may be necessary to insure that § 121a.550 is effectively implemented.

(20 U.S.C. 1412(5)(B))

Comment. Under section 612(5)(B) of the statute, the requirement to educate handicapped children with nonhandicapped children also applies to children in public and private institutions or other care facilities. Each State educational agency must insure that each applicable agency and institution in the State implements this requirement. Regardless of other reasons for institutional placement, no child in an institution who is capable of education in a regular public school setting may be denied access to an education in that setting.

§ 121a.555 Technical assistance and training activities.

Each State educational agency shall carry out activities to insure that teachers and administrators in all public agencies:

(a) Are fully informed about their responsibilities for implementing § 121a.550, and

(b) Are provided with technical assistance and training necessary to assist them in this effort.

(20 U.S.C. 1412(5)(B))

§ 121a.556 Monitoring activities.

(a) The State educational agency shall carry out activities to insure that § 121a.550 is implemented by each public agency.

(b) If there is evidence that a public agency makes placements that are inconsistent with § 121a.550 of this subpart, the State educational agency:

(1) Shall review the public agency's justification for its actions, and

(2) Shall assist in planning and implementing any necessary corrective action.

(20 U.S.C. 1412(5)(B))

CONFIDENTIALITY OF INFORMATION

§ 121a.560 Definitions.

As used in this subpart:

"Destruction" means physical destruction or removal of personal identifiers from information so that the information is no longer personally identifiable.

"Education records" means the type of records covered under the definition of "education records" in Part 99 of this title (the regulations implementing the Family Educational Rights and Privacy Act of 1974).

"Participating agency" means any agency or institution which collects, maintains, or uses personally identifiable information, or from which information is obtained, under this part.

(20 U.S.C. 1412(2)(D); 1417(c))

§ 121a.561 Notice to parents.

(a) The State educational agency shall give notice which is adequate to fully inform parents about the requirements under § 121a.128 of Subpart B, including:

(1) A description of the extent to which the notice is given in the native languages of the various population groups in the State;

(2) A description of the children on whom personally identifiable information is maintained, the types of information sought, the methods the State intends to use in gathering the information (including the sources from whom information is gathered), and the uses to be made of the information;

(3) A summary of the policies and procedures which participating agencies must follow regarding storage, disclosure to third parties, retention, and destruction of personally identifiable information; and

(4) A description of all of the rights of parents and children regarding this information, including the rights under section 438 of the General Education Provisions Act and Part 99 of this title (the Family Educational Rights and Privacy Act of 1974, and implementing regulations).

(b) Before any major identification, location, or evaluation activity, the notice must be published or announced in newspapers or other media, or both, with circulation adequate to notify parents throughout the State of the activity.

(20 U.S.C. 1412(2)(D); 1417(c))

§ 121a.562 Access rights.

(a) Each participating agency shall permit parents to inspect and review any education records relating to their children which are collected, maintained, or used by the agency under this part. The agency shall comply with a request without unnecessary delay and before any meeting regarding an individualized education program or hearing relating to the identification, evaluation, or placement of the child, and in no case more than 45 days after the request has been made.

(b) The right to inspect and review education records under this section includes:

(1) The right to a response from the participating agency to reasonable requests for explanations and interpretations of the records;

(2) The right to request that the agency provide copies of the records containing the information if failure to provide those copies would effectively prevent the parent from exercising the right to inspect and review the records; and

(3) The right to have a representative of the parent inspect and review the records.

(c) An agency may presume that the parent has authority to inspect and review records relating to his or her child unless the agency has been advised that the parent does not have the authority under applicable State law governing such matters as guardianship, separation, and divorce.

(20 U.S.C. 1412(2)(D); 1417(c))

§ 121a.563   Record of access.

Each participating agency shall keep a record of parties obtaining access to education records collected, maintained, or used under this part (except access by parents and authorized employees of the participating agency), including the name of the party, the date access was given, and the purpose for which the party is authorized to use the records.

(20 U.S.C. 1412(2)(D); 1417(c))

§ 121a.564   Records on more than one child.

If any education record includes information on more than one child, the parents of those children shall have the right to inspect and review only the information relating to their child

or to be informed of that specific information.

(20 U.S.C. 1412(2)(D); 1417(c))

§ 121a.565   List of types and locations of information.

Each participating agency shall provide parents on request a list of the types and locations of education records collected, maintained, or used by the agency.

(20 U.S.C. 1412(2)(D); 1417(c))

§ 121a.566   Fees.

(a) A participating education agency may charge a fee for copies of records which are made for parents under this part if the fee does not effectively prevent the parents from exercising their right to inspect and review those records.

(b) A participating agency may not charge a fee to search for or to retrieve information under this part.

(20 U.S.C. 1412(2)(D); 1417(c))

§ 121a.567   Amendment of records at parent's request.

(a) A parent who believes that information in education records collected, maintained, or used under this part is inaccurate or misleading or violates the privacy or other rights of the child, may request the participating agency which maintains the information to amend the information.

(b) The agency shall decide whether to amend the information in accordance with the request within a reasonable period of time of receipt of the request.

(c) If the agency decides to refuse to amend the information in accordance with the request it shall inform the parent of the refusal, and advise the parent of the right to a hearing under § 121a.568.

(20 U.S.C. 1412(2)(D); 1417(c))

§ 121a.568   Opportunity for a hearing.

The agency shall, on request, provide an opportunity for a hearing to challenge information in education records to insure that it is not inaccurate, misleading, or otherwise in violation of the privacy or other rights of the child.

(20 U.S.C. 1412(2)(D); 1417(c))

§ 121a.569 Result of hearing.

(a) If, as a result of the hearing, the agency decides that the information is inaccurate, misleading or otherwise in violation of the privacy or other rights of the child, it shall amend the information accordingly and so inform the parent in writing.

(b) If, as a result of the hearing, the agency decides that the information is not inaccurate, misleading, or otherwise in violation of the privacy of other rights of the child, it shall inform the parent of the right to place in the records it maintains on the child a statement commenting on the information or setting forth any reasons for disagreeing with the decision of the agency.

(c) Any explanation placed in the records of the child under this section must:

(1) Be maintained by the agency as part of the records of the child as long as the record or contested portion is maintained by the agency; and

(2) If the records of the child or the contested portion is disclosed by the agency to any party, the explanation must also be disclosed to the party.

(20 U.S.C. 1412(2)(D); 1417(c))

§ 121a.570 Hearing procedures.

A hearing held under § 121a.568 of this subpart must be conducted according to the procedures under § 99.22 of this title.

(20 U.S.C. 1412(2)(D); 1417(c))

§ 121a.571 Consent.

(a) Parental consent must be obtained before personally identifiable information is:

(1) Disclosed to anyone other than officials of participating agencies collecting or using the information under this part, subject to paragraph (b) of this section; or

(2) Used for any purpose other than meeting a requirement under this part.

(b) An educational agency or institution subject to Part 99 of this title may not release information from education records to participating agencies without parental consent unless authorized to do so under Part 99 of this title.

(c) The State educational agency shall include policies and procedures in its annual program plan which are used in the event that a parent refuses to provide consent under this section.

(20 U.S.C. 1412(2)(D); 1417(c))

§ 121a.572 Safeguards.

(a) Each participating agency shall protect the confidentiality of personally identifiable information at collection, storage, disclosure, and destruction stages.

(b) One official at each participating agency shall assume responsibility for insuring the confidentiality of any personally identifiable information.

(c) All persons collecting or using personally identifiable information must receive training or instruction regarding the State's policies and procedures under § 121a.129 of Subpart B and Part 99 of this title.

(d) Each participating agency shall maintain, for public inspection, a current listing of the names and positions of those employees within the agency who may have access to personally identifiable information.

(20 U.S.C. 1412(2)(D); 1417(c))

§ 121a.573 Destruction of information.

(a) The public agency shall inform parents when personally identifiable information collected, maintained, or used under this part is no longer needed to provide educational services to the child.

(b) The information must be destroyed at the request of the parents. However, a permanent record of a student's name, address, and phone number, his or her grades, attendance record, classes attended, grade level completed, and year completed may be maintained without time limitation.

(20 U.S.C. 1412(2)(D); 1417(c))

Comment. Under § 121a.573, the personally identifiable information on a handicapped child may be retained permanently unless the parents request that it be destroyed. Destruction of records is the best protection against improper and unauthorized disclosure. However, the records may be needed for other purposes. In informing parents about their rights under this section, the agency should remind them that the records may be needed by the child or the parents for social security benefits or other purposes. If the parents request that the information be destroyed, the agency may retain the information in paragraph (b).

§ 121a.574   Children's rights.

The State educational agency shall include policies and procedures in its annual program plan regarding the extent to which children are afforded rights of privacy similar to those afforded to parents, taking into consideration the age of the child and type or severity of disability.

(20 U.S.C. 1412(2)(D); 1417(c))

Comment. Note that under the regulations for the Family Educational Rights and Privacy Act (45 CFR 99.4(a)), the rights of parents regarding education records are transferred to the student at age 18.

§ 121a.575   Enforcement.

The State educational agency shall describe in its annual program plan the policies and procedures, including sanctions, which the State uses to insure that its policies and procedures are followed and that the requirements of the Act and the regulations in this part are met.

(20 U.S.C. 1412(2)(D); 1417(c))

§ 121a.576   Office of Education.

If the Office of Education or its authorized representatives collect any personally identifiable information regarding handicapped children which is not subject to 5 U.S.C. 552a (The Privacy Act of 1974), the Commissioner shall apply the requirements of 5 U.S.C. section 552a (b) (1)–(2), (4)–(11); (c); (d); (e)(1); (2); (3)(A), (B), and (D), (5)–(10); (h); (m); and (n), and the regulations implementing those provisions in Part 5b of this title.

(20 U.S.C. 1412(2)(D); 1417(c))

OFFICE OF EDUCATION PROCEDURES

§ 121a.580   Opportunity for a hearing.

The Commissioner gives a State educational agency reasonable notice and an opportunity for a hearing before taking any of the following actions:

(a) Disapproval of a State's annual program plan under § 121a.113 of Subpart B.

(b) Withholding payments from a State under § 121a.590 or under section 434(c) of the General Education Provisions Act.

(c) Waiving the requirement under § 121a.589 of this subpart regarding supplementing and supplanting with funds provided under Part B of the Act.

(20 U.S.C. 1232c(c); 1413(a)(9)(B); 1413(c); 1416)

§§ 121a.581–121a.588   [Reserved]

§ 121a.589   Waiver of requirement regarding supplementing and supplanting with Part B funds.

(a) Under sections 613(a)(9)(B) and 614(a)(2)(B)(ii) of the Act, State and local educational agencies must insure that Federal funds provided under Part B of the Act are used to supplement the level of State and local funds expended for the education of handicapped children, and in no case to supplant those State and local funds. Beginning with funds appropriated for fiscal year 1979 and for each following fiscal year, the nonsupplanting requirement only applies to funds allocated to local educational agencies. (See § 121a.372.)

(b) If the State provides clear and convincing evidence that all handicapped children have available to them a free appropriate public education, the Commissioner may waive in part the requirement under sections 613(a)(9)(B) and 614(a)(2)(B)(ii) of the Act if the Commissioner concurs with the evidence provided by the State.

(c) If a State wishes to request a waiver, it must inform the Commissioner in writing. The Commissioner then provides the State with a finance and membership report form which provides the basis for the request.

(d) In its request for a waiver, the State shall include the results of a special study made by the State to obtain evidence of the availability of a free appropriate public education to all handicapped children. The special study must include statements by a representative sample of organizations which deal with handicapped children, and parents and teachers of handicapped children, relating to the following areas:

(1) The adequacy and comprehensiveness of the State's system for locating, identifying, and evaluating handicapped children, and

(2) The cost to parents, if any, for education for children enrolled in public and private day schools, and in public and private residential schools and institutions, and

(3) The adequacy of the State's due process procedures.

(e) In its request for a waiver, the State shall include finance data relating to the availability of a free appropriate public education for all handicapped children, including:

(1) The total current expenditures for regular education programs and special education programs by function and by source of funds (State, local, and Federal) for the previous school year, and

(2) The full-time equivalent membership of students enrolled in regular programs and in special programs in the previous school year.

(f) The Commissioner considers the information which the State provides under paragraphs (d) and (e) of this section, along with any additional information he may request, or obtain through on-site reviews of the State's education programs and records, to determine if all children have available to them a free appropriate public education, and if so, the extent of the waiver.

(g) The State may request a hearing under §§ 121a.580–121a.583 with regard to any final action by the Commissioner under this section.

(20 U.S.C. 1411(c)(3); 1413(a)(9)(B))

Subpart F—State Administration

STATE EDUCATIONAL AGENCY RESPONSIBILITIES: GENERAL

§ 121a.600 Responsibility for all educational programs.

(a) The State educational agency is responsible for insuring:

(1) That the requirements of this part are carried out; and

(2) That each educational program for handicapped children administered within the State, including each program administered by any other public agency:

(i) Is under the general supervision of the persons responsible for educational programs for handicapped children in the State educational agency, and

(ii) Meets education standards of the State educational agency (including the requirements of this part).

(b) The State must comply with paragraph (a) of this section through State statute, State regulation, signed agreement between respective agency officials, or other documents.

(20 U.S.C. 1412(6))

Comment. The requirement in § 121a.600(a) is taken essentially verbatim from section 612(6) of the statute and reflects the desire of the Congress for a central point of responsibility and accountability in the education of handicapped children within each State. With respect to State educational agency responsibility, the Senate Report on Pub. L. 94–142 includes the following statements:

This provision is included specifically to assure a single line of responsibility with regard to the education of handicapped children, and to assure that in the implementation of all provisions of this Act and in carrying out the right to education for handicapped children, the State educational agency shall be the responsible agency * * *.

Without this requirement, there is an abdication of responsibility for the education of handicapped children. Presently, in many States, responsibility is divided, depending upon the age of the handicapped child, sources of funding, and type of services delivered. While the Committee understands that different agencies may, in fact, deliver services, the responsibility must remain in a central agency overseeing the education of handicapped children, so that failure to deliver services or the violation of the rights of handicapped children is squarely the responsibility of one agency. (Senate Report No. 94-168, p. 24 (1975))

In meeting the requirements of this section, there are a number of acceptable options which may be adopted, including the following:

(1) Written agreements are developed between respective State agencies concerning State educational agency standards and monitoring. These agreements are binding on the local or regional counterparts of each State agency.

(2) The Governor's Office issues an administrative directive establishing the State educational agency responsibility.

(3) State law, regulation, or policy designates the State educational agency as responsible for establishing standards for all educational programs for the handicapped, and includes responsibility for monitoring.

(4) State law mandates that the State educational agency is responsible for all educational programs.

USE OF FUNDS

§ 121a.620   Federal funds for State administration.

A State may use five percent of the total State allotment in any fiscal year under Part B of the Act, or $200,000, whichever is greater, for administrative costs related to carrying out sections 612 and 613 of the Act. However, this amount cannot be greater than the amount which the State may use under § 121a.704 or § 121a.705, as the case may be.

(20 U.S.C. 1411 (b), (c))

§ 121a.621   Allowable costs.

(a) The State educational agency may use funds under § 121a.620 of this subpart for:

(1) Administration of the annual program plan and for planning at the State level, including planning, or assisting in the planning, of programs or projects for the education of handicapped children;

(2) Approval, supervision, monitoring, and evaluation of the effectiveness of local programs and projects for the education of handicapped children;

(3) Technical assistance to local educational agencies with respect to the requirements of this part;

(4) Leadership services for the program supervision and management of special education activities for handicapped children; and

(5) Other State leadership activities and consultative services.

(b) The State educational agency shall use the remainder of its funds under § 121a.620 in accordance with § 121a.370 of Subpart C.

(20 U.S.C. 1411 (b), (c))

STATE ADVISORY PANEL

§ 121a.650   Establishment.

(a) Each State shall establish, in accordance with the provisions of this subpart, a State advisory panel on the education of handicapped children.

(b) The advisory panel must be appointed by the Governor or any other official authorized under State law to make those appointments.

(c) If a State has an existing advisory panel that can perform the functions in § 121a.652, the State may modify the existing panel so that it fulfills all of the requirements of this subpart, instead of establishing a new advisory panel.

(20 U.S.C. 1413(a)(12))

§ 121a.651   Membership.

(a) The membership of the State advisory panel must be composed of persons involved in or concerned with the education of handicapped children. The membership must include at least one person representative of each of the following groups:

(1) Handicapped individuals.

(2) Teachers of handicapped children.

(3) Parents of handicapped children.

(4) State and local educational officials.

(5) Special education program administrators.

(b) The State may expand the advisory panel to include additional persons in the groups listed in paragraph (a) of this section and representatives of other groups not listed.

(20 U.S.C. 1413(a)(12))

Comment. The membership of the State advisory panel, as listed in paragraphs (a) (1)–(5), is required in section 613(a)(12) of the Act. As indicated in paragraph (b), the composition of the panel and the number of members may be expanded at the discretion of the State. In adding to the membership, consideration could be given to having:

(1) An appropriate balance between professional groups and consumers (i.e., parents, advocates, and handicapped individuals);

(2) Broad representation within the consumer-advocate groups, to insure that the interests and points of view of various parents, advocates and handicapped individuals are appropriately represented;

(3) Broad representation within professional groups (e.g., (a) regular education personnel, (b) special educators, including teachers, teacher trainers, and administrators, who can properly represent various dimensions in the education of handicapped children, and (c) appropriate related services personnel); and

(4) Representatives from other State advisory panels (such as vocational education).

If a State elects to maintain a small advisory panel (e.g., 10-15 members), the panel itself could take steps to insure that it (1) consults with and receives inputs from various consumer and special interest professional groups, and (2) establishes committees for particular short-term purposes composed of representatives from those input groups.

§ 121a.652   Advisory panel functions.

The State advisory panel shall:

(a) Advise the State educational agency of unmet needs within the State in the education of handicapped children;

(b) Comment publicly on the State annual program plan and rules or regulations proposed for issuance by the State regarding the education of handicapped children and the procedures for distribution of funds under this part; and

(c) Assist the State in developing and reporting such information and evaluations as may assist the Commissioner in the performance of his responsibilities under section 618.

(20 U.S.C. 1413(a)(12))

§ 121a.653   Advisory panel procedures.

(a) The advisory panel shall meet as often as necessary to conduct its business.

(b) By July 1 of each year, the advisory panel shall submit an annual report of panel activities and suggestions to the State educational agency. This report must be made available to the public in a manner consistent with

other public reporting requirements under this part.

(c) Official minutes must be kept on all panel meetings and shall be made available to the public on request.

(d) All advisory panel meetings and agenda items must be publicly announced prior to the meeting, and meetings must be open to the public.

(e) Interpreters and other necessary services must be provided at panel meetings for panel members or participants. The State may pay for these services from funds under § 121a.620.

(f) The advisory panel shall serve without compensation but the State must reimburse the panel for reasonable and necessary expenses for attending meetings and performing duties. The State may use funds under § 121a.620 for this purpose.

(20 U.S.C. 1413(a)(12))

Subpart G—Allocation of Funds; Reports

ALLOCATIONS

§ 121a.700   Special definition of the term State.

For the purposes of § 121a.701, § 121a.702, and §§ 121a.704-121a.708, the term "State" does not include Guam, American Samoa, the Virgin Islands, and the Trust Territory of the Pacific Islands.

(20 U.S.C. 1411(a)(2))

§ 121a.701   State entitlement; formula.

(a) The maximum amount of the grant to which a State is entitled under section 611 of the Act in any fiscal year is equal to the number of handicapped children aged three through 21 in the State who are receiving special education and related services, multiplied by the applicable percentage, under paragraph (b) of this section, of the average per pupil expenditure in public elementary and secondary schools in the United States.

(b) For the purposes of the formula in paragraph (a) of this section, the applicable percentage of the average per pupil expenditure in public elementary and secondary schools in the United States for each fiscal year is:

(1) 1978—5 percent,
(2) 1979—10 percent,
(3) 1980—20 percent,
(4) 1981—30 percent, and
(5) 1982, and for each fiscal year after 1982, 40 percent.

(20 U.S.C. 1411(a)(1))

(c) For the purposes of this section, the average per pupil expenditure in public elementary and secondary schools in the United States, means the aggregate expenditures during the second fiscal year preceding the fiscal year for which the computation is made (or if satisfactory data for that year are not available at the time of computation, then during the most recent preceding fiscal year for which satisfactory data are available) of all local educational agencies in the United States (which, for the purpose of this section, means the fifty States and the District of Columbia), plus any direct expenditures by the State for operation of those agencies (without regard to the source of funds from which either of those expenditures are made), divided by the aggregate number of children in average daily attendance to whom those agencies provided free public education during that preceding year.

(20 U.S.C. 1411(a)(4))

§ 121a.702 Limitations and exclusions.

(a) In determining the amount of a grant under § 121a.701 of this subpart, the Commissioner may not count:

(1) Handicapped children in a State to the extent that the number of those children is greater than 12 percent of the number of all children aged five through 17 in the State; and

(2) [Reserved]

(3) Handicapped children who are counted under section 121 of the Elementary and Secondary Education Act of 1965.

(b) For the purposes of paragraph (a) of this section, the number of children aged five through 17 in any State shall be determined by the Commissioner on the basis of the most recent satisfactory data available to him.

(20 U.S.C. 1411(a)(5))

[42 FR 42476, Aug. 23, 1977, as amended at 42 FR 65083, Dec. 29, 1977]

§ 121a.703 Ratable reductions.

(a) *General.* If the sums appropriated for any fiscal year for making payments to States under section 611 of the Act are not sufficient to pay in full the total amounts to which all States are entitled to receive for that fiscal year, the maximum amount which all States are entitled to receive for that fiscal year shall be ratably reduced. In case additional funds become available for making payments for any fiscal year during which the preceding sentence is applicable, those reduced amounts shall be increased on the same basis they were reduced.

(20 U.S.C. 1411(g)(1))

(b) *Reporting dates for local educational agencies and reallocations.* (1) In any fiscal year in which the State entitlements have been ratably reduced, and in which additional funds have not been made available to pay in full the total of the amounts under paragraph (a) of this section, the State educational agency shall fix dates before which each local educational agency shall report to the State the amount of funds available to it under this part which it estimates it will expend.

(2) The amounts available under paragraph (a)(1) of this section, or any amount which would be available to any other local educational agency if it were to submit an application meeting the requirements of this part, which the State educational agency determines will not be used for the period of its availability, shall be available for allocation to those local educational agencies, in the manner provided in § 121a.707, which the State educational agency determines will need and be able to use additional funds to carry out approved programs.

(20 U.S.C. 1411(g)(2))

§ 121a.704 Hold harmless provision.

No State shall receive less than the amount it received under Part B of the Act for fiscal year 1977.

(20 U.S.C. 1411(a)(1))

§ 121a.705 Within-State distribution: Fiscal year 1978.

Of the funds received under § 121a.701 of this subpart by any State for fiscal year 1978:

(a) 50 percent may be used by the State in accordance with the provisions of § 121a.620 of Subpart F and § 121a.370 of Subpart C, and

(b) 50 percent shall be distributed to local educational agencies in the State in accordance with § 121a.707.

(20 U.S.C. 1411(b)(1))

§ 121a.706 Within-State distribution: Fiscal year 1979 and after.

Of the funds received under § 121a.701 by any State for fiscal year 1979, and for each fiscal year after fiscal year 1979:

(a) 25 percent may be used by the State in accordance with § 121a.620 of Subpart F and § 121a.370 of Subpart C, and

(b) 75 percent shall be distributed to the local educational agencies in the State in accordance with § 121a.707.

(20 U.S.C. 1411(c)(1))

§ 121a.707 Local educational agency entitlements; formula.

From the total amount of funds available to all local educational agencies, each local educational agency is entitled to an amount which bears the same ratio to the total amount as the number of handicapped children aged three through 21 in that agency who are receiving special education and related services bears to the aggregate number of handicapped children aged three through 21 receiving special education and related services in all local educational agencies which apply to the State educational agency for funds under Part B of the Act.

(20 U.S.C. 1411(d))

§ 121a.708 Reallocation of local educational agency funds.

If a State educational agency determines that a local educational agency is adequately providing a free appropriate public education to all handicapped children residing in the area served by the local agency with State and local funds otherwise available to the local agency, the State educational agency may reallocate funds (or portions of those funds which are not required to provide special education and related services) made available to the local agency under § 121a.707, to other local educational agencies within the State which are not adequately providing special education and related services to all handicapped children residing in the areas served by the other local educational agencies.

(20 U.S.C. 1414(e))

§ 121a.709 Payments to Secretary of Interior.

(a) The Commissioner is authorized to make payments to the Secretary of the Interior according to the need for that assistance for the education of handicapped children on reservations serviced by elementary and secondary schools operated for Indian children by the Department of the Interior.

(b) The amount of those payments for any fiscal year shall not exceed one percent of the aggregate amounts available to all States for that fiscal year under Part B of the Act.

(20 U.S.C. 1411(f)(1))

§ 121a.710 Entitlements to jurisdictions.

(a) The jurisdictions to which this section applies are Guam, American Samoa, the Virgin Islands, and the Trust Territory of the Pacific Islands.

(b) Each jurisdiction under paragraph (a) of this section is entitled to a grant for the purposes set forth in section 601(c) of the Act. The amount to which those jurisdictions are so entitled for any fiscal year shall not exceed an amount equal to 1 percent of the aggregate of the amounts available to all States under this part for that fiscal year. Funds appropriated for those jurisdictions shall be allocated proportionately among them on the basis of the number of children aged three through twenty-one in each jurisdiction. However, no jurisdiction shall receive less than $150,000, and other allocations shall be ratably reduced if necessary to insure that each jurisdiction receives at least that amount.

(c) The amount expended for administration by each jurisdiction under this section shall not exceed 5 percent of the amount allotted to the jurisdiction for any fiscal year, or $35,000, whichever is greater.

(20 U.S.C. 1411(e))

REPORTS

§ 121a.750 Annual report of children served—report requirement.

(a) The State educational agency shall report to the Commissioner no later than February 1 of each year the number of handicapped children aged three through 21 residing in the State who are receiving special education and related services.

(20 U.S.C. 1411(a)(3))

(b) The State educational agency shall submit the report on forms provided by the Commissioner.

(20 U.S.C. 1411(a)(3))

Comment. It is very important to understand that this report and the requirements that relate to it are solely for allocation purposes. The population of children the State may count for allocation purposes may differ from the population of children to whom the State must make available a free appropriate public education. For example, while section 611(a)(5) of the Act limits the number of children who may be counted for allocation purposes to 12 percent of the general school population aged five through seventeen, a State might find that 14 percent (or some other percentage) of its children are handicapped. In that case, the State must make free appropriate public education available to all of those handicapped children.

[42 FR 42476, Aug. 23, 1977, as amended at 45 FR 7551, Feb. 4, 1980]

§ 121a.751 Annual report of children served—information required in the report.

(a) In its report, the State educational agency shall include a table which shows:

(1) The number of handicapped children receiving special education and related services on December 1 of that school year;

(2) The number of those handicapped children within each disability category, as defined in the definition of "handicapped children" in § 121a.5 of Subpart A; and

(3) The number of those handicapped children within each of the following age groups:

(i) Three through five;

(ii) Six through seventeen; and

(iii) Eighteen through twenty-one.

(b) A child must be counted as being in the age group corresponding to his or her age on the date of the count: December 1.

(20 U.S.C. 1411(a)(3); 1411(a)(5)(A)(ii); 1418(b))

(c) The State educational agency may not report a child under more than one disability category.

(d) If a handicapped child has more than one disability, the State educational agency shall report that child in accordance with the following procedure:

(1) A child who is both deaf and blind must be reported as "deaf-blind."

(2) A child who has more than one disability (other than a deaf-blind child) must be reported as "multihandicapped."

(20 U.S.C. 1411(a)(3); 1411(a)(5)(A)(ii); 1418(b))

[42 FR 42476, Aug. 23, 1977, as amended at 45 FR 7551, Feb. 4, 1980]

§ 121a.752 Annual report of children served—certification.

The State educational agency shall include in its report a certification signed by an authorized official of the agency that the information provided is an accurate and unduplicated count of handicapped children receiving special education and related services on the dates in question.

(20 U.S.C. 1411(a)(3); 1417(b))

§ 121a.753 Annual report of children served—criteria for counting children.

(a) The State educational agency may include handicapped children in its report who are enrolled in a school or program which is operated or supported by a public agency, and which either:

(1) Provides them with both special education and related services; or

(2) Provides them only with special education if they do not need related services to assist them in benefitting from that special education.

(b) The State educational agency may not include handicapped children in its report who:

(1) Are not enrolled in a school or program operated or supported by a public agency;

(2) Are not provided special education that meets State standards;

(3) Are not provided with a related service that they need to assist them in benefitting from special education;

(4) Are counted by a State agency under section 121 of the Elementary and Secondary Education Act of 1965, as amended; or

(5) Are receiving special education funded solely by the Federal Government. However, the State may count children covered under § 121a.186(b) of Subpart B.

(20 U.S.C. 1411(a)(3); 1417(b))

Comment. 1. Under paragraph (a), the State may count handicapped children in a Head Start or other preschool program operated or supported by a public agency if those children are provided special education that meets State standards.

2. "Special education," by statutory definition, must be at no cost to parents. As of September 1, 1978, under the free appropriate public education requirement, both special education and related services must be at no cost to parents.

There may be some situations, however, where a child receives special education from a public source at no cost, but whose parents pay for the basic or regular education. This child may be counted. The Office of Education expects that there would only be limited situations where special education would be clearly separate from regular education—generally, where speech therapy is the only special education required by the child. For example, the child might be in a regular program in a parochial or other private school but receiving speech therapy in a program funded by the local educational agency. Allowing these children to be counted will provide incentives (in addition to complying with the legal requirement in section 613(a)(4)(A) of the Act regarding private schools) to public agencies to provide services to children in private schools, since funds are generated in part on the basis of the number of children provided special education and related services. Agencies should understand, however, that where a handicapped child is placed in or referred to a public or private school for educational purposes, special education includes the entire educational program provided to the child. In that case, parents may not be charged for any part of the child's education.

A State may not count Indian children on or near reservations and children on military facilities if it provides them no special education. If a State or local educational agency is responsible for serving these children, and does provide them special education and related services, they may be counted.

§ 121a.754 Annual report of children served—other responsibilities of the State educational agency.

In addition to meeting the other requirements in this subpart, the State educational agency shall:

(a) Establish procedures to be used by local educational agencies and other educational institutions in counting the number of handicapped children receiving special education and related services;

(b) Set dates by which those agencies and institutions must report to the State educational agency to insure that the State complies with § 121a.750(a);

(c) Obtain certification from each agency and institution that an unduplicated and accurate count has been made;

(d) Aggregate the data from the count obtained from each agency and institution, and prepare the reports required under this subpart; and

(e) Insure that documentation is maintained which enables the State and the Commissioner to audit the accuracy of the count.

(20 U.S.C. 1411(a)(3); 1417(b))

Comment. States should note that the data required in the annual report of children served are not to be transmitted to the Commissioner in personally identifiable form. States are encouraged to collect these data in non-personally identifiable form.

APPENDIX A—[RESERVED]

APPENDIX B—INDEX TO PART 121a

ADMINISTRATION

See: Monitoring.

Related Services.

SECTION 504 OF THE REHABILITATION ACT OF 1973 (29 U.S.C. § 794)

"No otherwise qualified handicapped individual in the United States, as defined in . . . this title, shall, solely by reason of his handicap, be excluded from the participation in, be denied the benefits of, or be subjected to discrimination under any program or activity receiving Federal financial assistance or under any program or activity conducted by any Executive agency or by the United States Postal Service. . . ."

Section 504 Regulations (34 C.F.R. Part 104)

These regulations were formerly cited as 45 C.F.R. Part 84.

PART 104—NONDISCRIMINATION ON THE BASIS OF HANDICAP IN PROGRAMS AND ACTIVITIES RECEIVING OR BENEFITING FROM FEDERAL FINANCIAL ASSISTANCE

Subpart G—Procedures

104.61 Procedures.

APPENDIX A—ANALYSIS OF FINAL REGULATION

APPENDIX B—GUIDELINES FOR ELIMINATING DISCRIMINATION AND DENIAL OF SERVICES ON THE BASIS OF RACE, COLOR, NATIONAL ORIGIN, SEX, AND HANDICAP IN VOCATIONAL EDUCATION PROGRAMS

AUTHORITY: Sec. 504, Rehabilitation Act of 1973, Pub. L. 93-112, 87 Stat. 394 (29 U.S.C. 794); sec. 111(a), Rehabilitation Act Amendments of 1974, Pub. L. 93-516, 88 Stat. 1619 (29 U.S.C. 706); sec. 606, Education of the Handicapped Act (20 U.S.C. 1405), as amended by Pub. L. 94-142, 89 Stat. 795.

SOURCE: 45 FR 30936, May 9, 1980, unless otherwise noted.

Subpart A—General Provisions

§ 104.1 Purpose.

The purpose of this part is to effectuate section 504 of the Rehabilitation Act of 1973, which is designed to eliminate discrimination on the basis of handicap in any program or activity receiving Federal financial assistance.

§ 104.2 Application.

This part applies to each recipient of Federal financial assistance from the Department of Education and to each program or activity that receives or benefits from such assistance.

§ 104.3 Definitions.

As used in this part, the term:

(a) "The Act" means the Rehabilitation Act of 1973, Pub. L. 93-112, as amended by the Rehabilitation Act Amendments of 1974, Pub. L. 93-516, 29 U.S.C. 794.

(b) "Section 504" means section 504 of the Act.

(c) "Education of the Handicapped Act" means that statute as amended by the Education for all Handicapped Children Act of 1975, Pub. L. 94-142, 20 U.S.C. 1401 et seq.

(d) "Department" means the Department of Education.

(e) "Assistant Secretary" means the Assistant Secretary for Civil Rights of the Department of Education.

(f) "Recipient" means any state or its political subdivision, any instrumentality of a state or its political subdivision, any public or private agency, institution, organization, or other entity, or any person to which Federal financial assistance is extended directly or through another recipient, including any successor, assignee, or transferee of a recipient, but excluding the ultimate beneficiary of the assistance.

(g) "Applicant for assistance" means one who submits an application, request, or plan required to be approved by a Department official or by a recipient as a condition to becoming a recipient.

(h) "Federal financial assistance" means any grant, loan, contract (other than a procurement contract or a contract of insurance or guaranty), or any other arrangement by which the Department provides or otherwise makes available assistance in the form of:

(1) Funds;

(2) Services of Federal personnel; or

(3) Real and personal property or any interest in or use of such property, including:

(i) Transfers or leases of such property for less than fair market value or for reduced consideration; and

(ii) Proceeds from a subsequent transfer or lease of such property if the Federal share of its fair market value is not returned to the Federal Government.

(i) "Facility" means all or any portion of buildings, structures, equipment, roads, walks, parking lots, or other real or personal property or interest in such property.

(j) "Handicapped person." (1) "Handicapped persons" means any person who (i) has a physical or mental impairment which substantially limits one or more major life activities, (ii) has a record of such an impairment, or (iii) is regarded as having such an impairment.

(2) As used in paragraph (j)(1) of this section, the phrase:

(i) "Physical or mental impairment" means (A) any physiological disorder or condition, cosmetic disfigurement, or anatomical loss affecting one or more of the following body systems:

neurological; musculoskeletal; special sense organs; respiratory, including speech organs; cardiovascular; reproductive, digestive, genito-urinary; hemic and lymphatic; skin; and endocrine; or (B) any mental or psychological disorder, such as mental retardation, organic brain syndrome, emotional or mental illness, and specific learning disabilities.

(ii) "Major life activities" means functions such as caring for one's self, performing manual tasks, walking, seeing, hearing, speaking, breathing, learning, and working.

(iii) "Has a record of such an impairment" means has a history of, or has been misclassified as having, a mental or physical impairment that substantially limits one or more major life activities.

(iv) "Is regarded as having an impairment" means (A) has a physical or mental impairment that does not substantially limit major life activities but that is treated by a recipient as constituting such a limitation; (B) has a physical or mental impairment that substantially limits major life activities only as a result of the attitudes of others toward such impairment; or (C) has none of the impairments defined in paragraph (j)(2)(i) of this section but is treated by a recipient as having such an impairment.

(k) "Qualified handicapped person" means:

(1) With respect to employment, a handicapped person who, with reasonable accommodation, can perform the essential functions of the job in question;

(2) With respect to public preschool elementary, secondary, or adult educational services, a handicappped person (i) of an age during which nonhandicapped persons are provided such services, (ii) of any age during which it is mandatory under state law to provide such services to handicapped persons, or (iii) to whom a state is required to provide a free appropriate public education under section 612 of the Education of the Handicapped Act; and

(3) With respect to postsecondary and vocational education services, a handicapped person who meets the academic and technical standards req-

uisite to admission or participation in the recipient's education program or activity;

(4) With respect to other services, a handicapped person who meets the essential eligibility requirements for the receipt of such services.

(l) "Handicap" means any condition or characteristic that renders a person a handicapped person as defined in paragraph (j) of this section.

§ 104.4 Discrimination prohibited.

(a) *General.* No qualified handicapped person shall, on the basis of handicap, be excluded from participation in, be denied the benefits of, or otherwise be subjected to discrimination under any program or activitiy which receives or benefits from Federal financial assistance.

(b) *Discriminatory actions prohibited.* (1) A recipient, in providing any aid, benefit, or service, may not, directly or through contractual, licensing, or other arrangements, on the basis of handicap:

(i) Deny a qualified handicapped person the opportunity to participate in or benefit from the aid, benefit, or service;

(ii) Afford a qualified handicapped person an opportunity to participate in or benefit from the aid, benefit, or service that is not equal to that afforded others;

(iii) Provide a qualified handicapped person with an aid, benefit, or service that is not as effective as that provided to others;

(iv) Provide different or separate aid, benefits, or services to handicapped persons or to any class of handicapped persons unless such action is necessary to provide qualified handicapped persons with aid, benefits, or services that are as effective as those provided to others;

(v) Aid or perpetuate discrimination against a qualified handicapped person by providing significant assistance to an agency, organization, or person that discriminates on the basis of handicap in providing any aid, benefit, or service to beneficiaries of the recipient's program;

(vi) Deny a qualified handicapped person the opportunity to participate as a member of planning or advisory boards; or

(vii) Otherwise limit a qualified handicapped person in the enjoyment of any right, privilege, advantage, or opportunity enjoyed by others receiving an aid, benefit, or service.

(2) For purposes of this part, aids, benefits, and services, to be equally effective, are not required to produce the identical result or level of achievement for handicapped and nonhandicapped persons, but must afford handicapped persons equal opportunity to obtain the same result, to gain the same benefit, or to reach the same level of achievement, in the most integrated setting appropriate to the person's needs.

(3) Despite the existence of separate or different programs or activities provided in accordance with this part, a recipient may not deny a qualified handicapped person the opportunity to participate in such programs or activities that are not separate or different.

(4) A recipient may not, directly or through contractual or other arrangements, utilize criteria or methods of administration (i) that have the effect of subjecting qualified handicapped persons to discrimination on the basis of handicap, (ii) that have the purpose or effect of defeating or substantially impairing accomplishment of the objectives of the recipient's program with respect to handicapped persons, or (iii) that perpetuate the discrimination of another recipient if both recipients are subject to common administrative control or are agencies of the same State.

(5) In determining the site or location of a facility, an applicant for assistance or a recipient may not make selections (i) that have the effect of excluding handicapped persons from, denying them the benefits of, or otherwise subjecting them to discrimination under any program or activity that receives or benefits from Federal financial assistance or (ii) that have the purpose or effect of defeating or substantially impairing the accomplishment of the objectives of the program or activity with respect to handicapped persons.

(6) As used in this section, the aid, benefit, or service provided under a program or activity receiving or benefiting from Federal financial assistance includes any aid, benefit, or service provided in or through a facility that has been constructed, expanded, altered, leased or rented, or otherwise acquired, in whole or in part, with Federal financial assistance.

(c) *Programs limited by Federal law.* The exclusion of nonhandicapped persons from the benefits of a program limited by Federal statute or executive order to handicapped persons or the exclusion of a specific class of handicapped persons from a program limited by Federal statute or executive order to a different class of handicapped persons is not prohibited by this part.

§ 104.5 Assurances required.

(a) *Assurances.* An applicant for Federal financial assistance for a program or activity to which this part applies shall submit an assurance, on a form specified by the Assistant Secretary, that the program will be operated in compliance with this part. An applicant may incorporate these assurances by reference in subsequent applications to the Department.

(b) *Duration of obligation.* (1) In the case of Federal financial assistance extended in the form of real property or to provide real property or structures on the property, the assurance will obligate the recipient or, in the case of a subsequent transfer, the transferee, for the period during which the real property or structures are used for the purpose for which Federal financial assistance is extended or for another purpose involving the provision of similar services or benefits.

(2) In the case of Federal financial assistance extended to provide personal property, the assurance will obligate the recipient for the period during which it retains ownership or possession of the property.

(3) In all other cases the assurance will obligate the recipient for the period during which Federal financial assistance is extended.

(c) *Covenants.* (1) Where Federal financial assistance is provided in the form of real property or interest in the property from the Department, the instrument effecting or recording this transfer shall contain a covenant running with the land to assure non-discrimination for the period during which the real property is used for a purpose for which the Federal financial assistance is extended or for another purpose involving the provision of similar services or benefits.

(2) Where no transfer of property is involved but property is purchased or improved with Federal financial assistance, the recipient shall agree to include the covenant described in paragraph (b)(2) of this section in the instrument effecting or recording any subsequent transfer of the property.

(3) Where Federal financial assistance is provided in the form of real property or interest in the property from the Department, the covenant shall also include a condition coupled with a right to be reserved by the Department to revert title to the property in the event of a breach of the covenant. If a transferee of real property proposes to mortgage or otherwise encumber the real property as security for financing construction of new, or improvement of existing, facilities on the property for the purposes for which the property was transferred, the Assistant Secretary may, upon request of the transferee and if necessary to accomplish such financing and upon such conditions as he or she deems appropriate, agree to forbear the exercise of such right to revert title for so long as the lien of such mortgage or other encumbrance remains effective.

§ 104.6 Remedial action, voluntary action, and self-evaluation.

(a) *Remedial action.* (1) If the Assistant Secretary finds that a recipient has discriminated against persons on the basis of handicap in violation of section 504 or this part, the recipient shall take such remedial action as the Assistant Secretary deems necessary to overcome the effects of the discrimination.

(2) Where a recipient is found to have discriminated against persons on the basis of handicap in violation of section 504 or this part and where another recipient exercises control over the recipient that has discriminated, the Assistant Secretary, where appro-

priate, may require either or both recipients to take remedial action.

(3) The Assistant Secretary may, where necessary to overcome the effects of discrimination in violation of section 504 or this part, require a recipient to take remedial action (i) with respect to handicapped persons who are no longer participants in the recipient's program but who were participants in the program when such discrimination occurred or (ii) with respect to handicapped persons who would have been participants in the program had the discrimination not occurred.

(b) *Voluntary action.* A recipient may take steps, in addition to any action that is required by this part, to overcome the effects of conditions that resulted in limited participation in the recipient's program or activity by qualified handicapped persons.

(c) *Self-evaluation.* (1) A recipient shall, within one year of the effective date of this part:

(i) Evaluate, with the assistance of interested persons, including handicapped persons or organizations representing handicapped persons, its current policies and practices and the effects thereof that do not or may not meet the requirements of this part;

(ii) Modify, after consultation with interested persons, including handicapped persons or organizations representing handicapped persons, any policies and practices that do not meet the requirements of this part; and

(iii) Take, after consultation with interested persons, including handicapped persons or organizations representing handicapped persons, appropriate remedial steps to eliminate the effects of any discrimination that resulted from adherence to these policies and practices.

(2) A recipient that employs fifteen or more persons shall, for at least three years following completion of the evaluation required under paragraph (c)(1) of this section, maintain on file, make available for public inspection, and provide to the Assistant Secretary upon request: (i) A list of the interested persons consulted, (ii) a description of areas examined and any problems identified, and (iii) a description of any modifications made and of any remedial steps taken.

§ 104.7 Designation of responsible employee and adoption of grievance procedures.

(a) *Designation of responsible employee.* A recipient that employs fifteen or more persons shall designate at least one person to coordinate its efforts to comply with this part.

(b) *Adoption of grievance procedures.* A recipient that employs fifteen or more persons shall adopt grievance procedures that incorporate appropriate due process standards and that provide for the prompt and equitable resolution of complaints alleging any action prohibited by this part. Such procedures need not be established with respect to complaints from applicants for employment or from applicants for admission to postsecondary educational institutions.

§ 104.8 Notice.

(a) A recipient that employs fifteen or more persons shall take appropriate initial and continuing steps to notify participants, beneficiaries, applications, and employees, including those with impaired vision or hearing, and unions or professional organizations holding collective bargaining or professional agreements with the recipient that it does not discriminate on the basis of handicap in violation of section 504 and this part. The notification shall state, where appropriate, that the recipient does not discriminate in admission or access to, or treatment or employment in, its programs and activities. The notification shall also include an identification of the responsible employee designated pursuant to § 104.7(a). A recipient shall make the initial notification required by this paragraph within 90 days of the effective date of this part. Methods of initial and continuing notification may include the posting of notices, publication in newspapers and magazines, placement of notices in recipients' publication, and distribution of memoranda or other written communications.

(b) If a recipient publishes or uses recruitment materials or publications containing general information that it makes available to participants, beneficiaries, applicants, or employees, it shall include in those materials or publications a statement of the policy described in paragraph (a) of this section. A recipient may meet the requirement of this paragraph either by including appropriate inserts in existing materials and publications or by revising and reprinting the materials and publications.

§ 104.9 Administrative requirements for small recipients.

The Assistant Secretary may require any recipient with fewer than fifteen employees, or any class of such recipients, to comply with §§ 104.7 and 104.8, in whole or in part, when the Assistant Secretary finds a violation of this part or finds that such compliance will not significantly impair the ability of the recipient or class of recipients to provide benefits or services.

§ 104.10 Effect of state or local law or other requirements and effect of employment opportunities.

(a) The obligation to comply with this part is not obviated or alleviated by the existence of any state or local law or other requirement that, on the basis of handicap, imposes prohibitions or limits upon the eligibility of qualified handicapped persons to receive services or to practice any occupation or profession.

(b) The obligation to comply with this part is not obviated or alleviated because employment opportunities in any occupation or profession are or may be more limited for handicapped persons than for nonhandicapped persons.

Subpart B—Employment Practices

§ 104.11 Discrimination prohibited.

(a) *General.* (1) No qualified handicapped person shall, on the basis of handicap, be subjected to discrimination in employment under any program or activity to which this part applies.

(2) A recipient that receives assistance under the Education of the Handicapped Act shall take positive steps to employ and advance in employment qualified handicapped persons in programs assisted under that Act.

(3) A recipient shall make all decisions concerning employment under any program or activity to which this

part applies in a manner which ensures that discrimination on the basis of handicap does not occur and may not limit, segregate, or classify applicants or employees in any way that adversely affects their opportunities or status because of handicap.

(4) A recipient may not participate in a contractual or other relationship that has the effect of subjecting qualified handicapped applicants or employees to discrimination prohibited by this subpart. The relationships referred to in this paragraph include relationships with employment and referral agencies, with labor unions, with organizations providing or administering fringe benefits to employees of the recipient, and with organizations providing training and apprenticeship programs.

(b) *Specific activities.* The provisions of this subpart apply to:

(1) Recruitment, advertising, and the processing of applications for employment;

(2) Hiring, upgrading, promotion, award of tenure, demotion, transfer, layoff, termination, right of return from layoff and rehiring;

(3) Rates of pay or any other form of compensation and changes in compensation;

(4) Job assignments, job classifications, organizational structures, position descriptions, lines of progression, and seniority lists;

(5) Leaves of absense, sick leave, or any other leave;

(6) Fringe benefits available by virtue of employment, whether or not administered by the recipient;

(7) Selection and financial support for training, including apprenticeship, professional meetings, conferences, and other related activities, and selection for leaves of absence to pursue training;

(8) Employer sponsored activities, including social or recreational programs; and

(9) Any other term, condition, or privilege of employment.

(c) A recipient's obligation to comply with this subpart is not affected by any inconsistent term of any collective bargaining agreement to which it is a party.

§ 104.12 Reasonable accommodation.

(a) A recipient shall make reasonable accommodation to the known physical or mental limitations of an otherwise qualified handicapped applicant or employee unless the recipient can demonstrate that the accommodation would impose an undue hardship on the operation of its program.

(b) Reasonable accommodation may include: (1) Making facilities used by employees readily accessible to and usable by handicapped persons, and (2) job restructuring, part-time or modified work schedules, acquisition or modification of equipment or devices, the provision of readers or interpreters, and other similar actions.

(c) In determining pursuant to paragraph (a) of this section whether an accommodation would impose an undue hardship on the operation of a recipient's program, factors to be considered include:

(1) The overall size of the recipient's program with respect to number of employees, number and type of facilities, and size of budget;

(2) The type of the recipient's operation, including the composition and structure of the recipient's workforce; and

(3) The nature and cost of the accommodation needed.

(d) A recipient may not deny any employment opportunity to a qualified handicapped employee or applicant if the basis for the denial is the need to make reasonable accommodation to the physical or mental limitations of the employee or applicant.

§ 104.13 Employment criteria.

(a) A recipient may not make use of any employment test or other selection criterion that screens out or tends to screen out handicapped persons or any class of handicapped persons unless: (1) The test score or other selection criterion, as used by the recipient, is shown to be job-related for the position in question, and (2) alternative job-related tests or criteria that do not screen out or tend to screen out as many handicapped persons are not shown by the Director to be available.

(b) A recipient shall select and administer tests concerning employment so as best to ensure that, when administered to an applicant or employee who has a handicap that impairs sensory, manual, or speaking skills, the test results accurately reflect the applicant's or employee's job skills, aptitude, or whatever other factor the test purports to measure, rather than reflecting the applicant's or employee's impaired sensory, manual, or speaking skills (except where those skills are the factors that the test purports to measure).

§ 104.14   Preemployment inquiries.

(a) Except as provided in paragraphs (b) and (c) of this section, a recipient may not conduct a preemployment medical examination or may not make preemployment inquiry of an applicant as to whether the applicant is a handicapped person or as to the nature or severity of a handicap. A recipient may, however, make preemployment inquiry into an applicant's ability to perform job-related functions.

(b) When a recipient is taking remedial action to correct the effects of past discrimination pursuant to § 84.6 (a), when a recipient is taking voluntary action to overcome the effects of conditions that resulted in limited participation in its federally assisted program or activity pursuant to § 84.6(b), or when a recipient is taking affirmative action pursuant to section 503 of the Act, the recipient may invite applicants for employment to indicate whether and to what extent they are handicapped, *Provided,* That:

(1) The recipient states clearly on any written questionnaire used for this purpose or makes clear orally if no written questionnaire is used that the information requested is intended for use solely in connection with its remedial action obligations or its voluntary or affirmative action efforts; and

(2) The recipient states clearly that the information is being requested on a voluntary basis, that it will be kept confidential as provided in paragraph (d) of this section, that refusal to provide it will not subject the applicant or employee to any adverse treatment, and that it will be used only in accordance with this part.

(c) Nothing in this section shall prohibit a recipient from conditioning an offer of employment on the results of a medical examination conducted prior to the employee's entrance on duty, *Provided,* That: (1) All entering employees are subjected to such an examination regardless of handicap, and (2) the results of such an examination are used only in accordance with the requirements of this part.

(d) Information obtained in accordance with this section as to the medical condition or history of the applicant shall be collected and maintained on separate forms that shall be accorded confidentiality as medical records, except that:

(1) Supervisors and managers may be informed regarding restrictions on the work or duties of handicapped persons and regarding necessary accommodations;

(2) First aid and safety personnel may be informed, where appropriate, if the condition might require emergency treatment; and

(3) Government officials investigating compliance with the Act shall be provided relevant information upon request.

Subpart C—Program Accessibility

§ 104.21   Discrimination prohibited.

No qualified handicapped person shall, because a recipient's facilities are inaccessible to or unusable by handicapped persons, be denied the benefits of, be excluded from participation in, or otherwise be subjected to discrimination under any program or activity to which this part applies.

§ 104.22   Existing facilities.

(a) *Program accessibility.* A recipient shall operate each program or activity to which this part applies so that the program or activity, when viewed in its entirety, is readily accessible to handicapped persons. This paragraph does not require a recipient to make each of its existing facilities or every part of a facility accessible to and usable by handicapped persons.

(b) *Methods.* A recipient may comply with the requirements of paragraph (a) of this section through such means as redesign of equipment, reassignment of classes or other services to accessible buildings, assignment of aides to beneficiaries, home visits, delivery of health, welfare, or other social services at alternate accessible sites, alteration of existing facilities and construction of new facilities in conformance with the requirements of § 104.23, or any other methods that result in making its program or activity accessible to handicapped persons. A recipient is not required to make structural changes in existing facilities where other methods are effective in achieving compliance with paragraph (a) of this section. In choosing among available methods for meeting the requirement of paragraph (a) of this section, a recipient shall give priority to those methods that offer programs and activities to handicapped persons in the most integrated setting appropriate.

(c) *Small health, welfare, or other social service providers.* If a recipient with fewer than fifteen employees that provides health, welfare, or other social services finds, after consultation with a handicapped person seeking its services, that there is no method of complying with paragraph (a) of this section other than making a significant alteration in its existing facilities, the recipient may, as an alternative, refer the handicapped person to other providers of those services that are accessible.

(d) *Time period.* A recipient shall comply with the requirement of paragraph (a) of this section within sixty days of the effective date of this part except that where structural changes in facilities are necessary, such changes shall be made within three years of the effective date of this part, but in any event as expeditiously as possible.

(e) *Transition plan.* In the event that structural changes to facilities are necessary to meet the requirement of paragraph (a) of this section, a recipient shall develop, within six months of the effective date of this part, a transition plan setting forth the steps necessary to complete such changes. The plan shall be developed with the assistance of interested persons, including handicapped persons or organizations representing handicapped persons. A copy of the transition plan shall be made available for public inspection. The plan shall, at a minimum:

(1) Identify physical obstacles in the recipient's facilities that limit the accessibility of its program or activity to handicappped persons;

(2) Describe in detail the methods that will be used to make the facilities accessible;

(3) Specify the schedule for taking the steps necessary to achieve full program accessibility and, if the time period of the transition plan is longer than one year, identify the steps of that will be taken during each year of the transition period; and

(4) Indicate the person responsible for implementation of the plan.

(f) *Notice.* The recipient shall adopt and implement procedures to ensure that interested persons, including persons with impaired vision or hearing, can obtain information as to the existence and location of services, activities, and facilities that are accessible to and usable   by handicapped persons.

§ 104.23   New construction.

(a) *Design and construction.* Each facility or part of a facility constructed by, on behalf of, or for the use of a recipient shall be designed and constructed in such manner that the facility or part of the facility is readily accessible to and usable by handicapped persons, if the construction was commenced after the effective date of this part.

(b) *Alteration.* Each facility or part of a facility which is altered by, on behalf of, or for the use of a recipient after the effective date of this part in a manner that affects or could affect the usability of the facility or part of the facility shall, to the maximum extent feasible, be altered in such manner that the altered portion of the facility is readily accessible to and usable by handicapped persons.

(c) *American National Standards Institute accessibility standards.* Design, construction, or alteration of facilities in conformance with the "American National Standard Specifications for Making Buildings and Facilities Accessible to, and Usable by, the Physically Handicapped," published by the American National Standards Institute, Inc. (ANSI A117.1-1961 (R1971)), which is incorporated by reference in this part, shall constitute compliance with paragraphs (a) and (b) of this section. Departures from particular requirements of those standards by the use of other methods shall be permitted when it is clearly evident that equivalent access to the facility or part of the facility is thereby provided. Incorporation by reference provisions approved by the Director of the Federal Register, May 27, 1975. Incorporated documents are on file at the Office of the Federal Register.

Copies of the standards are obtainable from American National Standards Institute, Inc., 1430 Broadway, New York, N.Y. 10018.

[45 FR 30936, May 9, 1980; 45 FR 37426, June 3, 1980]

Subpart D—Preschool, Elementary, and Secondary Education

§ 104.31 Application of this subpart.

Subpart D applies to preschool, elementary, secondary, and adult education programs and activities that receive or benefit from Federal financial assistance and to recipients that operate, or that receive or benefit from Federal financial assistance for the operation of, such programs or activities.

§ 104.32 Location and notification.

A recipient that operates a public elementary or secondary education program shall annually:

(a) Undertake to identify and locate every qualified handicapped person residing in the recipient's jurisdiction who is not receiving a public education; and

(b) Take appropriate steps to notify handicapped persons and their parents or guardians of the recipient's duty under this subpart.

§ 104.33 Free appropriate public education.

(a) *General.* A recipient that operates a public elementary or secondary education program shall provide a free appropriate public education to each qualified handicapped person who is in the recipient's jurisdiction, regardless of the nature or severity of the person's handicap.

(b) *Appropriate education.* (1) For the purpose of this subpart, the provision of an appropriate education is the provision of regular or special education and related aids and services that (i) are designed to meet individual educational needs of handicapped persons as adequately as the needs of nonhandicapped persons are met and (ii) are based upon adherence to procedures that satisfy the requirements of §§ 104.34, 104.35, and 104.36.

(2) Implementation of an individualized education program developed in accordance with the Education of the Handicapped Act is one means of meeting the standard established in paragraph (b)(1)(i) of this section.

(3) A recipient may place a handicapped person in or refer such person to a program other than the one that it operates as its means of carrying out the requirements of this subpart. If so, the recipient remains responsible for ensuring that the requirements of this subpart are met with respect to any handicapped person so placed or referred.

(c) *Free education—*(1) *General.* For the purpose of this section, the provision of a free education is the provision of educational and related services without cost to the handicapped person or to his or her parents or guardian, except for those fees that are imposed on non-handicapped persons or their parents or guardian. It may consist either of the provision of free services or, if a recipient places a handicapped person in or refers such person to a program not operated by the recipient as its means of carrying out the requirements of this subpart, of payment for the costs of the program. Funds available from any public or private agency may be used to meet the requirements of this subpart. Nothing in this section shall be construed to relieve an insurer or similar third party from an otherwise valid obligation to provide or pay for services provided to a handicapped person.

(2) *Transportation.* If a recipient places a handicapped person in or refers such person to a program not operated by the recipient as its means of carrying out the requirements of this subpart, the recipient shall ensure that adequate transportation to and from the program is provided at no greater cost than would be incurred by the person or his or her parents or

guardian if the person were placed in the program operated by the recipient.

(3) *Residential placement.* If placement in a public or private residential program is necessary to provide a free appropriate public education to a handicapped person because of his or her handicap, the program, including non-medical care and room and board, shall be provided at no cost to the person or his or her parents or guardian.

(4) *Placement of handicapped persons by parents.* If a recipient has made available, in conformance with the requirements of this section and § 104.34, a free appropriate public education to a handicapped person and the person's parents or guardian choose to place the person in a private school, the recipient is not required to pay for the person's education in the private school. Disagreements between a parent or guardian and a recipient regarding whether the recipient has made such a program available or otherwise regarding the question of financial responsibility are subject to the due process procedures of § 104.36.

(d) *Compliance.* A recipient may not exclude any qualified handicapped person from a public elementary or secondary education after the effective date of this part. A recipient that is not, on the effective date of this regulation, in full compliance with the other requirements of the preceding paragraphs of this section shall meet such requirements at the earliest practicable time and in no event later than September 1, 1978.

§ 104.34 Educational setting.

(a) *Academic setting.* A recipient to which this subpart applies shall educate, or shall provide for the education of, each qualified handicapped person in its jurisdiction with persons who are not handicapped to the maximum extent appropriate to the needs of the handicapped person. A recipient shall place a handicapped person in the regular educational environment operated by the recipient unless it is demonstrated by the recipient that the education of the person in the regular environment with the use of supplementary aids and services cannot be achieved satisfactorily. Whenever a re-

cipient places a person in a setting other than the regular educational environment pursuant to this paragraph, it shall take into account the proximity of the alternate setting to the person's home.

(b) *Nonacademic settings.* In providing or arranging for the provision of nonacademic and extracurricular services and activities, including meals, recess periods, and the services and activities set forth in § 104.37(a)(2), a recipient shall ensure that handicapped persons participate with nonhandicapped persons in such activities and services to the maximum extent appropriate to the needs of the handicapped person in question.

(c) *Comparable facilities.* If a recipient, in compliance with paragraph (a) of this section, operates a facility that is identifiable as being for handicapped persons, the recipient shall ensure that the facility and the services and activities provided therein are comparable to the other facilities, services, and activities of the recipient.

§ 104.35 Evaluation and placement.

(a) *Preplacement evaluation.* A recipient that operates a public elementary or secondary education program shall conduct an evaluation in accordance with the requirements of paragraph (b) of this section of any person who, because of handicap, needs or is believed to need special education or related services before taking any action with respect to the initial placement of the person in a regular or special education program and any subsequent significant change in placement.

(b) *Evaluation procedures.* A recipient to which this subpart applies shall establish standards and procedures for the evaluation and placement of persons who, because of handicap, need or are believed to need special education or related services which ensure that:

(1) Tests and other evaluation materials have been validated for the specific purpose for which they are used and are administered by trained personnel in conformance with the instructions provided by their producer;

(2) Tests and other evaluation materials include those tailored to assess

specific areas of educational need and not merely those which are designed to provide a single general intelligence quotient; and

(3) Tests are selected and administered so as best to ensure that, when a test is administered to a student with impaired sensory, manual, or speaking skills, the test results accurately reflect the student's aptitude or achievement level or whatever other factor the test purports to measure, rather than reflecting the student's impaired sensory, manual, or speaking skills (except where those skills are the factors that the test purports to measure).

(c) *Placement procedures.* In interpreting evaluation data and in making placement decisions, a recipient shall (1) draw upon information from a variety of sources, including aptitude and achievement tests, teacher recommendations, physical condition, social or cultural background, and adaptive behavior, (2) establish procedures to ensure that information obtained from all such sources is documented and carefully considered, (3) ensure that the placement decision is made by a group of persons, including persons knowledgeable about the child, the meaning of the evaluation data, and the placement options, and (4) ensure that the placement decision is made in conformity with § 104.34.

(d) *Reevaluation.* A recipient to which this section applies shall establish procedures, in accordance with paragraph (b) of this section, for periodic reevaluation of students who have been provided special education and related services. A reevaluation procedure consistent with the Education for the Handicapped Act is one means of meeting this requirement.

§ 104.36   Procedural safeguards.

A recipient that operates a public elementary or secondary education program shall establish and implement, with respect to actions regarding the identification, evaluation, or educational placement of persons who, because of handicap, need or are believed to need special instruction or related services, a system of procedural safeguards that includes notice, an opportunity for the parents or guardian of the person to examine relevant records, an impartial hearing with opportunity for participation by the person's parents or guardian and representation by counsel, and a review procedure. Compliance with the procedural safeguards of section 615 of the Education of the Handicapped Act is one means of meeting this requirement.

§ 104.37   Nonacademic services.

(a) *General.* (1) A recipient to which this subpart applies shall provide nonacademic and extracurricular services and activities in such manner as is necessary to afford handicapped students an equal opportunity for participation in such services and activities.

(2) Nonacademic and extracurricular services and activities may include counseling services, physical recreational athletics, transportation, health services, recreational activities, special interest groups or clubs sponsored by the recipients, referrals to agencies which provide assistance to handicapped persons, and employment of students, including both employment by the recipient and assistance in making available outside employment.

(b) *Counseling services.* A recipient to which this subpart applies that provides personal, academic, or vocational counseling, guidance, or placement services to its students shall provide these services without discrimination on the basis of handicap. The recipient shall ensure that qualified handicapped students are not counseled toward more restrictive career objectives than are nonhandicapped students with similar interests and abilities.

(c) *Physical education and athletics.* (1) In providing physical education courses and athletics and similar programs and activities to any of its students, a recipient to which this subpart applies may not discriminate on the basis of handicap. A recipient that offers physical education courses or that operates or sponsors interscholastic, club, or intramural athletics shall provide to qualified handicapped students an equal opportunity for participation in these activities.

(2) A recipient may offer to handi-

capped students physical education and athletic activities that are separate or different from those offered to nonhandicapped students only if separation or differentiation is consistent with the requirements of § 104.34 and only if no qualified handicapped student is denied the opportunity to compete for teams or to participate in courses that are not separate or different.

§ 104.38 Preschool and adult education programs.

A recipient to which this subpart applies that operates a preschool education or day care program or activity or an adult education program or activity may not, on the basis of handicap, exclude qualified handicapped persons from the program or activity and shall take into account the needs of such persons in determining the aid, benefits, or services to be provided under the program or activity.

§ 104.39 Private education programs.

(a) A recipient that operates a private elementary or secondary education program may not, on the basis of handicap, exclude a qualified handicapped person from such program if the person can, with minor adjustments, be provided an appropriate education, as defined in § 104.33(b)(1), within the recipient's program.

(b) A recipient to which this section applies may not charge more for the provision of an appropriate education to handicapped persons than to nonhandicapped persons except to the extent that any additional charge is justified by a substantial increase in cost to the recipient.

(c) A recipient to which this section applies that operates special education programs shall operate such programs in accordance with the provisions of §§ 104.35 and 104.36. Each recipient to which this section applies is subject to the provisions of §§ 104.34, 104.37, and 104.38.

Subpart E—Postsecondary Education

§ 104.41 Application of this subpart.

Subpart E applies to postsecondary education programs and activities, including postsecondary vocational education programs and activities, that receive or benefit from Federal financial assistance and to recipients that operate, or that receive or benefit from Federal financial assistance for the operation of, such programs or activities.

§ 104.42 Admissions and recruitment.

(a) *General.* Qualified handicapped persons may not, on the basis of handicap, be denied admission or be subjected to discrimination in admission or recruitment by a recipient to which this subpart applies.

(b) *Admissions.* In administering its admission policies, a recipient to which this subpart applies:

(1) May not apply limitations upon the number or proportion of handicapped persons who may be admitted;

(2) May not make use of any test or criterion for admission that has a disproportionate, adverse effect on handicapped persons or any class of handicapped persons unless (i) the test or criterion, as used by the recipient, has been validated as a predictor of success in the education program or activity in question and (ii) alternate tests or criteria that have a less disproportionate, adverse effect are not shown by the Assistant Secretary to be available.

(3) Shall assure itself that (i) admissions tests are selected and administered so as best to ensure that, when a test is administered to an applicant who has a handicap that impairs sensory, manual, or speaking skills, the test results accurately reflect the applicant's aptitude or achievement level or whatever other factor the test purports to measure, rather than reflecting the applicant's impaired sensory, manual, or speaking skills (except where those skills are the factors that the test purports to measure); (ii) admissions tests that are designed for persons with impaired sensory, manual, or speaking skills are offered as often and in as timely a manner as are other admissions tests; and (iii) admissions tests are administered in facilities that, on the whole, are accessible to handicapped persons; and

(4) Except as provided in paragraph (c) of this section, may not make

preadmission inquiry as to whether an applicant for admission is a handicapped person but, after admission, may make inquiries on a confidential basis as to handicaps that may require accommodation.

(c) *Preadmission inquiry exception.* When a recipient is taking remedial action to correct the effects of past discrimination pursuant to § 104.6(a) or when a recipient is taking voluntary action to overcome the effects of conditions that resulted in limited participation in its federally assisted program or activity pursuant to § 104.6(b), the recipient may invite applicants for admission to indicate whether and to what extent they are handicapped, *Provided,* That:

(1) The recipient states clearly on any written questionnaire used for this purpose or makes clear orally if no written questionnaire is used that the information requested is intended for use solely in connection with its remedial action obligations or its voluntary action efforts; and

(2) The recipient states clearly that the information is being requested on a voluntary basis, that it will be kept confidential, that refusal to provide it will not subject the applicant to any adverse treatment, and that it will be used only in accordance with this part.

(d) *Validity studies.* For the purpose of paragraph (b)(2) of this section, a recipient may base prediction equations on first year grades, but shall conduct periodic validity studies against the criterion of overall success in the education program or activity in question in order to monitor the general validity of the test scores.

§ 104.43   Treatment of students; general.

(a) No qualified handicapped student shall, on the basis of handicap, be excluded from participation in, be denied the benefits of, or otherwise be subjected to discrimination under any academic, research, occupational training, housing, health insurance, counseling, financial aid, physical education, athletics, recreation, transportation, other extracurricular, or other postsecondary education program or activity to which this subpart applies.

(b) A recipient to which this subpart applies that considers participation by students in education programs or activities not operated wholly by the recipient as part of, or equivalent to, an education program or activity operated by the recipient shall assure itself that the other education program or activity, as a whole, provides an equal opportunity for the participation of qualified handicapped persons.

(c) A recipient to which this subpart applies may not, on the basis of handicap, exclude any qualified handicapped student from any course, course of study, or other part of its education program or activity.

(d) A recipient to which this subpart applies shall operate its programs and activities in the most integrated setting appropriate.

§ 104.44   Academic adjustments.

(a) *Academic requirements.* A recipient to which this subpart applies shall make such modifications to its academic requirements as are necessary to ensure that such requirements do not discriminate or have the effect of discriminating, on the basis of handicap, against a qualified handicapped applicant or student. Academic requirements that the recipient can demonstrate are essential to the program of instruction being pursued by such student or to any directly related licensing requirement will not be regarded as discriminatory within the meaning of this section. Modifications may include changes in the length of time permitted for the completion of degree requirements, substitution of specific courses required for the completion of degree requirements, and adaptation of the manner in which specific courses are conducted.

(b) *Other rules.* A recipient to which this subpart applies may not impose upon handicapped students other rules, such as the prohibition of tape recorders in classrooms or of dog guides in campus buildings, that have the effect of limiting the participation of handicapped students in the recipient's education program or activity.

(c) *Course examinations.* In its course examinations or other procedures for evaluating students' academic achievement in its program, a recipient to which this subpart applies shall provide such methods for evaluating the achievement of students who have a handicap that impairs sensory, manual, or speaking skills as will best ensure that the results of the evaluation represent the student's achievement in the course, rather than reflecting the student's impaired sensory, manual, or speaking skills (except where such skills are the factors that the test purports to measure).

(d) *Auxiliary aids.* (1) A recipient to which this subpart applies shall take such steps as are necessary to ensure that no handicapped student is denied the benefits of, excluded from participation in, or otherwise subjected to discrimination under the education program or activity operated by the recipient because of the absence of educational auxiliary aids for students with impaired sensory, manual, or speaking skills.

(2) Auxiliary aids may include taped texts, interpreters or other effective methods of making orally delivered materials available to students with hearing impairments, readers in libraries for students with visual impairments, classroom equipment adapted for use by students with manual impairments, and other similar services and actions. Recipients need not provide attendants, individually prescribed devices, readers for personal use or study, or other devices or services of a personal nature.

§ 104.45   Housing.

(a) *Housing provided by the recipient.* A recipient that provides housing to its nonhandicapped students shall provide comparable, convenient, and accessible housing to handicapped students at the same cost as to others. At the end of the transition period provided for in Subpart C, such housing shall be available in sufficient quantity and variety so that the scope of handicapped students' choice of living accommodations is, as a whole, comparable to that of nonhandicapped students.

(b) *Other housing.* A recipient that assists any agency, organization, or person in making housing available to any of its students shall take such action as may be necessary to assure itself that such housing is, as a whole,

made available in a manner that does not result in discrimination on the basis of handicap.

§ 104.46   Financial and employment assistance to students.

(a) *Provision of financial assistance.* (1) In providing financial assistance to qualified handicapped persons, a recipient to which this subpart applies may not (i), on the basis of handicap, provide less assistance than is provided to nonhandicapped persons, limit eligibility for assistance, or otherwise discriminate or (ii) assist any entity or person that provides assistance to any of the recipient's students in a manner that discriminates against qualified handicapped persons on the basis of handicap.

(2) A recipient may administer or assist in the administration of scholarships, fellowships, or other forms of financial assistance established under wills, trusts, bequests, or similar legal instruments that require awards to be made on the basis of factors that discriminate or have the effect of discriminating on the basis of handicap only if the overall effect of the award of scholarships, fellowships, and other forms of financial assistance is not discriminatory on the basis of handicap.

(b) *Assistance in making available outside employment.* A recipient that assists any agency, organization, or person in providing employment opportunities to any of its students shall assure itself that such employment opportunities, as a whole, are made available in a manner that would not violate Subpart B if they were provided by the recipient.

(c) *Employment of students by recipients.* A recipient that employs any of its students may not ao so in a manner that violates Subpart B.

§ 104.47   Nonacademic services.

(a) *Physical education and athletics.* (1) In providing physical education courses and athletics and similar programs and activities to any of its students, a recipient to which this subpart applies may not discriminate on the basis of handicap. A recipient that offers physical education courses or that operates or sponsors intercollegiate, club, or intramural athletics shall provide to qualified handicapped students an equal opportunity for participation in these activities.

(2) A recipient may offer to handicapped students physical education and athletic activities that are separate or different only if separation or differentiation is consistent with the requirements of § 104.43(d) and only if no qualified handicapped student is denied the opportunity to compete for teams or to participate in courses that are not separate or different.

(b) *Counseling and placement services.* A recipient to which this subpart applies that provides personal, academic, or vocational counseling, guidance, or placement services to its students shall provide these services without discrimination on the basis of handicap. The recipient shall ensure that qualified handicapped students are not counseled toward more restrictive career objectives than are non-handicapped students with similar interests and abilities. This requirement does not preclude a recipient from providing factual information about licensing and certification requirements that may present obstacles to handicapped persons in their pursuit of particular careers.

(c) *Social organizations.* A recipient that provides significant assistance to fraternities, sororities, or similar organizations shall assure itself that the membership practices of such organizations do not permit discrimination otherwise prohibited by this subpart.

Subpart F—Health, Welfare, and Social Services

§ 104.51 **Application of this subpart.**

Subpart F applies to health, welfare, and other social service programs and activities that receive or benefit from Federal financial assistance and to recipients that operate, or that receive or benefit from Federal financial assistance for the operation of, such programs or activities.

§ 104.52 **Health, welfare, and other social services.**

(a) *General.* In providing health, welfare, or other social services or benefits, a recipient may not, on the basis of handicap:

(1) Deny a qualified handicapped person these benefits or services;

(2) Afford a qualified handicapped person an opportunity to receive benefits or services that is not equal to that offered nonhandicapped persons;

(3) Provide a qualified handicapped person with benefits or services that are not as effective (as defined in § 104.4(b)) as the benefits or services provided to others;

(4) Provide benefits or services in a manner that limits or has the effect of limiting the participation of qualified handicapped persons; or

(5) Provide different or separate benefits or services to handicapped persons except where necessary to provide qualified handicapped persons with benefits and services that are as effective as those provided to others.

(b) *Notice.* A recipient that provides notice concerning benefits or services or written material concerning waivers of rights or consent to treatment shall take such steps as are necessary to ensure that qualified handicapped persons, including those with impaired sensory or speaking skills, are not denied effective notice because of their handicap.

(c) *Emergency treatment for the hearing impaired.* A recipient hospital that provides health services or benefits shall establish a procedure for effective communication with persons with impaired hearing for the purpose of providing emergency health care.

(d) *Auxiliary aids.* (1) A recipient to which this subpart applies that employs fifteen or more persons shall provide appropriate auxiliary aids to persons with impaired sensory, manual, or speaking skills, where necessary to afford such persons an equal opportunity to benefit from the service in question.

(2) The Assistant Secretary may require recipients with fewer than fifteen employees to provide auxiliary aids where the provision of aids would not significantly impair the ability of the recipient to provide its benefits or services.

(3) For the purpose of this paragraph, auxiliary aids may include

brailled and taped material, interpreters, and other aids for persons with impaired hearing or vision.

§ 104.53 Drug and alcohol addicts.

A recipient to which this subpart applies that operates a general hospital or outpatient facility may not discriminate in admission or treatment against a drug or alcohol abuser or alcoholic who is suffering from a medical condition, because of the person's drug or alcohol abuse or alcoholism.

§ 104.54 Education of institutionalized persons.

A recipient to which this subpart applies and that operates or supervises a program or activity for persons who are institutionalized because of handicap shall ensure that each qualified handicapped person, as defined in § 104.3(k)(2), in its program or activity is provided an appropriate education, as defined in § 104.33(b). Nothing in this section shall be interpreted as altering in any way the obligations of recipients under Subpart D.

Subpart G—Procedures

§ 104.61 Procedures.

The procedural provisions applicable to title VI of the Civil Rights Act of 1964 apply to this part. These procedures are found in §§ 100.6–100.10 and Part 101 of this title.

APPENDIX A—ANALYSIS OF FINAL REGULATION

SUBPART A—GENERAL PROVISIONS

Definitions—1. *"Recipient"*. Section 104.23 contains definitions used throughout the regulation.

One comment requested that the regulation specify that nonpublic elementary and secondary schools that are not otherwise recipients do not become recipients by virtue of the fact their students participate in certain federally funded programs. The Secretary believes it unnecessary to amend the regulation in this regard, because almost identical language in the Department's regulations implementing title VI and title IX of the Education Amendments of 1972 has consistently been interpreted so as not to render such schools recipients. These schools, however, are indirectly subject to the substantive requirements of this regulation through the application of § 104.4(b)(iv), which prohibits recipients from assisting agencies that discriminate on the basis of handicap in providing services to beneficiaries of the recipients' programs.

2. *"Federal financial assistance"*. In § 104.3(h), defining federal financial assistance, a clarifying change has been made: procurement contracts are specifically excluded. They are covered, however, by the Department of Labor's regulation under section 503. The Department has never considered such contracts to be contracts of assistance; the explicit exemption has been added only to avoid possible confusion.

The proposed regulation's exemption of contracts of insurance or guaranty has been retained. A number of comments argued for its deletion on the ground that section 504, unlike title VI and title IX, contains no statutory exemption for such contracts. There is no indication, however, in the legislative history of the Rehabilitation Act of 1973 or of the amendments to that Act in 1974, that Congress intended section 504 to have a broader application, in terms of federal financial assistance, than other civil rights statutes. Indeed, Congress directed that section 504 be implemented in the same manner as titles VI and IX. In view of the long established exemption of contracts of insurance or guaranty under title VI, we think it unlikely that Congress intended section 504 to apply to such contracts.

3. *"Handicapped person"*. Section 104.3(j), which defines the class of persons protected under the regulation, has not been substantially changed. The definition of handicapped person in paragraph (j)(1) conforms to the statutory definition of handicapped person that is applicable to section 504, as set forth in section 111(a) of the Rehabilitation Act Amendments of 1974, Pub. L. 93-516.

The first of the three parts of the statutory and regulatory definition includes any person who has a physical or mental impairment that substantially limits one or more major life activities. Paragraph (j)(2)(i) further defines physical or mental impairments. The definition does not set forth a list of specific diseases and conditions that constitute physical or mental impairments because of the difficulty of ensuring the comprehensiveness of any such list. The term includes, however, such diseases and conditions as orthopedic, visual, speech, and hearing impairments, cerebral palsy, epilepsy, muscular dystrophy, multiple sclerosis, cancer, heart disease, diabetes, mental retardation, emotional illness, and, as discussed below, drug addiction and alcoholism.

It should be emphasized that a physical or mental impairment does not constitute a handicap for purposes of section 504 unless its severity is such that it results in a substantial limitation of one or more major life activities. Several comments observed the lack of any definition in the proposed regulation of the phrase "substantially limits." The Department does not believe that a definition of this term is possible at this time.

A related issue raised by several comments is whether the definition of handicapped person is unreasonably broad. Comments suggested narrowing the definition in various ways. The most common recommendation was that only "traditional" handicaps be covered. The Department continues to believe, however, that it has no flexibility within the statutory definition to limit the term to persons who have those severe, permanent, or progressive conditions that are most commonly regarded as handicaps. The Department intends, however, to give particular attention in its enforcement of section 504 to eliminating discrimination against persons with the severe handicaps that were the focus of concern in the Rehabilitation Act of 1973.

The definition of handicapped person also includes specific limitations on what persons are classified as handicapped under the regulation. The first of the three parts of the definition specifies that only physical and mental handicaps are included. Thus, environmental, cultural, and economic disadvantage are not in themselves covered; nor are prison records, age, or homosexuality. Of course, if a person who has any of these characteristics also has a physical or mental handicap, the person is included within the definition of handicapped person.

In paragraph (j)(2)(i), physical or mental impairment is defined to include, among other impairments, specific learning disabilities. The Department will interpret the term as it is used in section 602 of the Education of the Handicapped Act, as amended. Paragraph (15) of section 602 uses the term "specific learning disabilities" to describe such conditions as perceptual handicaps, brain injury, minimal brain dysfunction, dyslexia, and developmental aphasia.

Paragraph (j)(2)(i) has been shortened, but not substantively changed, by the deletion of clause (C), which made explicit the inclusion of any condition which is mental or physical but whose precise nature is not at present known. Clauses (A) and (B) clearly comprehend such conditions.

The second part of the statutory and regulatory definition of handicapped person includes any person who has a record of a physical or mental impairment that substantially limits a major life activity. Under the definition of "record" in paragraph (j)(2)(iii), persons who have a history of a handicapping condition but no longer have the condition, as well as persons who have been incorrectly classified as having such a condition, are protected from discrimination under section 504. Frequently occurring examples of the first group are persons with histories of mental or emotional illness, heart disease, or cancer; of the second group, persons who have been misclassified as mentally retarded.

The third part of the statutory and regulatory definition of handicapped person includes any person who is regarded as having a physical or mental impairment that substantially limits one or more major life activities. It includes many persons who are ordinarily considered to be handicapped but who do not technically fall within the first two parts of the statutory definition, such as persons with a limp. This part of the definition also includes some persons who might not ordinarily be considered handicapped, such as persons with disfiguring scars, as well as persons who have no physical or mental impairment but are treated by a recipient as if they were handicapped.

4. *Drug addicts and alcoholics.* As was the case during the first comment period, the issue of whether to include drug addicts and alcoholics within the definition of handicapped person was of major concern to many commenters. The arguments presented on each side of the issue were similar during the two comment periods, as was the preference of commenters for exclusion of this group of persons. While some comments reflected misconceptions about the implications of including alcoholics and drug addicts within the scope of the regulation, the Secretary understands the concerns that underlie the comments on this question and recognizes that application of section 504 to active alcoholics and drug addicts presents sensitive and difficult questions that must be taken into account in interpretation and enforcement.

The Secretary has carefully examined the issue and has obtained a legal opinion from the Attorney General. That opinion concludes that drug addiction and alcoholism are "physical or mental impairments" within the meaning of section 7(6) of the Rehabilitation Act of 1973, as amended, and that drug addicts and alcoholics are therefore handicapped for purposes of section 504 if their impairment substantially limits one of their major life activities. The Secretary therefore believes that he is without authority to exclude these conditions from the definition. There is a medical and legal consensus that alcoholism and drug addiction are diseases, although there is disagreement as to whether they are primarily mental or physical. In addition, while Congress did not focus specifically on the problems of drug addiction and alcoholism in enacting section 504, the committees that considered the Rehabilitation Act of 1973 were made aware of the Department's long-standing practice of treating addicts and alcoholics as handicapped individuals eligible for rehabilitation services under the Vocational Rehabilitation Act.

The Secretary wishes to reassure recipients that inclusion of addicts and alcoholics within the scope of the regulation will not lead to the consequences feared by many commenters. It cannot be emphasized too strongly that the statute and the regulation apply only to discrimination against qualified handicapped persons solely by reason of their handicap. The fact that drug addiction and alcoholism may be handicaps does not mean that these conditions must be ignored in determining whether an individual is qualified for services or employment opportunities. On the contrary, a recipient may hold a drug addict or alcoholic to the same standard of performance and behavior to which it holds others, even if any unsatisfactory performance or behavior is related to the person's drug addiction or alcoholism. In other words, while an alcoholic or drug addict may not be denied services or disqualified from employment solely because of his or her condition, the behavioral manifestations of the condition may be taken into account in determining whether he or she is qualified.

With respect to the employment of a drug addict or alcoholic, if it can be shown that the addiction or alcoholism prevents successful performance of the job, the person need not be provided the employment opportunity in question. For example, in making employment decisions, a recipient may judge addicts and alcoholics on the same basis it judges all other applicants and employees. Thus, a recipient may consider—for all applicants including drug addicts and alcoholics—past personnel records, absenteeism, disruptive, abusive, or dangerous behavior, violations of rules and unsatisfactory work performance. Moreover, employers may enforce rules prohibiting the possession or use of alcohol or drugs in the work-place, provided that such rules are enforced against all employees.

With respect to other services, the implications of coverage, of alcoholics and drug addicts are two-fold: first, no person may be excluded from services solely by reason of the presence or history of these conditions; second, to the extent that the manifestations of the condition prevent the person from meeting the basic eligibility requirements of the program or cause substantial interference with the operation of the program, the condition may be taken into consideration. Thus, a college may not exclude an addict or alcoholic as a student, on the basis of addiction or alcoholism, if the person can successfully participate in the education program and complies with the rules of the college and if his or her behav-

ior does not impede the performance of other students.

Of great concern to many commenters was the question of what effect the inclusion of drug addicts and alcoholics as handicapped persons would have on school disciplinary rules prohibiting the use or possession of drugs or alcohol by students. Neither such rules nor their application to drug addicts or alcoholics is prohibited by this regulation, provided that the rules are enforced evenly with respect to all students.

5. *"Qualified handicapped person."* Paragraph (k) of § 104.3 defines the term "qualified handicapped person." Throughout the regulation, this term is used instead of the statutory term "otherwise qualified handicapped person." The Department believes that the omission of the word "otherwise" is necessary in order to comport with the intent of the statute because, read literally, "otherwise" qualified handicapped persons include persons who are qualified except for their handicap, rather than in spite of their handicap. Under such a literal reading, a blind person possessing all the qualifications for driving a bus except sight could be said to be "otherwise qualified" for the job of driving. Clearly, such a result was not intended by Congress. In all other respects, the terms "qualified" and "otherwise qualified" are intended to be interchangeable.

Section 104.3(k)(1) defines a qualified handicapped person with respect to employment as a handicapped person who can, with reasonable accommodation, perform the essential functions of the job in question. The term "essential functions" does not appear in the corresponding provision of the Department of Labor's section 503 regulation, and a few commenters objected to its inclusion on the ground that a handicapped person should be able to perform all job tasks. However, the Department believes that inclusion of the phrase is useful in emphasizing that handicapped persons should not be disqualified simply because they may have difficulty in performing tasks that bear only a marginal relationship to a particular job. Further, we are convinced that inclusion of the phrase is not inconsistent with the Department of Labor's application of its definition.

Certain commenters urged that the definition of qualified handicapped person be amended so as explicitly to place upon the employer the burden of showing that a particular mental or physical characteristic is essential. Because the same result is achieved by the requirement contained in paragraph (a) of § 104.13, which requires an employer to establish that any selection criterion that tends to screen out handicapped persons is job-related, that recommendation has not been followed.

Section 104.3(k)(2) defines qualified

handicapped person, with respect to preschool, elementary, and secondary programs, in terms of age. Several commenters recommended that eligibility for the services be based upon the standard of substantial benefit, rather than age, because of the need of many handicapped children for early or extended services if they are to have an equal opportunity to benefit from education programs. No change has been made in this provision, again because of the extreme difficulties in administration that would result from the choice of the former standard. Under the remedial action provisions of § 104.6(a)(3), however, persons beyond the age limits prescribed in § 104.3(k)(2) may in appropriate cases be required to be provided services that they were formerly denied because of a recipient's violation of section 504.

Section 104.3(k)(2) states that a handicapped person is qualified for preschool, elementary, or secondary services if the person is of an age at which nonhandicapped persons are eligible for such services or at which state law mandates the provision of educational services to handicapped persons. In addition, the extended age ranges for which recipients must provide full educational opportunity to all handicapped persons in order to be eligible for assistance under the Education of the Handicapped Act—generally, 3-18 as of September 1978, and 3-21 as of September 1980 are incorporated by reference in this paragraph.

Section 104.3(k)(3) defines qualified handicapped person with respect to postsecondary educational programs. As revised, the paragraph means that both academic and technical standards must be met by applicants to these programs. The term "technical standards" refers to all nonacademic admissions criteria that are essential to participation in the program in question.

6. *General prohibitions against discrimination.* Section 104.4 contains general prohibitions against discrimination applicable to all recipients of assistance from this Department.

Paragraph (b)(1)(i) prohibits the exclusion of qualified handicapped persons from aids, benefits, or services, and paragraph (ii) requires that equal opportunity to participate or benefit be provided. Paragraph (iii) requires that services provided to handicapped persons be as effective as those provided to the nonhandicapped. In paragraph (iv), different or separate services are prohibited except when necessary to provide equally effective benefits.

In this context, the term "equally effective," defined in paragraph (b)(2), is intended to encompass the concept of equivalent, as opposed to identical, services and to acknowledge the fact that in order to meet the individual needs of handicapped persons to the same extent that the corresponding needs of nonhandicapped persons are met, adjustments to regular programs or the provision of different programs may sometimes be necessary. This standard parallels the one established under title VI of Civil Rights Act of 1964 with respect to the provision of educational services to students whose primary language is not English. See *Lau* v. *Nichols,* 414 U.S. 563 (1974). To be equally effective, however, an aid, benefit, or service need not produce equal results; it merely must afford an equal opportunity to achieve equal results.

It must be emphasized that, although separate services must be required in some instances, the provision of unnecessarily separate or different services is discriminatory. The addition to paragraph (b)(2) of the phrase "in the most integrated setting appropriate to the person's needs" is intended to reinforce this general concept. A new paragraph (b)(3) has also been added to § 104.4, requiring recipients to give qualified handicapped persons the option of participating in regular programs despite the existence of permissibly separate or different programs. The requirement has been reiterated in §§ 104.38 and 104.47 in connection with physical education and athletics programs.

Section 104.4(b)(1)(v) prohibits a recipient from supporting another entity or person that subjects participants or employees in the recipient's program to discrimination on the basis of handicap. This section would, for example, prohibit financial support by a recipient to a community recreational group or to a professional or social organization that discriminates against handicapped persons. Among the criteria to be considered in each case are the substantiality of the relationship between the recipient and the other entity, including financial support by the recipient, and whether the other entity's activities relate so closely to the recipient's program or activity that they fairly should be considered activities of the recipient itself. Paragraph (b)(1)(vi) was added in response to comment in order to make explicit the prohibition against denying qualified handicapped persons the opportunity to serve on planning and advisory boards responsible for guiding federally assisted programs or activities.

Several comments appeared to interpret § 104.4(b)(5), which proscribes discriminatory site selection, to prohibit a recipient that is located on hilly terrain from erecting any new buildings at its present site. That, of course, is not the case. This paragraph is not intended to apply to construction of additional buildings at an existing site. Of course, any such facilities must be made accessible in accordance with the requirements of § 104.23.

7. *Assurances of compliance.* Section 104.5(a) requires a recipient to submit to the

Assistant Secretary an assurance that each of its programs and activities receiving or benefiting from Federal financial assistance from this Department will be conducted in compliance with this regulation. Many commenters also sought relief from the paperwork requirements imposed by the Department's enforcement of its various civil rights responsibilities by requesting the Department to issue one form incorporating title VI, title IX, and section 504 assurances. The Secretary is sympathetic to this request. While it is not feasible to adopt a single civil rights assurance form at this time, the Office for Civil Rights will work toward that goal.

8. *Private rights of action.* Several comments urged that the regulation incorporate provision granting beneficiaries a private right of action against recipients under section 504. To confer such a right is beyond the authority of the executive branch of Government. There is, however, case law holding that such a right exists. *Lloyd* v. *Regional Transportation Authority,* 548 F. 2d 1277 (7th Cir. 1977); *see Hairston* v. *Drosick,* Civil No. 75-0691 (S.D. W. Va., Jan. 14, 1976); *Gurmankin* v. *Castanzo,* 411 F. Supp. 982 (E.D. Pa. 1976); *cf. Lau* v. *Nichols, supra.*

9. *Remedial action.* Where there has been a finding of discrimination, § 104.6 requires a recipient to take remedial action to overcome the effects of the discrimination. Actions that might be required under paragraph (a)(1) include provision of services to persons previously discriminated against, reinstatement of employees and development of a remedial action plan. Should a recipient fail to take required remedial action, the ultimate sanctions of court action or termination of Federal financial assistance may be imposed.

Paragraph (a)(2) extends the responsibility for taking remedial action to a recipient that exercises control over a noncomplying recipient. Paragraph (a)(3) also makes clear that handicapped persons who are not in the program at the time that remedial action is required to be taken may also be the subject of such remedial action. This paragraph has been revised in response to comments in order to include persons who would have been in the program if discriminatory practices had not existed. Paragraphs (a) (1), (2), and (3) have also been amended in response to comments to make plain that, in appropriate cases, remedial action might be required to redress clear violations of the statute itself that occurred before the effective date of this regulation.

10. *Voluntary action.* In § 104.6(b), the term "voluntary action" has been substituted for the term "affirmative action" because the use of the latter term led to some confusion. We believe the term "voluntary action" more accurately reflects the purpose

of the paragraph. This provision allows action, beyond that required by the regulation, to overcome conditions that led to limited participation by handicapped persons, whether or not the limited participation was caused by any discriminatory actions on the part of the recipient. Several commenters urged that paragraphs (a) and (b) be revised to require remedial action to overcome effects of prior discriminatory practices regardless of whether there has been an express finding of discrimination. The self-evaluation requirement in paragraph (c) accomplishes much the same purpose.

11. *Self-evaluation.* Paragraph (c) requires recipients to conduct a self-evaluation in order to determine whether their policies or practices may discriminate against handicapped persons and to take steps to modify any discriminatory policies and practices and their effects. The Department received many comments approving of the addition to paragraph (c) of a requirement that recipients seek the assistance of handicapped persons in the self-evaluation process. This paragraph has been further amended to require consultation with handicapped persons or organizations representing them before recipients undertake the policy modifications and remedial steps prescribed in paragraphs (c) (ii) and (iii).

Paragraph (c)(2), which sets forth the recordkeeping requirements concerning self-evaluation, now applies only to recipients with fifteen or more employees. This change was made as part of an effort to reduce unnecessary or counterproductive administrative obligations on small recipients. For those recipients required to keep records, the requirements have been made more specific; records must include a list of persons consulted and a description of areas examined, problems identified, and corrective steps taken. Moreover, the records must be made available for public inspection.

12. *Grievance procedure.* Section 104.7 requires recipients with fifteen or more employees to designate an individual responsible for coordinating its compliance efforts and to adopt a grievance procedure. Two changes were made in the section in response to comment. A general requirement that appropriate due process procedures be followed has been added. It was decided that the details of such procedures could not at this time be specified because of the varied nature of the persons and entities who must establish the procedures and of the programs to which they apply. A sentence was also added to make clear that grievance procedures are not required to be made available to unsuccessful applicants for employment or to applicants for admission to colleges and universities.

The regulation does not require that grievance procedures be exhausted before recourse is sought from the Department.

However, the Secretary believes that it is desirable and efficient in many cases for complainants to seek resolution of their complaints and disputes at the local level and therefore encourages them to use available grievance procedures.

A number of comments asked whether compliance with this section or the notice requirements of § 104.8 could be coordinated with comparable action required by the title IX regulation. The Department encourages such efforts.

13. *Notice.* Section 104.8 (formerly § 84.9) sets forth requirements for dissemination of statements of nondiscrimination policy by recipients.

It is important that both handicapped persons and the public at large be aware of the obligations of recipients under section 504. Both the Department and recipients have responsibilities in this regard. Indeed the Department intends to undertake a major public information effort to inform persons of their rights under section 504 and this regulation. In § 104.8 the Department has sought to impose a clear obligation on major recipients to notify beneficiaries and employees of the requirements of section 504, without dictating the precise way in which this notice must be given. At the same time, we have avoided imposing requirements on small recipients (those with fewer than fifteen employees) that would create unnecessary and counterproductive paper work burdens on them and unduly stretch the enforcement resources of the Department.

Section 104.8(a), as simplified, requires recipients with fifteen or more employees to take appropriate steps to notify beneficiaries and employees of the recipient's obligations under section 504. The last sentence of § 104.8(a) has been revised to list possible, rather than required, means of notification. Section 104.8(b) requires recipients to include a notification of their policy of nondiscrimination in recruitment and other general information materials.

In response to a number of comments, § 104.8 has been revised to delete the requirements of publication in local newspapers, which has proved to be both troublesome and ineffective. Several commenters suggested that notification on separate forms be allowed until present stocks of publications and forms are depleted. The final regulation explicitly allows this method of compliance. The separate form should, however, be included with each significant publication or form that is distributed.

Section 104 which prohibited the use of materials that might give the impression that a recipient excludes qualified handicapped persons from its program, has been deleted. The Department is convinced by the comments that this provision is unnecessary and difficult to apply. The Department encourages recipients, however, to include in their recruitment and other general information materials photographs of handicapped persons and ramps and other features of accessible buildings.

Under new § 104.9 the Assistant Secretary may, under certain circumstances, require recipients with fewer than fifteen employees to comply with one or more of these requirements. Thus, if experience shows a need for imposing notice or other requirements on particular recipients or classes of small recipients, the Department is prepared to expand the coverage of these sections.

14. *Inconsistent State laws.* Section 104.10(a) states that compliance with the regulation is not excused by state or local laws limiting the eligibility of qualified handicapped persons to receive services or to practice an occupation. The provision thus applies only with respect to state or local laws that unjustifiably differentiate on the basis of handicap.

Paragraph (b) further points out that the presence of limited employment opportunities in a particular profession, does not excuse a recipient from complying with the regulation. Thus, a law school could not deny admission to a blind applicant because blind lawyers may find it more difficult to find jobs than do nonhandicapped lawyers.

SUBPART B—EMPLOYMENT PRACTICES

Subpart B prescribes requirements for nondiscrimination in the employment practices of recipients of Federal financial assistance administered by the Department. This subpart is consistent with the employment provisions of the Department's regulation implementing title IX of the Education Amendments of 1972 (34 CFR, Part 106) and the regulation of the Department of Labor under section 503 of the Rehabilitation Act, which requires certain Federal contractors to take affirmative action in the employment and advancement of qualified handicapped persons. All recipients subject to title IX are also subject to this regulation. In addition, many recipients subject to this regulation receive Federal procurement contracts in excess of $2,500 and are therefore also subject to section 503.

15. *Discriminatory practices.* Section 104.11 sets forth general provisions with respect to discrimination in employment. A new paragraph (a)(2) has been added to clarify the employment obligations of recipients that receive Federal funds under Part B of the Education of the Handicapped Act, as amended (EHA). Section 606 of the EHA obligates elementary or secondary school systems that receive EHA funds to take

positive steps to employ and advance in employment qualified handicapped persons. This obligation is similar to the nondiscrimination requirement of section 504 but requires recipients to take additional steps to hire and promote handicapped persons. In enacting section 606 Congress chose the words "positive steps" instead of "affirmative action" advisedly and did not intend section 606 to incorporate the types of activities required under Executive Order 11246 (affirmative action on the basis of race, color, sex, or national origin) or under sections 501 and 503 of the Rehabilitation Act of 1973.

Paragraph (b) of § 104.11 sets forth the specific aspects of employment covered by the regulation. Paragraph (c) provides that inconsistent provisions of collective bargaining agreements do not excuse noncompliance.

16. *Reasonable accommodation.* The reasonable accommodation requirement of § 104.12 generated a substantial number of comments. The Department remains convinced that its approach is both fair and effective. Moreover, the Department of Labor reports that it has experienced little difficulty in administering the requirements of reasonable accommodation. The provision therefore remains basically unchanged from the proposed regulation.

Section 104.12 requires a recipient to make reasonable accommodation to the known physical or mental limitations of a handicapped applicant or employee unless the recipient can demonstrate that the accommodation would impose an undue hardship on the operation of its program. Where a handicapped person is not qualified to perform a particular job, where reasonable accommodation does not overcome the effects of a person's handicap, or where reasonable accommodation causes undue hardship to the employer, failure to hire or promote the handicapped person will not be considered discrimination.

Section 104.12(b) lists some of the actions that constitute reasonable accommodation. The list is neither all-inclusive nor meant to suggest that employers must follow all of the actions listed.

Reasonable accommodation includes modification of work schedules, including part-time employment, and job restructuring. Job restructuring may entail shifting nonessential duties to other employees. In other cases, reasonable accommodation may include physical modifications or relocation of particular offices or jobs so that they are in facilities or parts of facilities that are accessible to and usable by handicapped persons. If such accommodations would cause undue hardship to the employer, they need not be made.

Paragraph (c) of this section sets forth the factors that the Office for Civil Rights will consider in determining whether an accommodation necessary to enable an applicant or employee to perform the duties of a job would impose an undue hardship. The weight given to each of these factors in making the determination as to whether an accommodation constitutes undue hardship will vary depending on the facts of a particular situation. Thus, a small day-care center might not be required to expend more than a nominal sum, such as that necessary to equip a telephone for use by a secretary with impaired hearing, but a large school district might be required to make available a teacher's aide to a blind applicant for a teaching job. The reasonable accommodation standard in § 104.12 is similar to the obligation imposed upon Federal contractors in the regulation implementing section 503 of the Rehabilitation Act of 1973, administered by the Department of Labor. Although the wording of the reasonable accommodation provisions of the two regulations is not identical, the obligation that the two regulations impose is the same, and the Federal Government's policy in implementing the two sections will be uniform. The Department adopted the factors listed in paragraph (c) instead of the "business necessity" standard of the Labor regulation because that term seemed inappropriate to the nature of the programs operated by the majority of institutions subject to this regulation, e.g., public school systems, colleges and universities. The factors listed in paragraph (c) are intended to make the rationale underlying the business necessity standard applicable to   understandable by recipients of ED funds.

17. *Tests and selection criteria.* Revised § 104.13(a) prohibits employers from using test or other selection criteria that screen out or tend to screen out handicapped persons unless the test or criterion is shown to be job-related and alternative tests or criteria that do not screen out or tend to screen out as many handicapped persons are not shown by the Assistant Secretary to be available. This paragraph is an application of the principle established under title VII of the Civil Rights Act of 1964 in *Griggs* v. *Duke Power Company,* 401 U.S. 424 (1971).

Under the proposed section, a statistical showing of adverse impact on handicapped persons was required to trigger an employer's obligation to show that employment criteria and qualifications relating to handicap were necessary. This requirement was changed because the small number of handicapped persons taking tests would make statistical showings of "disproportionate, adverse effect" difficult and burdensome. Under the altered, more workable provision, once it is shown that an employment test substantially limits the opportunities of handicapped persons, the employer must show the test to be job-related. A recipient is no longer limited to using predictive validity studies as the method for demonstrating that a test or other selection criterion is in fact job-related. Nor, in all cases, are predictive validity studies sufficient to demonstrate that a test or criterion is job-related. In addition, § 104.13(a) has been revised to place the burden on the Assistant Secretary, rather than the recipient, to identify alternate tests.

Section 104.13(b) requires that a recipient take into account that some tests and criteria depend upon sensory, manual, or speaking skills that may not themselves be necessary to the job in question but that may make the handicapped person unable to pass the test. The recipient must select and administer tests so as best to ensure that the test will measure the handicapped person's ability to perform on the job rather than the person's ability to see, hear, speak, or perform manual tasks, except, of course, where such skills are the factors that the test purports to measure. For example, a person with a speech impediment may be perfectly qualified for jobs that do not or need not, with reasonable accommodation, require ability to speak clearly. Yet, if given an oral test, the person will be unable to perform in a satisfactory manner. The test results will not, therefore, predict job performance but instead will reflect impaired speech.

18. *Preemployment inquiries.* Section 104.14, concerning preemployment inquiries, generated a large number of comments. Commenters representing handicapped persons strongly favored a ban on preemployment inquiries on the ground that such inquiries are often used to discriminate against handicapped persons and are not necessary to serve any legitimate interests of employers. Some recipients, on the other hand, argued that preemployment inquiries are necessary to determine qualifications of the applicant, safety hazards caused by a particular handicapping condition, and accommodations that might be required.

The Secretary has concluded that a general prohibition of preemployment inquiries is appropriate. However, a sentence has been added to paragraph (a) to make clear that an employer may inquire into an applicant's ability to perform job-related tasks but may not ask if the person has a handicap. For example, an employer may not ask on an employment form if an applicant is visually impaired but may ask if the person has a current driver's license (if that is a necessary qualification for the position in question). Similarly, employers may make inquiries about an applicant's ability to perform a job safely. Thus, an employer may not ask if an applicant is an epileptic but may ask whether the person can perform a particular job without endangering other employees.

Section 104.14(b) allows preemployment inquiries only if they are made in conjunction with required remedial action to correct past discrimination, with voluntary action to overcome past conditions that have limited the participation of handicapped persons, or with obligations under section 503 of the Rehabilitation Act of 1973. In these instances, paragraph (b) specifies certain safeguards that must be followed by the employer.

Finally, the revised provision allows an employer to condition offers of employment to handicapped persons on the results of medical examinations, so long as the examinations are administered to all employees in a nondiscriminatory manner and the results are treated on a confidential basis.

19. *Specific acts of Discrimination.* Sections 104.15 (recruitment), 104.16 (compensation), 104.17 (job classification and structure) and 104.18 (fringe benefits) have been deleted from the regulation as unnecessarily duplicative of § 104.11 (discrimination prohibited). The deletion of these sections in no way changes the substantive obligations of employers subject to this regulation from those set forth in the July 16 proposed regulation. These deletions bring the regulation closer in form to the Department of Labor's section 503 regulation.

A proposed section, concerning fringe benefits, had allowed for differences in benefits or contributions between handicapped and nonhandicapped persons in situations only where such differences could be justified on an actuarial basis. Section 104.11 simply bars discrimination in providing fringe benefits and does not address the issue of actuarial differences. The Department believes that currently available data and experience do not demonstrate a basis for promulgating a regulation specifically allowing for differences in benefits or contributions.

SUBPART C—PROGRAM ACCESSIBILITY

In general, Subpart C prohibits the exclusion of qualified handicapped persons from federally assisted programs or activities because a recipient's facilities are inaccessible or unusable.

20. *Existing facilities.* Section 104.22 maintains the same standard for nondiscrimination in regard to existing facilities as was included in the proposed regulation. The section states that a recipient's program or activity, when viewed in its entirety, must be readily accessible to and usable by handicapped persons. Paragraphs (a) and (b) make clear that a recipient is not required to make each of its existing facilities accessible to handicapped persons if its program as a whole is accessible. Accessibility to the recipient's program or activity may be achieved by a number of means, including redesign of equipment, reassignment of

classes or other services to accessible buildings, and making aides available to beneficiaries. In choosing among methods of compliance, recipients are required to give priority consideration to methods that will be consistent with provision of services in the most appropriate integrated setting. Structural changes in existing facilities are required only where there is no other feasible way to make the recipient's program accessible.

Under § 104.22, a university does not have to make all of its existing classroom buildings accessible to handicapped students if some of its buildings are already accessible and if it is possible to reschedule or relocate enough classes so as to offer all required courses and a reasonable selection of elective courses in accessible facilities. If sufficient relocation of classes is not possible using existing facilities, enough alterations to ensure program accessibility are required. A university may not exclude a handicapped student from a specifically requested course offering because it is not offered in an accessible location, but it need not make every section of that course accessible.

Commenters representing several institutions of higher education have suggested that it would be appropriate for one postsecondary institution in a geographical area to be made accessible to handicapped persons and for other colleges and universities in that area to participate in that school's program, thereby developing an educational consortium for the postsecondary education of handicapped students. The Department believes that such a consortium, when developed and applied only to handicapped persons, would not constitute compliance with § 104.22, but would discriminate against qualified handicapped persons by restricting their choice in selecting institutions of higher education and would, therefore, be inconsistent with the basic objectives of the statute.

Nothing in this regulation, however, should be read as prohibiting institutions from forming consortia for the benefit of all students. Thus, if three colleges decide that it would be cost-efficient for one college to offer biology, the second physics, and the third chemistry to all students at the three colleges, the arrangement would not violate section 504. On the other hand, it would violate the regulation if the same institutions set up a consortium under which one college undertook to make its biology lab accessible, another its physics lab, and a third its chemistry lab, and under which mobility-impaired handicapped students (but not other students) were required to attend the particular college that is accessible for the desired courses.

Similarly, while a public school district need not make each of its buildings completely accessible, it may not make only one facility or part of a facility accessible if the result is to segregate handicapped students in a single setting.

All recipients that provide health, welfare, or other social services may also comply with § 104.22 by delivering services at alternate accessible sites or making home visits. Thus, for example, a pharmacist might arrange to make home deliveries of drugs. Under revised § 104.22(c), small providers of health, welfare, and social services (those with fewer than fifteen employees) may refer a beneficiary to an accessible provider of the desired service, but only if no means of meeting the program accessibility requirement other than a significant alteration in existing facilities is available. The referring recipient has the responsibility of determining that the other provider is in fact accessible and willing to provide the service.

A recent change in the tax law may assist some recipients in meeting their obligations under this section. Under section 2122 of the Tax Reform Act of 1976, recipients that pay federal income tax are eligible to claim a tax deduction of up to $25,000 for architectural and transportation modifications made to improve accessibility for handicapped persons. See 42 FR 17870 (April 4, 1977), adopting 26 CFR 7.190.

Several commenters expressed concern about the feasibility of compliance with the program accessibility standard. The Secretary believes that the standard is flexible enough to permit recipients to devise ways to make their programs accessible short of extremely expensive or impractical physical changes in facilities. Accordingly, the section does not allow for waivers. The Department is ready at all times to provide technical assistance to recipients in meeting their program accessibility responsibilities. For this purpose, the Department is establishing a special technical assistance unit. Recipients are encouraged to call upon the unit staff for advice and guidance both on structural modifications and on other ways of meeting the program accessibility requirement.

Paragraph (d) has been amended to require recipients to make all nonstructural adjustments necessary for meeting the program accessibility standard within sixty days. Only where structural changes in facilities are necessary will a recipient be permitted up to three years to accomplish program accessibility. It should be emphasized that the three-year time period is not a waiting period and that all changes must be accomplished as expeditiously as possible. Further, it is the Department's belief, after consultation with experts in the field, that outside ramps to buildings can be constructed quickly and at relatively low cost. Therefore, it will be expected that such structural additions will be made promptly to comply with § 104.22(d).

The regulation continues to provide, as did the proposed version, that a recipient planning to achieve program accessibility by making structural changes must develop a transition plan for such changes within six months of the effective date of the regulation. A number of commenters suggested extending that period to one year. The secretary believes that such an extension is unnecessary and unwise. Planning for any necessary structural changes should be undertaken promptly to ensure that they can be completed within the three-year period. The elements of the transition plan as required by the regulation remain virtually unchanged from the proposal but § 104.22(d) now includes a requirement that the recipient make the plan available for public inspection.

Several commenters expressed concern that the program accessibility standard would result in the segregation of handicapped persons in educational institutions. The regulation will not be applied to permit such a result. See § 104.4(c)(2)(iv), prohibiting unnecessarily separate treatment; § 104.35, requiring that students in elementary and secondary schools be educated in the most integrated setting appropriate to their needs; and new § 104.43(d), applying the same standard to postsecondary education.

We have received some comments from organizations of handicapped persons on the subject of requiring, over an extended period of time, a barrier-free environment—that is, requiring the removal of all architectural barriers in existing facilities. The Department has considered these comments but has decided to take no further action at this time concerning these suggestions, believing that such action should only be considered in light of experience in implementing the program accessibility standard.

21. *New construction.* Section 104.23 requires that all new facilities, as well as alterations that could affect access to and use of existing facilities, be designed and constructed in a manner so as to make the facility accessible to and usable by handicapped persons. Section 104.23(a) has been amended so that it applies to each newly constructed facility if the construction was commenced after the effective date of the regulation. The words "if construction has commenced" will be considered to mean "if groundbreaking has taken place." Thus, a recipient will not be required to alter the design of a facility that has progressed beyond groundbreaking prior to the effective date of the regulation.

Paragraph (b) requires certain alterations to conform to the requirement of physical accessibility in paragraph (a). If an alteration is undertaken to a portion of a building the accessibility of which could be improved by the manner in which the alter-

ation is carried out, the alteration must be made in that manner. Thus, if a doorway or wall is being altered, the door or other wall opening must be made wide enough to accommodate wheelchairs. On the other hand, if the alteration consists of altering ceilings, the provisions of this section are not applicable because this alteration cannot be done in a way that affects the accessibility of that portion of the building. The phrase "to the maximum extent feasible" has been added to allow for the occasional case in which the nature of an existing facility is such as to make it impractical or prohibitively expensive to renovate the building in a manner that results in its being entirely barrier-free. In all such cases, however, the alteration should provide the maximum amount of physical accessibility feasible.

As proposed, § 104.23(c) required compliance with the American National Standards Institute (ANSI) standard on building accessibility as the minimum necessary for compliance with the accessibility requirement of §§104.23 (a) and (b). The reference to the ANSI standard created some ambiguity, since the standard itself provides for waivers where other methods are equally effective in providing accessibility to the facility. Moreover, the Secretary does not wish to discourage innovation in barrier-free construction by requiring absolute adherence to a rigid design standard. Accordingly, § 104.23 (c) has been revised to permit departures from particular requirements of the ANSI standard where the recipient can demonstrate that equivalent access to the facility is provided.

Section 104.23(d) of the proposed regulation, providing for a limited deferral of action concerning facilities that are subject to section 502 as well as section 504 of the Act, has been deleted. The Secretary believes that the provision is unnecessary and inappropriate to this regulation. The Department will, however, seek to coordinate enforcement activities under this regulation with those of the Architectural and Transportation Barriers Compliance Board.

SUBPART D—PRESCHOOL, ELEMENTARY, AND SECONDARY EDUCATION

Subpart D sets forth requirements for nondiscrimination in preschool, elementary, secondary, and adult education programs and activities, including secondary vocational education programs. In this context, the term "adult education" refers only to those educational programs and activities for adults that are operated by elementary and secondary schools.

The provisions of Subpart D apply to state and local educational agencies. Although the subpart applies, in general, to both public and private education programs and activities that are federally assisted, §§ 104.32 and 104.33 apply only to public programs and § 104.39 applies only to private programs; §§ 104.35 and 104.36 apply both to public programs and to those private programs that include special services for handicapped students.

Subpart B generally conforms to the standards established for the education of handicapped persons in *Mills* v. *Board of Education of the District of Columbia*, 348 F. Supp. 866 (D.D.C. 1972), *Pennsylvania Association for Retarded Children* v. *Commonwealth of Pennsylvania*, 344 F. Supp. 1257 (E.D. 1971), 343 F. Supp. 279 (E.D. Pa. 1972), and *Lebanks* v. *Spears*, 60, F.R.D. 135 (E.D. La. 1973), as well as in the Education of the Handicapped Act, as amended by Pub. L. 94-142 (the EHA).

The basic requirements common to those cases, to the EHA, and to this regulation are (1) that handicapped persons, regardless of the nature or severity of their handicap, be provided a free appropriate public education, (2) that handicapped students be educated with nonhandicapped students to the maximum extent appropriate to their needs, (3) that educational agencies undertake to identify and locate all unserved handicapped children, (4) that evaluation procedures be improved in order to avoid the inappropriate education that results from the misclassification of students, and (5) that procedural safeguard be established to enable parents and guardians to influence decisions regarding the evaluation and placement of their children. These requirements are designed to ensure that no handicapped child is excluded from school on the basis of handicap and, if a recipient demonstrates that placement in a regular educational setting cannot be achieved satisfactorily, that the student is provided with adequate alternative services suited to the student's needs without additional cost to the student's parents or guardian. Thus, a recipient that operates a public school system must either educate handicapped children in its regular program or provide such children with an appropriate alternative education at public expense.

It is not the intention of the Department, except in extraordinary circumstances, to review the result of individual placement and other educational decisions, so long as the school district complies with the "process" requirements of this subpart (concerning identification and location, evaluation, and due process procedures). However, the Department will place a high priority on investigating cases which may involve exclusion of a child from the education system or a pattern or practice of discriminatory placements or education.

22. *Location and notification.* Section 104.32 requires public schools to take steps annually to identify and locate handicapped children who are not receiving an education and to publicize to handicapped children

and their parents the rights and duties established by section 504 and this regulation. This section has been shortened without substantive change.

23. *Free appropriate public education.* Under § 104.33(a), a recipient is responsible for providing a free appropriate public education to each qualified handicapped person who is in the recipient's jurisdiction. The word "in" encompasses the concepts of both domicile and actual residence. If a recipient places a child in a program other than its own, it remains financially responsible for the child, whether or not the other program is operated by another recipient or educational agency. Moreover, a recipient may not place a child in a program that is inappropriate or that otherwise violates the requirements of Subpart D. And in no case may a recipient refuse to provide services to a handicapped child in its jurisdiction because of another person's or entity's failure to assume financial responsibility.

Section 104.33(b) concerns the provision of appropriate educational services to handicapped children. To be appropriate, such services must be designed to meet handicapped children's individual educational needs to the same extent that those of nonhandicapped children are met. An appropriate education could consist of education in regular classes, education in regular classes with the use of supplementary services, or special education and related services. Special education may include specially designed instruction in classrooms, at home, or in private or public institutions and may be accompanied by such related services as developmental, corrective, and other supportive services (including psychological, counseling, and medical diagnostic services). The placement of the child must, however, be consistent with the requirements of § 104.34 and be suited to his or her educational needs.

The quality of the educational services provided to handicapped students must equal that of the services provided to nonhandicapped students; thus, handicapped students' teachers must be trained in the instruction of persons with the handicap in question and appropriate materials and equipment must be available. The Department is aware that the supply of adequately trained teachers may, at least at the outset of the imposition of this requirement, be insufficient to meet the demand of all recipients. This factor will be considered in determining the appropriateness of the remedy for noncompliance with this section. A new § 104.33(b)(2) has been added, which allows this requirement to be met through the full implementation of an individualized education program developed in accordance with the standards of the EHA.

Paragraph (c) of § 104.33 sets forth the specific financial obligations of a recipient.

If a recipient does not itself provide handicapped persons with the requisite services, it must assume the cost of any alternate placement. If, however, a recipient offers adequate services and if alternate placement is chosen by a student's parent or guardian, the recipient need not assume the cost of the outside services. (If the parent or guardian believes that his or her child cannot be suitably educated in the recipient's program, he or she may make use of the procedures established in § 104.36.) Under this paragraph, a recipient's obligation extends beyond the provision of tuition payments in the case of placement outside the regular program. Adequate transportation must also be provided. Recipients must also pay for psychological services and those medical services necessary for diagnostic and evaluative purposes.

If the recipient places a student, because of his or her handicap, in a program that necessitates his or her being away from home, the payments must also cover room and board and nonmedical care (including custodial and supervisory care). When residential care is necessitated not by the student's handicap but by factors such as the student's home conditions, the recipient is not required to pay the cost of room and board.

Two new sentences have been added to paragraph (c)(1) to make clear that a recipient's financial obligations need not be met solely through its own funds. Recipients may rely on funds from any public or private source including insurers and similar third parties.

The EHA requires a free appropriate education to be provided to handicapped children "no later than September 1, 1978," but section 504 contains no authority for delaying enforcement. To resolve this problem, a new paragraph (d) has been added to § 104.33. Section 104.33(d) requires recipients to achieve full compliance with the free appropriate public education requirements of § 104.33 as expeditiously as possible, but in no event later than September 1, 1978. The provision also makes clear that, as of the effective date of this regulation, no recipient may exclude a qualified handicapped child from its educational program. This provision against exclusion is consistent with the order of providing services set forth in section 612(3) of the EHA, which places the highest priority on providing services to handicapped children who are not receiving an education.

24. *Educational setting.* Section 104.34 prescribes standards for educating handicapped persons with nonhandicapped persons to the maximum extent appropriate to the needs of the handicapped person in question. A handicapped student may be removed from the regular educational setting only where the recipient can show that the needs of the student would, on balance, be served by placement in another setting.

Although under § 104.34, the needs of the handicapped person are determinative as to proper placement, it should be stressed that, where a handicapped student is so disruptive in a regular classroom that the education of other students is significantly impaired, the needs of the handicapped child cannot be met in that environment. Therefore, regular placement would not be appropriate to his or her needs and would not be required by § 104.34.

Among the factors to be considered in placing a child is the need to place the child as close to home as possible. A new sentence has been added to paragraph (a) requiring recipients to take this factor into account. As pointed out in several comments, the parents' right under § 104.36 to challenge the placement of their child extends not only to placement in special classes or separate schools but also to placement in a distant school and, in particular, to residential placement. An equally appropriate educational program may exist closer to home; this issue may be raised by the parent or guardian under §§ 104.34 and 104.36.

New paragraph (b) specified that handicapped children must also be provided nonacademic services in as integrated a setting as possible. This requirement is especially important for children whose educational needs necessitate their being solely with other handicapped children during most of each day. To the maximum extent appropriate, children in residential settings are also to be provided opportunities for participation with other children.

Section 104.34(c) requires that any facilities that are identifiable as being for handicapped students be comparable in quality to other facilities of the recipient. A number of comments objected to this section on the basis that it encourages the creation and maintenance of such facilities. This is not the intent of the provision. A separate facility violates section 504 unless it is indeed necessary to the provision of an appropriate education to certain handicapped students. In those instances in which such facilities are necessary (as might be the case, for example, for severely retarded persons), this provision requires that the educational services provided be comparable to those provided in the facilities of the recipient that are not identifiable as being for handicapped persons.

25. *Evaluation and placement.* Because the failure to provide handicapped persons with an appropriate education is so frequently the result of misclassification or misplacement, § 104.33(b)(1) makes compliance with its provisions contingent upon adherence to certain procedures designed to ensure appropriate classification and placement. These procedures, delineated in

§§ 104.35 and 104.36, are concerned with testing and other evaluation methods and with procedural due process rights.

Section 104.35(a) requires that an individual evaluation be conducted before any action is taken with respect either to the initial placement of a handicapped child in a regular or special education program or to any subsequent significant change in that placement. Thus, a full reevaluation is not required every time an adjustment in placement is made. "Any action" includes denials of placement.

Paragraphs (b) and (c) of § 104.35 establish procedures designed to ensure that children are not misclassified, unnecessarily labeled as being handicapped, or incorrectly placed because of inappropriate selection, administration, or interpretation of evaluation materials. This problem has been extensively documented in "Issues in the Classification of Children," a report by the Project on Classification of Exceptional Children, in which the HEW Interagency Task Force participated. The provisions of these paragraphs are aimed primarily at abuses in the placement process that result from misuse of, or undue or misplaced reliance on, standardized scholastic aptitude tests.

Paragraph (b) has been shortened but not substantively changed. The requirement in former subparagraph (1) that recipients provide and administer evaluation materials in the native language of the student has been deleted as unnecessary, since the same requirement already exists under title VI and is more appropriately covered under that statute. Paragraphs (1) and (2) are, in general, intended to prevent misinterpretation and similar misuse of test scores and, in particular, to avoid undue reliance on general intelligence tests. Subparagraph (3) requires a recipient to administer tests to a student with impaired sensory, manual, or speaking skills in whatever manner is necessary to avoid distortion of the test results by the impairment. Former subparagraph (4) has been deleted as unnecessarily repetitive of the other provisions of this paragraph.

Paragraph (c) requires a recipient to draw upon a variety of sources in the evaluation process so that the possibility of error in classification is minimized. In particular, it requires that all significant factors relating to the learning process, including adaptive behavior, be considered. (Adaptive behavior is the effectiveness with which the individual meets the standards of personal independence and social responsibility expected of his or her age and cultural group.) Information from all sources must be documented and considered by a group of persons, and the procedure must ensure that the child is placed in the most integrated setting appropriate.

The proposed regulation would have required a complete individual reevaluation of the student each year. The Department has concluded that it is inappropriate in the section 504 regulation to require full reevaluations on such a rigid schedule. Accordingly, § 104.35(c) requires periodic reevaluations and specifies that reevaluations in accordance with the EHA will constitute compliance. The proposed regulation implementing the EHA allows reevaluation at three-year intervals except under certain specified circumstances.

Under § 104.36, a recipient must establish a system of due process procedures to be afforded to parents or guardians before the recipient takes any action regarding the identification, evaluation, or educational placement of a person who, because of handicap, needs or is believed to need special education or related services. This section has been revised. Because the due process procedures of the EHA, incorporated by reference in the proposed section 504 regulation, are inappropriate for some recipients not subject to that Act, the section now specifies minimum necessary procedures: notice, a right to inspect records, an impartial hearing with a right to representation by counsel, and a review procedure. The EHA procedures remain one means of meeting the regulation's due process requirements, however, and are recommended to recipients as a model.

26. *Nonacademic services.* Section 104.37 requires a recipient to provide nonacademic and extracurricular services and activities in such manner as is necessary to afford handicapped students an equal opportunity for participation. Because these services and activities are part of a recipient's education program, they must, in accordance with the provisions of § 104.34, be provided in the most integrated setting appropriate.

Revised paragraph (c)(2) does permit separation or differentiation with respect to the provision of physical education and athletics activities, but only if qualified handicapped students are also allowed the opportunity to compete for regular teams or participate in regular activities. Most handicapped students are able to participate in one or more regular physical education and athletics activities. For example, a student in a wheelchair can participate in regular archery course, as can a deaf student in a wrestling course.

Finally, the one-year transition period provided in a proposed section was deleted in response to the almost unanimous objection of commenters to that provision.

27. *Preschool and adult education.* Section 104.38 prohibits discrimination on the basis of handicap in preschool and adult education programs. Former paragraph (b), which emphasized that compensatory programs for disadvantaged children are subject to section 504, has been deleted as unnecessary, since it is comprehended by paragraph (a).

28. *Private education.* Section 104.39 sets forth the requirements applicable to recipients that operate private education programs and activities. The obligations of these recipients have been changed in two significant respects: first, private schools are subject to the evaluation and due process provisions of the subpart only if they operate special education programs; second, under § 104.39(b), they may charge more for providing services to handicapped students than to nonhandicapped students to the extent that additional charges can be justified by increased costs.

Paragraph (a) of § 104.39 is intended to make clear that recipients that operate private education programs and activities are not required to provide an appropriate education to handicapped students with special educational needs if the recipient does not offer programs designed to meet those needs. Thus, a private school that has no program for mentally retarded persons is neither required to admit such a person into its program nor to arrange or pay for the provision of the person's education in another program. A private recipient without a special program for blind students, however, would not be permitted to exclude, on the basis of blindness, a blind applicant who is able to participate in the regular program with minor adjustments in the manner in which the program is normally offered.

Subpart E—Postsecondary Education

Subpart E prescribes requirements for nondiscrimination in recruitment, admission, and treatment of students in postsecondary education programs and activities, including vocational education.

29. *Admission and recruitment.* In addition to a general prohibition of discrimination on the basis of handicap in § 104.42(a), the regulation delineates, in § 104.42(b), specific prohibitions concerning the establishment of limitations on admission of handicapped students, the use of tests or selection criteria, and preadmission inquiry. Several changes have been made in this provision.

Section 104.42(b) provides that postsecondary educational institutions may not use any test or criterion for admission that has a disproportionate, adverse effect on handicapped persons unless it has been validated as a predictor of academic success and alternate tests or criteria with a less disproportionate, adverse effect are shown by the Department to be available. There are two significant changes in this approach from the July 16 proposed regulation.

First, many commenters expressed concern that § 104.42(b)(2)(ii) could be interpreted to require a "global search" for alternate tests that do not have a disproportionate, adverse impact on handicapped persons. This was not the intent of the provision and, therefore, it has been amended to place

the burden on the Assistant Secretary for Civil Rights, rather than on the recipient, to identify alternate tests.

Second, a new paragraph (d), concerning validity studies, has been added. Under the proposed regulation, overall success in an education program, not just first-year grades, was the criterion against which admissions tests were to be validated. This approach has been changed to reflect the comment of professional testing services that use of first year grades would be less disruptive of present practice and that periodic validity studies against overall success in the education program would be sufficient check on the reliability of first-year grades.

Section 104.42(b)(3) also requires a recipient to assure itself that admissions tests are selected and administered to applicants with impaired sensory, manual, or speaking skills in such manner as is necessary to avoid unfair distortion of test results. Methods have been developed for testing the aptitude and achievement of persons who are not able to take written tests or even to make the marks required for mechanically scored objective tests; in addition, methods for testing persons with visual or hearing impairments are available. A recipient, under this paragraph, must assure itself that such methods are used with respect to the selection and administration of any admissions tests that it uses.

Section 104.42(b)(3)(iii) has been amended to require that admissions tests be administered in facilities that, on the whole, are accessible. In this context, "on the whole" means that not all of the facilities need be accessible so long as a sufficient number of facilities are available to handicapped persons.

Revised § 104.42(b)(4) generally prohibits preadmission inquiries as to whether an applicant has a handicap. The considerations that led to this revision are similar to those underlying the comparable revision of § 104.14 on preemployment inquiries. The regulation does, however, allow inquiries to be made, after admission but before enrollment, as to handicaps that may require accommodation.

New paragraph (c) parallels the section on preemployment inquiries and allows postsecondary institutions to inquire about applicants' handicaps before admission, subject to certain safeguards, if the purpose of the inquiry is to take remedial action to correct past discrimination or to take voluntary action to overcome the limited participation of handicapped persons in postsecondary educational institutions.

Proposed § 104.42(c), which would have allowed different admissions criteria in certain cases for handicapped persons, was widely misinterpreted in comments from both handicapped persons and recipients. We have concluded that the section is unnecessary, and it has been deleted.

30. *Treatment of students.* Section 104.43 contains general provisions prohibiting the discriminatory treatment of qualified handicapped applicants. Paragraph (b) requires recipients to ensure that equal opportunities are provided to its handicapped students in education programs and activities that are not operated by the recipient. The recipient must be satisfied that the outside education program or activity as a whole is nondiscriminatory. For example, a college must ensure that discrimination on the basis of handicap does not occur in connection with teaching assignments of student teachers in elementary or secondary schools not operated by the college. Under the "as a whole" wording, the college could continue to use elementary or secondary school systems that discriminate if, and only if, the college's student teaching program, when viewed in its entirety, offered handicapped student teachers the same range and quality of choice in student teaching assignments afforded nonhandicapped students.

Paragraph (c) of this section prohibits a recipient from excluding qualified handicapped students from any course, course of study, or other part of its education program or activity. This paragraph is designed to eliminate the practice of excluding handicapped persons from specific courses and from areas of concentration because of factors such as ambulatory difficulties of the student or assumptions by the recipient that no job would be available in the area in question for a person with that handicap.

New paragraph (d) requires postsecondary institutions to operate their programs and activities so that handicapped students are provided services in the most integrated setting appropriate. Thus, if a college had several elementary physics classes and had moved one such class to the first floor of the science building to accommodate students in wheelchairs, it would be a violation of this paragraph for the college to concentrate handicapped students with no mobility impairments in the same class.

31. *Academic adjustments.* Paragraph (a) of § 104.44 requires that a recipient make certain adjustments to academic requirements and practices that discriminate or have the effect of discriminating on the basis of handicap. This requirement, like its predecessor in the proposed regulation, does not obligate an institution to waive course or other academic requirements. But such institutions must accommodate those requirements to the needs of individual handicapped students. For example, an institution might permit an otherwise qualified handicapped student who is deaf to substitute an art appreciation or music history course for a required course in music appreciation or could modify the manner in which the music appreciation course is con-

ducted for the deaf student. It should be stressed that academic requirements that can be demonstrated by the recipient to be essential to its program of instruction or to particular degrees need not be changed.

Paragraph (b) provides that postsecondary institutions may not impose rules that have the effect of limiting the participation of handicapped students in the education program. Such rules include prohibition of tape recorders or braillers in classrooms and dog guides in campus buildings. Several recipients expressed concern about allowing students to tape record lectures because the professor may later want to copyright the lectures. This problem may be solved by requiring students to sign agreements that they will not release the tape recording or transcription or otherwise hinder the professor's ability to obtain a copyright.

Paragraph (c) of this section, concerning the administration of course examinations to students with impaired sensory, manual, or speaking skills, parallels the regulation's provisions on admissions testing (§ 104.42(b)) and will be similarly interpreted.

Under § 104.44(d), a recipient must ensure that no handicapped student is subject to discrimination in the recipient's program because of the absence of necessary auxiliary educational aids. Colleges and universities expressed concern about the costs of compliance with this provision.

The Department emphasizes that recipients can usually meet this obligation by assisting students in using existing resources for auxiliary aids such as state vocational rehabilitation agencies and private charitable organizations. Indeed, the Department anticipates that the bulk of auxiliary aids will be paid for by state and private agencies, not by colleges or universities. In those circumstances where the recipient institution must provide the educational auxiliary aid, the institution has flexibility in choosing the methods by which the aids will be supplied. For example, some universities have used students to work with the institution's handicapped students. Other institutions have used existing private agencies that tape texts for handicapped students free of charge in order to reduce the number of readers needed for visually impaired students.

As long as no handicapped person is excluded from a program because of the lack of an appropriate aid, the recipient need not have all such aids on hand at all times. Thus, readers need not be available in the recipient's library at all times so long as the schedule of times when a reader is available is established, is adhered to, and is sufficient. Of course, recipients are not required to maintain a complete braille library.

32. *Housing.* Section 104.45(a) requires

postsecondary institutions to provide housing to handicapped students at the same cost as they provide it to other students and in a convenient, accessible, and comparable manner. Commenters, particularly blind persons pointed out that some handicapped persons can live in any college housing and need not wait to the end of the transition period in Subpart C to be offered the same variety and scope of housing accommodations given to nonhandicapped persons. The Department concurs with this position and will interpret this section accordingly.

A number of colleges and universities reacted negatively to paragraph (b) of this section. It provides that, if a recipient assists in making off-campus housing available to its students, it should develop and implement procedures to assure itself that off-campus housing, as a whole, is available to handicapped students. Since postsecondary institutions are presently required to assure themselves that off-campus housing is provided in a manner that does not discriminate on the basis of sex (§ 106.32 of the title IX regulation), they may use the procedures developed under title IX in order to comply with § 104.45(b). It should be emphasized that not every off-campus living accommodation need be made accessible to handicapped persons.

33. *Health and insurance.* A proposed section, providing that recipients may not discriminate on the basis of handicap in the provision of health related services, has been deleted as duplicative of the general provisions of § 104.43. This deletion represents no change in the obligation of recipients to provide nondiscriminatory health and insurance plans. The Department will continue to require that nondiscriminatory health services be provided to handicapped students. Recipients are not required, however, to provide specialized services and aids to handicapped persons in health programs. If, for example, a college infirmary treats only simple disorders such as cuts, bruises, and colds, its obligation to handicapped persons is to treat such disorders for them.

34. *Financial assistance.* Section 104.46(a), prohibiting discrimination in providing financial assistance, remains substantively the same. It provides that recipients may not provide less assistance to or limit the eligibility of qualified handicapped persons for such assistance, whether the assistance is provided directly by the recipient or by another entity through the recipient's sponsorship. Awards that are made under wills, trusts, or similar legal instruments in a discriminatory manner are permissible, but only if the overall effect of the recipient's provision of financial assistance is not discriminatory on the basis of handicap.

It will not be considered discriminatory to deny, on the basis of handicap, an athletic scholarship to a handicapped person if the handicap renders the person unable to qualify for the award. For example, a student who has a neurological disorder might be denied a varsity football scholarship on the basis of his inability to play football, but a deaf person could not, on the basis of handicap, be denied a scholarship for the school's diving team. The deaf person could, however, be denied a scholarship on the basis of comparative diving ability.

Commenters on § 104.46(b), which applies to assistance in obtaining outside employment for students, expressed similar concerns to those raised under § 104.43(b), concerning cooperative programs. This paragraph has been changed in the same manner as § 104.43(b) to include the "as a whole" concept and will be interpreted in the same manner as § 104.43(b).

35. *Nonacademic services.* Section 104.47 establishes nondiscrimination standards for physical education and athletics counseling and placement services, and social organizations. This section sets the same standards as does § 104.38 of Subpart D, discussed above, and will be interpreted in a similar fashion.

SUBPART F—HEALTH, WELFARE, AND SOCIAL SERVICES

Subpart F applies to recipients that operate health, welfare, and social service programs. The Department received fewer comments on this subpart than on others.

Although many commented that Subpart F lacked specificity, these commenters provided neither concrete suggestions nor additions. Nevertheless, some changes have been made, pursuant to comment, to clarify the obligations of recipients in specific areas. In addition, in an effort to reduce duplication in the regulation, the section governing recipients providing health services has been consolidated with the section regulating providers of welfare and social services. Since the separate provisions that appeared in the proposed regulation were almost identical, no substantive change should be inferred from their consolidation.

Several commenters asked whether Subpart F applies to vocational rehabilitation agencies whose purpose is to assist in the rehabilitation of handicapped persons. To the extent that such agencies receive financial assistance from the Department, they are covered by Subpart F and all other relevant subparts of the regulation. Nothing in this regulation, however, precludes such agencies from servicing only handicapped persons. Indeed, § 104.4(c) permits recipients to offer services or benefits that are limited by federal law to handicapped persons or classes of handicapped persons.

Many comments suggested requiring state social service agencies to take an active role in the enforcement of section 504 with regard to local social service providers. The Department believes that the possibility for federal-state cooperation in the administration and enforcement of section 504 warrants further consideration.

A number of comments also discussed whether section 504 should be read to require payment of compensation to institutionalized handicapped patients who perform services for the institution in which they reside. The Department of Labor has recently issued a proposed regulation under the Fair Labor Standards Act (FLSA) that covers the question of compensation for institutionalized persons. 42 FR 15224 (March 18, 1977). This Department will seek information and comment from the Department of Labor concerning that agency's experience administering the FLSA regulation.

36. *Health, welfare, and other social service providers.* Section 104.52(a) has been expanded in several respects. The addition of new paragraph (a)(2) is intended to make clear the basic requirement of equal opportunity to receive benefits or services in the health, welfare, and social service areas. The paragraph parallels §§ 104.4(b)(ii) and 104.43(b). New paragraph (a)(3) requires the provision of effective benefits or services, as defined in § 104.4(b)(2) (i.e., benefits or services which "afford handicapped persons equal opportunity to obtain the same result (or) to gain the same benefit * * *").

Section 104.52(a) also includes provisions concerning the limitation of benefits or services to handicapped persons and the subjection of handicapped persons to different eligibility standards. One common misconception about the regulation is that it would require specialized hospitals and other health care providers to treat all handicapped persons. The regulation makes no such requirement. Thus, a burn treatment center need not provide other types of medical treatment to handicapped persons unless it provides such medical services to nonhandicapped persons. It could not, however, refuse to treat the burns of a deaf person because of his or her deafness.

Commenters had raised the question of whether the prohibition against different standards of eligibility might preclude recipients from providing special services to handicapped persons or classes of handicapped persons. The regulation will not be so interpreted, and the specific section in question has been eliminated. Section 104.4(c) makes clear that special programs for handicapped persons are permitted.

A new paragraph (a)(5) concerning the provision of different or separate services or benefits has been added. This provision prohibits such treatment unless necessary to provide qualified handicapped persons with benefits and services that are as effective as those provided to others.

Section 104.52(b) has been amended to cover written material concerning waivers of rights or consent to treatment as well as general notices concerning health benefits or services. The section requires the recipient to ensure that qualified handicapped persons are not denied effective notice because of their handicap. For example, recipients could use several different types of notice in order to reach persons with impaired vision or hearing, such as brailled messages, radio spots, and tactile devices on cards or envelopes to inform blind persons of the need to call the recipient for further information.

Section 104.52(c) is a new section requiring recipient hospitals to establish a procedure for effective communication with persons with impaired hearing for the purpose of providing emergency health care. Although it would be appropriate for a hospital to fulfill its responsibilities under this section by having a full-time interpreter for the deaf on staff, there may be other means of accomplishing the desired result of assuring that some means of communication is immediately available for deaf persons needing emergency treatment.

Section 104.52(c), also a new provision, requires recipients with fifteen or more employees to provide appropriate auxiliary aids for persons with impaired sensory, manual, or speaking skills. Further, the Assistant Secretary may require a small provider to furnish auxiliary aids where the provision of aids would not adversely affect the ability of the recipient to provide its health benefits or service.

37. *Treatment of Drug Addicts and Alcoholics.* Section 104.53 is a new section that prohibits discrimination in the treatment and admission of drug and alcohol addicts to hospitals and outpatient facilities. Section 104.53 prohibits discrimination against drug abusers by operators of outpatient facilities, despite the fact that section 407 pertains only to hospitals, because of the broader application of section 504. This provision does not mean that all hospitals and outpatient facilities must treat drug addiction and alcoholism. It simply means, for example, that a cancer clinic may not refuse to treat cancer patients simply because they are also alcoholics.

38. *Education of institutionalized persons.* The regulation retains § 104.54 of the proposed regulation that requires that an appropriate education be provided to qualified handicapped persons who are confined to residential institutions or day care centers.

SUBPART G—PROCEDURES

In § 104.61, the Secretary has adopted the title VI complaint and enforcement procedures for use in implementing section 504 until such time as they are superseded by the issuance of a consolidated procedural regulation applicable to all of the civil rights statutes and executive orders administered by the Department.

APPENDIX B—GUIDELINES FOR ELIMINATING DISCRIMINATION AND DENIAL OF SERVICES ON THE BASIS OF RACE, COLOR, NATIONAL ORIGIN, SEX, AND HANDICAP IN VOCATIONAL EDUCATION PROGRAMS

NOTE: For the text of these guidelines, see 34 CFR, Part 100, Appendix B.

LEGAL ORGANIZATIONS

American Bar Association
Commission on the Mentally
 Disabled
1800 M St., N.W.
Washington, DC 20036

American Civil Liberties Union
22 East 40th St.
New York, NY 10016

Children's Defense Fund
1520 New Hampshire Ave., N.W.
Washington, DC 20036

Education Law Center
605 Broad St.
Suite 800
Newark, NJ 07102

Education Law Center
225 S. 15th St.
Philadelphia, PA 19102

Mental Health Law Project
1220 19th St., N.W.
Washington, DC 20036

National Center for Law and the
 Deaf/Legal Defense Fund
7th and Florida Ave., N.W.
Washington, DC 20002

National Center for Law and
 the Handicapped
1235 N. Eddy St.
South Bend, IN 46617

National Juvenile Law Center
3701 Lindell Blvd.
St. Louis, MO 63108

National Juvenile Law Center
693 Mission St.
San Francisco, CA 94102

Western Center for Law and
 the Handicapped
849 S. Broadway
Los Angeles, CA 90014

Center for Law and Education
14 Appian Way
Cambridge, MA 02138

For Legal Services:
Legal Services Corporation
733 15th St., N.W.
Washington, DC 20005

For Federal Violations:
U.S. Department of Education
Office for Civil Rights
400 Maryland Ave., S.W.
Washington, DC 20202

For Advocacy Organizations:
Council for Exceptional
    Children
1920 Association Dr.
Reston, VA 22091

INDEX